A DAUGHTER'S TALE

A
Daughter's Tale

The Memoir of
Winston Churchill's Youngest Child

MARY SOAMES

RANDOM HOUSE

NEW YORK

Published in the United States by Random House,
an imprint of The Random House Publishing Group,
a division of Random House, Inc., New York.

RANDOM HOUSE and colophon are registered
trademarks of Random House, Inc.

Originally published in Great Britain by Doubleday, an imprint of
Transworld Publishers, a Random House Group Company, in 2011.

LIBRARY OF CONGRESS CATALOGING-IN-PUBLICATION DATA
Soames, Mary.
A daughter's tale: the memoir of Winston Churchill's
youngest child / by Mary Soames.
p. cm.
Includes bibliographical references.
ISBN 978-0-8129-9333-2
eISBN 978-0-679-64518-4
1. Soames, Mary—Childhood and youth.   2. Churchill, Winston,
1874–1965.   3. Churchill, Clementine, Lady, 1885–1977.
4. Soames, Mary—Family.   5. Great Britain—History—
George VI, 1936–1952.   6. World War, 1939–1945—Great Britain.
7. Great Britain—Biography.   I. Title.
DA566.9.S57A3 2012   941.084092—dc23   2011037070
[B]

Printed in the United States of America on acid-free paper

www.atrandom.com

246897531

FIRST U.S. EDITION

Book design by Barbara M. Bachman

CONTENTS

Note on Sources

———

THE TEXT QUOTES EXTENSIVELY FROM THE AUTHOR'S PERSONAL diaries, which remain in her possession, as do letters from the author to her parents. Letters from Winston Churchill up to his resignation in July 1945 are held in the Chartwell Papers, Churchill Archives Centre, Churchill College, Cambridge. Letters from Clementine Churchill are held in the Baroness Spencer–Churchill Papers, also in the Churchill Archives Centre, Churchill College, Cambridge. Papers in these collections are not cited individually in the endnotes.

The author's letter to David Lloyd George, 20 September 1937, is held in the Lloyd George Papers, Parliamentary Archives, Westminster. The author's letter to W. Averell Harriman, 13 May 1941, is held in the Library of Congress, Washington, D.C.

A DAUGHTER'S TALE

Prelude

As the 1920s began, conditions seemed set fair, professionally and personally, for Winston Churchill and his family. From the summer of 1917, when Winston had returned to office as Minister of Munitions after the debacle of the 1915 Dardanelles campaign had cost him his place in Asquith's Coalition government, he had served in various ministries and permutations of Lloyd George's Coalition governments, and in early 1921 he was appointed Secretary of State for the Colonies. Winston was in his forty-seventh year and Clementine, whom he had married in 1908, ten years younger: their family consisted of Diana, aged twelve years; Randolph, ten; Sarah, seven; and Marigold, rising three.

But 1921 was to be a year of heavy tidings for the Churchill family. In early January, Blanche, the redoubtable Countess of Airlie, died. Clementine had never been really fond of her grandmother, but her death brought back memories of childhood summer holidays at Airlie Castle with her so dearly beloved sister Kitty (who had died aged only sixteen), and the twins, Nellie and Bill. Later that month the death in a railway accident of a distant Londonderry kinsman of Winston's, Lord Herbert Vane-Tempest, brought shock and regret if not grief; his unexpected demise wrought changes in Winston's fortunes, the consequences of which belong to a later chapter.

Then, in the spring, stark tragedy struck. In April, Bill Hozier, Clementine's only brother, aged thirty-three, shot himself in a hotel bedroom in Paris. And at the end of May, Lady Randolph Churchill, the beautiful and celebrated Jennie—in predictably high heels—fell down a staircase: a month later, after amputation of her leg, and a sudden haemorrhage, she died, in her sixty-eighth year. She had become a legend in her own lifetime, and her death was widely mourned. Her sons, Winston and Jack, grieved deeply; and if their wives, Clementine and Goonie, had had their reservations in the past about Belle Maman's extravagances and vagaries, the undaunted spirit with which she met the difficulties in her life, and her great courage in her last weeks, commanded their true and loving admiration.

A quieter departure was the death in early August of Thomas Walden, who had been Lord Randolph's manservant: he had accompanied Winston to the South African war, enlisting in the Imperial Light Horse, and continued in service with him after the war. He was indeed a family treasure, and his departure was a cause of great sadness for Winston.

But the worst blow in this already dark year was yet to come. Winston and Clementine's youngest child, Marigold, had been born four days after the Armistice in 1918. A chubby, redheaded, lively baby, "the Duckadilly" was the pet of the family. Reading her parents' letters to each other during Marigold's brief infancy, one perceives from passing references that she was markedly prone to sore throats and catching colds, so probably earlier action should have been taken when the child developed symptoms while in seaside lodgings, along with Diana, Randolph, and Sarah, at Broadstairs in Kent in early August. The nursery party, in the charge of a young French nanny, Mlle. Rose, was due to travel north to join Winston and Clementine for a lovely family holiday in Scotland, staying with the Duke and Duchess of Westminster: but the plan collapsed when Marigold became ill, with what developed rapidly into septicaemia of the throat. Tragically, the nanny failed to recognize the seriousness of the child's condition, and it was only after prompting by the lodging-house landlady that Clementine was sent for. She rushed immediately to Broadstairs, to be joined shortly by Winston, and a London specialist was sent for—

but alas, to no avail: the adored "Duckadilly" died with her distraught parents at her side on the evening of 23 August. She was two years and nine months old.

Many years later my father told me that when Marigold died, Clementine gave a succession of wild shrieks like an animal in mortal pain. My mother never got over Marigold's death, and her very existence was a forbidden subject in the family: Clementine battened down her grief and marched on. I was about twelve, I think, when I asked my mother who was the tubby little girl wearing a sun hat and holding a spade in the small photograph on her bedroom desk—and she told me: the picture had been taken on the beach at Broadstairs a week or two before Marigold's death. But it was many more years before I discovered that my mother regularly visited the pathetic little grave in the vastness of a London cemetery, with its beautiful memorial cross by Eric Gill: she never invited me to accompany her. It was only during our many conversations at the time when I was beginning work on her biography—this was in the 1960s—that she at last brought herself to open up to me about Marigold.

AFTER THIS TRAGEDY, life of course took up its rhythm again as Clementine responded to the imperatives of the other three children's needs and claims, and of her total involvement in Winston's career. This deep grief had brought them very close, and early in the following year Clementine found that she was with child once more. At first she and Winston kept this news to themselves. Clementine was in Cannes, holidaying and playing tennis—including taking part in the club tournament—when her expectations were confirmed: they had been out there together, but Winston had returned to London at the end of the parliamentary recess. Winston was rather anxious, but on 3 February Clementine wrote reassuringly: "Don't think I am doing too much . . . after playing I go to my Bunny [bed] & eschew the Casino & its heat and tobacco smoke, not to speak of its financial danger." She ended her letter: "Goodbye Darling—Kiss the two red-haired kittens

[Diana and Sarah] for me. I wonder if the new one will have red hair. Shall we have a bet about it: 'Rouge ou Noir'?"

In the last lap of her pregnancy, Clementine and the children spent some weeks at Frinton, from where she wrote to Winston on 8 August: "I feel quite excited at the approach of a new kitten, only 5 weeks now and a new being—perhaps a genius—anyhow very precious to us— will make its appearance & demand our attention. Darling, I hope it will be like you." But painful thoughts of the beloved Duckadilly were much in her mind—"Three days from now August the 11th our Marigold began to fade; She died on the 23rd." Winston too had sad thoughts of those days, and was tender and understanding: "I think a gt deal of the coming kitten," he wrote on 10 August, "& about you my sweet pet. I feel it will enrich yr life and brighten our home to have the nursery started again. I pray to God to watch over us all."

Winston and Clementine's last child, Mary, was born at their London home, 2 Sussex Square, early on the morning of 15 September.

IN 2002, IN MY eighty-first year, I received a letter from a ninety-two-year-old lady, Mrs. Alida Harvie, who reminded me that our paths had crossed way back in 1942 when, for a few weeks, we were both at the ATS OCTU (Officer Cadet Training Unit) at Windsor. Her father, Sir Harry Brittain, was for some time a parliamentary colleague of my father, and in 1921, soon after Marigold's death, the Brittains, accompanied by their daughter Alida, had met Winston and Clementine at some political occasion. In conversation with Lady Brittain, Clementine said: "We are not planning to have any more children"—to which Lady Brittain replied: "Oh! Never say that—the next little one may prove the greatest joy to you all."

So many years on, I felt grateful that Mrs. Harvie should have wished me to know this story; and I am moved and humbled to realize that perhaps I was, for my parents, the child of consolation.

CHAPTER I

Chartwell Child

———————

SEPTEMBER 1922 SAW ANOTHER EVENT OF EVEN GREATER IMPORtance to the Churchills' family life than the birth of the "Benjamin"—myself. In the very week I was born, Winston made an offer for Chartwell Manor, near Westerham in Kent. Three years earlier, Winston and Clementine had sold a charming old house and property, Lullenden, near East Grinstead in Sussex, which they had bought in the latter part of the First World War, chiefly to get their (and Winston's brother Jack's) children out of London and away from the zeppelin raids. It had been a real haven for everybody, but the small farm proved a real money loser, and in 1919 they had most regretfully sold it. Since then the whole family had greatly missed their country life. Long school holidays were spent in rented houses, but these were no substitute for one's own home, and Winston and Clementine were soon on the lookout for another "country basket" (as Clementine called it). One major problem stood between them and their dream house: money—or rather, the lack of it. However, in January 1921 a totally unforeseen event dramatically changed their financial situation: the death, already noted, of Lord Herbert Vane-Tempest. He was childless, and through the tortuous processes of entail his considerable fortune, in the form of the Garron Towers estate in Ireland, passed to Winston. Now the remote hope of a "country basket" became a bright possibility, and Winston and Clementine kept their eyes and ears open.

Presently Winston saw Chartwell. About twenty-five miles from London, it was a dilapidated and unprepossessing Victorian house built round a much older core, standing on a hilltop commanding the most sensational view to the south over the Weald of Kent. Below the house the hillside falls away to a lake, fed by a spring—the Chartwell—and alongside the whole valley ran a wide belt of beech woods sheltering the property from the north and east. Winston fell—at once and forever—in love with this beautiful place. He, of course, hastened to show it to Clementine, whose first reaction was enthusiastic—"I can think of nothing but that heavenly tree-crowned Hill," she had written to him in July 1921. But on subsequent visits she became aware of several major defects in its condition, and soon realized that the cost of making the house habitable would be significantly higher than the original estimates. Furthermore—perhaps most serious of all the drawbacks—she feared the house and property would be too much for them to run and maintain. Time would prove her right in both these judgements. However, to all her arguments Winston was deaf—although for a time he went "quiet" on the plan to buy this place which had so beguiled him. Then, during the second half of September, while Clementine was fully occupied with their new baby, Winston presented her with a fait accompli—his offer for Chartwell had been accepted. Clementine, contrary to Winston's earnest hope, never came to share his love of Chartwell—and never quite forgave him for his (totally untypical) lack of candour with her at the time of its purchase.

The autumn of 1922 was an eventful one both for the Churchills domestically and for the country politically. While Winston lay very ill from an emergency appendectomy in October, the famous and fateful meeting of the Conservative party at the Carlton Club put an end to the Coalition: Lloyd George and his government resigned, and were succeeded by Bonar Law and a Conservative administration. Parliament was dissolved, and at the ensuing general election in November the Conservatives won a large majority over the Liberals, the latter fatally divided between the followers of Lloyd George (Winston among them) and of Asquith.

Winston's seat in Dundee, which he had represented for fourteen years, was gallantly fought by Clementine and a band of devoted supporters until Winston, still in a very weak condition after his operation, arrived late in the campaign. It was here that I made my first entry into politics, at the age of seven weeks, when in the local newspaper a photograph of my mother arriving by train from London for the campaign bore the unhelpful (and, in the circumstances, churlish) caption: "Mrs Churchill and her *unbaptized infant* [my italics] arrive in Dundee." A further ill omen was their local address in Dudhope Terrace. Winston was roundly defeated, thereby evoking his rueful comment that he found himself "without an office, without a seat, without a party and without an appendix."

After all these events and calamities, Winston (liberated from the ties of government and Parliament) and Clementine took themselves and their brood off to five sunshine months in Cannes, where they rented the Villa Rêve d'Or. Winston recovered his health, painted, and pondered his future; Clementine loved the warmth and played a lot of tennis; and I (after my first singularly unsuccessful foray into politics) lay cocooned in my pram.

I WAS NEARLY TWO YEARS old when our family moved into a rehabilitated and largely rebuilt Chartwell, after all the usual hazards and hindrances, compromises, and final ill will between architect and clients which seem inevitably to accompany such enterprises.

Winston, with the three "Big Ones," Diana, Randolph, and Sarah, formed the pioneer party, moving in with a basic survival kit and minimal staff support in the Easter holidays: Winston wrote his first letter to Clementine from Chartwell on 17 April 1924. But it would be nearly another two months before she, Nana Whyte (who will figure very prominently in my story), "Baby Bud" (me), and the rest of the household took up residence. The first weekend guests signed the visitors' book in the last weekend of June.

My first memory is snapshot-clear, and must be from that summer. I am lying in my big pram under the great yew tree on the lawn in front of the arcaded windows of the new dining room. Woken up from my midmorning siesta, I am greatly bored: I start jiggling (I am really too big now for the pram), and (securely held by my harness) manage to rock my "boat." Now I try a back-and-forth movement: this is great fun—except suddenly the pram pitches forward on to its handle, and I slide down, held awkwardly suspended by my straps. Suddenly grown-ups, clutching white table napkins, are running towards me—a luncheon party was in progress, and my plight had been observed: I am rescued, taken into the dining room, consoled, and made much of. I think dining-room life is very agreeable, and plan to join it as soon as may be!

At this point I must introduce Nana. After the trauma of Marigold's death, and the departure of Mlle. Rose, Clementine was much shaken in her confidence, and, fully aware that her life with Winston would always mean frequent absences from her children, cast about to find a more mature nanny/nursery governess figure to take charge of them. As chance would have it, she did not have far to look: her own first cousin, Maryott Whyte, was a trained Norland nurse—then, as now, the ne plus ultra in terms of child care. Maryott, known as "Moppet," was the younger daughter of Lady Maude Whyte, a daughter of the Earl and Countess of Airlie and so Clementine's aunt. Lady Maude Ogilvy had made a late, and—since she had next to no money herself—improvident marriage to Theodore Whyte, himself an impoverished gentleman land agent. The Whytes had four children—Madeline, Mark (who would be killed aged nineteen in Flanders in 1918), Maryott, and Felix. The two girls were well educated, but, unlike their female cousins (or indeed the majority of their female social contemporaries), knew that they must earn their living. Madeline was an intellectual artisan, learning carpentry and working at the famous

Doves Press. Here, under the tutelage of Cobden Sanderson, she became an expert in bookbinding, a craft she subsequently taught herself for many years. Moppet was sensible and intelligent, but less eccentric than her elder sister: she elected to train as a children's nurse and, at the time her cousin Clementine Churchill was looking round for someone to take charge of her lively nursery/schoolroom, was aged twenty-six and in one of her early posts after completing her Norland training.

So cousin Moppet, or Nana—as she was to all of us children—was recruited, and came to our family in October 1921. Randolph was then in his second year at Sandroyd, a preparatory school in Surrey, and the two girls were day pupils at Notting Hill High School. After my arrival on the scene nearly a year later, Nana's attention was largely focused on myself: she was enchanted to be in charge of a baby again, and with Randolph and Diana rapidly outgrowing the confines of the nursery, her dominion principally embraced Sarah and the "Baby Bud." Nana, while observing her professional position in the household, was nevertheless from the start on a different footing from all the previous nannies, as Clementine's first cousin and the social equal of her employers: when I was christened, she was my godmother.

I cannot think of any reason for my being named Mary. My only godfather, Victor Cazalet,* considerably annoyed my mother by suggesting I should be called "Victoria," and went so far as to have that name engraved on the elegant pale blue velvet case which enclosed his present to me (the almost statutory christening gift at that time: an "add-a-pearl" necklace—to which the recipient's benefactors were meant to do just that at regular intervals). I only discovered this fontside disagreement years later when, on examining the velvet case, I made out that MARY had been very firmly superimposed on an only partially successful erasure of VICTORIA. I was rather sorry; I felt I would have liked to be Victoria (Vicky to personal friends, of course).

---

* Victor's family at Fairlawne had long bee n friends of Clementine, and he would soon be our neighbour at Chartwell. Victor was at this time also a political friend and supporter of Winston.

But plain old Mary had clearly been under discussion for some time before my christening at the end of November, because in a letter from school on 1 October Randolph wrote: "What is the baby going to be christened? I do hope it will be Mary. . . ."

A "Benjamin's" life is one of contrasts, especially when there is a wide age gap between oneself and older siblings, as in my case: Sarah was nearly eight years old, Randolph eleven, and Diana thirteen when I appeared on the family scene. One finds oneself alternately in the roles of new cuddly toy and real little bore—to be discarded rapidly when a more pressing or suitable-to-age attraction presents itself. Soon after our family's arrival at Chartwell, our father caused to be constructed in the first fork of the great lime in the front drive a wonderful tree house—from which, of course, I was excluded. Access to this aerial retreat was by means of a rope ladder, which would be swiftly pulled up to preserve the privacy of the members of this elite club. The older children and their visiting cousins would spend hours aloft, and I remember at age four or five wandering disconsolately round the tree, gazing up, trying to catch the loudly whispered secrets and yearning to know the cause for the gales of uproarious laughter, quite often punctuated by stern commands down to me to "Go and find Nana." I remember I very often took refuge in the office, whose windows looked out on the drive, where I found delightful (and apparently appreciative) company in the secretaries, who indulgently allowed me to play with the typewriters and pinch treasury tags and paper clips: I think they must have sometimes wished for the protection of a rope ladder too! Presently Nana would appear and bear me off to my quarters.

The nursery wing had been purposely built as part of the major construction work in the rehabilitation of Chartwell. Comprising three floors and an attic, it faced due south, overlooking the gardens and the beautiful Weald. On the ground floor, a long room combined both schoolroom and nursery life: there was a large open log fireplace (where we made buttered toast), and glazed doors opened out on to the garden. Behind this big front room were a bathroom, and a kitchen/

pantry which produced elevenses, teas (delicious drop scones made on the stovetop), and our various pets' meals; luncheon and Nana's supper were brought from the main kitchen by the nurserymaid.

The upper floors were connected by a very steep, narrow staircase, with blue linoleum-covered treads "nosed" with thick rubber. At first I scrambled laboriously down and up this precipice, but was soon negotiating it at high speed, taking two and three steps at a time: I had some horrific tumbles.

On the first floor Sarah had her room—a lovely bed-sitter (evolving over the years from schoolgirl's den to debutante's "bower") which also communicated via a door onto the Pink Terrace with Mama's Blue Sitting Room. Diana and Randolph from the first had their bedrooms in the main part of the house. On the second floor was the night nursery, with its adjoining bathroom: this was Nana's and my abode until I was about ten, when I was promoted to the attic and my first bed-sitter.

Only vestigial traces of the nursery staircase remain now, as sometime in the midthirties, when I was in my teens and had melded into grown-up domestic life, Nana and I migrated to the top floor of the main house. Then my father pierced through the thick wall and took possession of the former night nursery for his bedroom. Later still, after the war, my mother colonized her former sitting room as a bedroom, penetrating into Sarah's former room on the same level to create a dressing room and bathroom. I explain all this in some detail, because today thousands of visitors troop through the house, some of whom may read this book and be puzzled by the present configuration of the rooms and the disappearance of the nursery wing which figured so strongly in my childhood life.

If the nursery wing was my "castle" (of which undoubtedly I was the "princess"), it was also the base from which I sallied forth into the wider world. To a small child it was mountainous territory, as Chartwell, being constructed on the side of a steep hill, is a house of confusingly many levels. Unlike most nursery quarters one reads of, mine were based on the garden floor, and I started my daily forays on the same level as the servants' hall, pantry, and kitchen. After calling on my numerous friends in those regions, I would then start on my uphill scramble to the upper floors—probably first visiting my mother, who, adorned with curlers and hairnet, face liberally greased, would usually be ensconced in bed, penned in by her breakfast tray or hidden behind *The Times.* I always remember a warm welcome, though at this point it took the physical form of a wave rather than a cuddle. Here I would remain while a succession of "callers" made their appearance: her lady's maid; a secretary with a message; or Papa, arriving suddenly and unceremoniously, clad in his (extremely mini) silk vest/nightshirt, clutching his copy of *The Times,* and usually protesting at some part of the leading article. This he would discuss with Mummie (who had usually already noticed the offending passage) before departing again, like a tempestuous gust of wind, for his own study-bedroom along the passage. I always, if visible, received en passant a warm hug or embrace during this visitation. A more ceremonious interlude was the daily conference with the cook, who, in spotless white overall and apron, bearing the menu book, would draw up a chair and seat herself at the bedside. During the long—and to me infinitely boring—dialogue which ensued, I would disappear from view under the desk (I was a lion in my den); or I would clamber onto the lower shelf of the great oak double-doored cupboard, retreating and burrowing into folds of satin underclothes— I remember how deliciously the silky gloom smelled. Needless to say, successive lady's maids greatly deplored this activity of "little Miss Mary"—and I don't remember liking any of them very much: a generally disapproving race I deemed them to be. On looking now at the cupboard (still in its exact place in my mother's bedroom), I realize I must have been very small to have hidden there, and that my freedom to roam at will all over the house began at a very early age.

But, as with all states of "liberty," there were certain strict rules. On my parents' floor, Papa's study-bedroom was the "Holy of Holies," and indeed that end of the landing was sacrosanct, and a "no-noise area": I remember hearing the "Big Ones" getting fearful wiggings for noise (especially whistling). In order to avoid this "no-go zone" I would invariably ascend to this floor by the back staircase (narrow and blue linoleumed, as in the nursery wing), from where I could reach my mother's room without trespassing on forbidden territory. By the same route I could also gain access to the visitors' rooms: they were meant to be out of bounds, but I seem to recall making sly visits when I saw the breakfast trays going up, and being the appreciative recipient of titbits (peeled peach segments and spoonfuls of sugar dunked in coffee were my favourite perks).

Downstairs, a general admonition was not to "bother the servants." This was open to a rather wide interpretation, but two areas were strictly off-limits to me: the servants' hall and the kitchen. The first ban was to protect the privacy of the occupants; the second was in part for obvious safety reasons (especially valid in those days when the kitchen was dominated by a large coal range, on which stood the perpetual huge stockpot, and large pans of boiling fat sizzled away). But the prime reason was that the cook was a potentate, addressed always as "Mrs."—*She* who must be approached at all times with care; *She* who must not be ruffled (and cooks, I learned, were perennially prone to ruffledom). As far as I knew, the only two people who had access to this sanctuary (apart from the footman fetching and carrying dishes) were my mother and the butler—another power to be conciliated, and always addressed by the children and other staff as "Mr."

In fact the servants were, I realize in retrospect, extremely kind and indulgent. The pantry staff would stand me on a wine case, wrap me in tea towels, and allow me to "help" them with the washing up: I would take liberal scoops of "soft soap" (like dark Vaseline) from a huge tin, creating a mountainous lather in the wooden sink (no stainless steel then), and proceed with this delectable task until I was so thoroughly soaked as to have to be dispatched back to the nursery.

One important domestic ceremonial, common to most private houses, was the stirring of the Christmas puddings, which always took place fairly late in November on the Sunday when the collect begins, "Stir up, we beseech thee, O Lord, the wills of thy faithful people . . . ," consequently known as "Stir-up Sunday." The great bowl full of rich mixture stood on the kitchen table most of that day, and everyone (exceptionally) was permitted to call in to give a stir with a huge wooden spoon; one was meant to make a wish at the same time. In my early years I would be hoisted onto the table, where, wielding the spoon with both hands and some help, I would have great trouble in selecting quickly just one wish from my long and varied running list of desires.

I suppose I must have been a bit older before I was allowed to roam freely by myself in the gardens, with their many hazards: but Nana was not a Scotswoman for nothing, and moreover daily outdoor exercise was most certainly a cardinal rule in a Norlander's training. Suitably clad for whatever the weather—wet or fine, warm or bitter—together we would set off. Chartwell's gardens offer endless opportunities for fun and freedom for children (as mine would in their turn discover), for there are wide-open spaces, and steep banks to roll down, and streams and lakes, and trees to climb. But I think it was more full of possibilities for fun and adventure in my childhood days, for then so much was still in the making.

Nana and I, with the dogs, would head straight for whatever works were in progress. Perhaps Papa was building a wall: when I was bigger I would volunteer to be his "bricklayer's mate," as did Sarah, and hand him the bricks—but this usually ended for me in tears as, soon becoming bored and inattentive, I would drop a brick on my plimsolled foot (I can assure those who have not had this experience that it is a most painful one). Papa would be vaguely sympathetic, but was engrossed in his task and thought me clumsy, and I would retreat howling to the nursery. For now, though, Nana and I would just make a social call, noting progress, and if I was lucky, old Kurn (the retired bricklayer who assisted my father and taught him his skill) would let me have a careful stir with his trowel of the pudding-mixture-like cement.

In the winter, more fun was to be had if Papa and his minions were wooding and making a bonfire, for Chartwell at this stage had many trees and much scrubland to be cleared. My father's task force would probably consist of the ubiquitous Kurn and a gardener taken off his proper task (this used to annoy my mother greatly), additionally assisted by any of the older children and possibly the literary assistant of the day, plus any stalwart guests. We all had our appointed tasks (I being allowed to cast suitably sized twigs on the blaze); Nana would fetch large potatoes from the kitchen and bake them in the embers—they tasted rather charcoally, but were delectably comforting to hold in one's freezing hands. Hot drinks would be brought out, and it was all the greatest fun.

Snow brought the possibility of tobogganing. Chartwell is ideally suited for this, with slopes graded to every degree of daring, but snow conditions suitable for "winter sports" occur so randomly in England that one always seems to be caught out and ill-prepared: however, large wooden pantry trays made wonderful substitute toboggans for those without the genuine article. If freeze-ups persisted long and hard enough, there was of course also skating on the lakes: none of my family was particularly expert, and I remember chiefly the wearisome doing up of ill-fitting boots, and the terrors of cracking ice and warning shrieks.

Springtime and summer brought their own train of activities and pleasures. We picked snowdrops and then primroses, Nana showing me how to tie the bunches with odd bits of wool from her knitting bag. Actually my fault of impatience made me a pretty poor picker—I think I left it mostly to Nana and Gladys, the nurserymaid, and amused myself by throwing sticks for the dogs.

At all seasons our walks often took us right down the hill to the farmyard. Our property ended just beyond the orchard, where on a level stretch were several service cottages, the garages, the old Victorian stables, and, later, a model woodshed designed and largely constructed by my father. The farm at the very bottom of the hill (which he acquired after the war) at this time belonged to the Jansen family, who lived in the very beautiful Queen Anne house—Mariners—about a quarter of a mile away. The farm manager was kindly disposed to us, as indeed were the Jansens, and we were allowed to visit the farmyard and its inhabitants; we were also allowed the freedom of their woods for walking and picnicking. I was much in favour during the

lambing season, as I undertook to bottle-feed any orphans. The lamb-
kins would be brought up from the farm and a wire-netting enclosure
constructed for them in the small orchard below the potting sheds.
(This area is now a large terrace with seats, commanding a panoramic
view over the Weald, my mother after the war having swept away the
greenhouses and potting sheds to a less prominent situation.) I think
we sometimes nurtured four or five lambs at a time. Needless to say,
these sweet orphans—mercifully for them—did not depend entirely
on my attentions: I think probably the head gardener's wife was my
"colleague" in lamb rearing. But this was a great and regular feature of
springtime life at Chartwell.

As my legs grew longer so did our walks, which soon included the
Belt (the protecting arms of beech woods which enclosed our lovely
valley). Sarah and I discovered an old dogs' cemetery; we uncovered
the gravestones and with pointed sticks cleaned the lettering, figuring
out the names of dear companions of generations of the Campbell-
Colquhoun family who had owned Chartwell before us. One epitaph
was particularly touching: "The faithful guardian of the pram."

Beyond the farmyard the dirt road led through fields to Puddle-
dock, a group of cottages at the bottom of the steep and narrow road
climbing up to the famous beauty spot of Toy's Hill: but at this stage
we had reached our limit, and turned back homewards through fields
which in those days were a hop garden. Many of the oast houses (including the ones at Chartwell Farm), now redeveloped as attractive
homes, still stand as reminders of what in those days was the principal
industry for this region. A great event each summer was the descent
on all the hop fields of thousands of pickers. Now, commercial crops
are largely harvested by migrant workers; then, whole families from
the East End of London, along with bands of gypsy families, would
come year after year to the same farms to pick the hops. The Londoners were accommodated in custom-built sheds, somewhat like army-
barrack dormitories; the gypsies lived in their caravans. The work was
very hard, but everyone had a good time. I was a bit too young to share
in all this, and somewhat overcome by such hordes of strangers. Many

years later, when Christopher and I were living at Chartwell Farm House, I found the remains of the foundations of the hop pickers' huts buried in the woodland opposite our house.

I HAVE ALREADY MENTIONED the dogs that accompanied Nana and me on our walks, and animals were a very important part of my life from the beginning. My father loved animals—this was a strong bond between us—whereas my mother tolerated them. Largely owing to the peripatetic nature of their life, it was not until after the war that my father had a dog of his own—a chocolate poodle—but he shared fully in the dramas which inevitably erupted from time to time involving my various pets.

There was animal life in abundance outside the house: goldfish in the water garden; geese, ornamental ducks, and black and white swans (the latter perpetually at war with each other) on the lakes; and a series of farm animals which usually proved unsatisfactory from a practical point of view. Winston's letters to Clementine from Chartwell in any of her absences were full of events relating to the animals' lives. Particularly vexatious were the regular predations of the foxes, which murdered swans with distressing regularity, despite elaborate measures taken to protect them. In all these animals and birds I took the liveliest interest, and even in my earliest letters to my father would report on them, as well as on my own nursery animals.

Brought up chiefly among grown-ups, I was compensated for the lack of companionship of children of my own age by a procession of pets. Starting with rabbits, I soon progressed to a nursery dog and cat; the orphan lambs; bantams; goats; budgerigars; a pair of canaries (Percy and Lucy); two orphan fox cubs (for a season only); and an exquisite little marmoset—which, however, succumbed quite soon, I fear, to indifferent care and draughts. Most companionable among my menagerie were, of course, my dogs—for to Punch, the beige pug, acquired when I was about four, was added in 1931 Jasper, an enchanting Blenheim spaniel given to me by Cousin Sunny (my father's kinsman, the ninth Duke of Marlborough), whose exceptionally beautiful and eccentric wife, Gladys, bred them in great numbers. To mark the Marlbrouckian connection—which my father, in an early history lesson, explained to me—my puppy's kennel name was Jasper, Prince of Mindleheim. I must have evidently been much impressed by my new dog's noble descent, for I wrote to my ducal cousin (somewhat muddling the degree of our consanguinity):

CHARTWELL
WESTERHAM, KENT
JULY 24TH 1931

Dear Uncle Sunny

I am sending you a snapshot of the little Blenheim you gave, he is such a darling and I love him very much. Do you think you could ask Cousin Gladys to let me have his pedigree he is admired wherever we go and people ask how he is bred, and I should so much like to have it.

Your affectionate niece,
Mary Churchill

Sadly, Jasper was run over by a motorcycle outside Chartwell gates when he was only three years old: I was heartbroken. But presently Nana gave me a rough-and-tumble Lakeland terrier called Paddy, who lived to a ripe old age.

My pug, Punch, had the distinction of having a poem written by my father in his honour. At one point he became desperately ill (distemper, I suppose), and both Sarah and I were in floods of tears: my father, greatly concerned for us in our anguish, composed this touching ditty, which was chanted by the family while Punch was ailing:

Oh, what is the matter with poor Puggy-wug?
Pet him and kiss him and give him a hug.
Run and fetch him a suitable drug,

Wrap him up tenderly all in a rug,
That is the way to cure Puggy-wug.

Happily, dear Punch recovered, and he too survived to a ripe and rather cantankerous old age: there is a snapshot of him looking very venerable in 1938.

The dog population at Chartwell was at various times augmented by Sarah's chocolate spaniel (not for nothing called Trouble), given her by her devoted beau Harry Llewellyn, and Randolph's fox terrier, Harvey—his name deriving from Dr. Johnson, who, referring to his patron Henry Hervey, said: "If you call a dog Hervey I shall love him." Considering my mother was not particularly animal-minded, I think on reflection she was very long-suffering, for the dogs strayed all over the house, and cocked their legs with impunity: I regret to say Punch was a bad offender in this respect. Even Papa rebelled on one occasion, writing to my mother in April 1935, while she was travelling abroad: "I have banished all the dogs from our part of the house. Punch is in the nursery. Trouble is with Arnold [the farm bailiff] and Harvey is with Howes [the chauffeur]. I really think you will have to buy a new strip of carpet outside my landing."

It was not only in the house that pet life was the cause of vexation. When I was about thirteen the two nanny goats acquired by my father as "nibblers" had in the natural course of events become a mini-flock, and were my especial charge; I used to get up very early in term time to feed them and picket out the adults to perform their allotted task of keeping the orchard grass short, their kids being free to scamper round. Sometimes, if I had carelessly picketed one within reach of an apple tree, I would return from school to find outraged grown-ups—and an apple tree whose bark had been neatly, expertly, and fatally "ringed." If Mama was at home, the worst of the storm broke at once: if she was away, it was almost worse waiting for it to brew up and explode on her return.

When we first went to Chartwell there were ponies, among them my father's polo ponies, and a rather old groom—Mr. Best—who had been the Campbell-Colquhouns' coachman and had stayed on with us. In 1926 there was a "crisis," the first—but certainly not the last—about the expense of running Chartwell, and a memorandum survives from Winston to Clementine proposing a series of draconian measures to effect economies: among the resolutions listed, all the ponies were to be sold ("except Energy and her foal"), and the groom dispensed with. I do not remember any polo ponies, so I think they must have all departed fairly soon; but there is a photograph of me at about that time on Judy, a piebald pony, whom I do remember, so she obviously escaped the "purge"—as did Mr. Best, who stayed on, finally retiring in about 1932. Judy lived to a venerable old age also, pensioned off out at grass.

There was always a nursery cat: the one I chiefly recall was a plebeian "moggy," very suitably called Tinker. There were others, but none made a mark outside our nursery world until the advent of Tango, the most beautifully and richly marked marmalade kitten. He was greatly admired by the whole household, and at first I used to carry him round to call on his fans, cradled in my arms; but as he grew to cat's estate, Tango perceived that the fleshpots of "upstairs" life were superior to those on offer in the nursery—as was (he evidently and snobbishly opined) the company: so he transferred himself to the upper regions of the house, where he was fulsomely welcomed by all, and became the apple of my father's eye. He had cream from a saucer (sitting in a chair or on the table), slept where he liked (mostly on beds—any visitor being regarded as particularly fortunate should the cat's choice fall on his or her bed), and was sketched and painted by the famous artist William Nicholson, who stayed a great deal while painting a conversation piece of my parents. Mr. Cat, as he came to be called, lived to an advanced age; when he died, in the week of the fall of Tobruk in 1942, the Prime Minister's staff kept this domestic sadness from him until the news from the battlefront was better.

ANOTHER GREAT SOURCE of concern, companionship, and occupation for me was my family of dolls: Kate, Christopher, Muriel Davina, and

Jane, acquired over a period of time and in no particular sequence (though they eventually assumed the above order), their sizes bearing little relation to their allotted ages. Kate, the eldest, was a "nice little girl," with flaxen hair in plaits (which really plaited); she looked charming, my French tutor Mme. L'Honoré having made her a very chic dress. Christopher was a "proper tomboy" in shorts and football boots; Muriel Davina (thus named, I think, for some distant relations of Nana's with whom I once stayed in Scotland), physically the largest of my "collection"—china-faced, with wonderful eyelashes—was perpetually about eighteen months old. Finally there was Jane—she must have been my first rag doll, and was much battered about, having lost one eye; having no hair, she always wore a bonnet, and she spent a lot of time in bed.

My "family" was of great importance to me. I was "Mrs. Davis" (and required to be addressed thus); the existence of Mr. Davis was wrapped in mystery: I thus was the precursor by half a century of that social-problem figure known as the Single Mother. My "nursery" was well provided with dolls' furniture, baths, bottles, perambulators, cots, and other equipment, and my children had a well-stocked wardrobe. I spent long happy hours organizing my family: bathing them, dressing them, feeding them, and accompanying all these procedures with my own running commentary, delivered out loud, along with a flood of instructions, scoldings, and admonitions, accompanied by frequent slappings or shakings administered as necessary. As I myself learned to read, the Davis nursery world enjoyed long sessions of being read aloud to—and of course its inhabitants all said their prayers.

Along with "Mr. Cat," my family of dolls had the great distinction (not enough appreciated by them or me at the time) of being drawn by William Nicholson—our beloved *cher maître,* as we all called him— who spent many hours in the nursery doing the portraits of the Davis family.

CHAPTER 2

A Widening World

———

Iₙ EARLY NOVEMBER 1924—THE SAME YEAR OUR FAMILY MOVED into Chartwell—my father became Chancellor of the Exchequer in Stanley Baldwin's newly elected Conservative government. Naturally, as I was aged just two years old, this important development in my father's career escaped my attention—but it considerably affected my life. In early January 1925 we moved out of No. 2 Sussex Square in Bayswater (where I had been born, but which I do not remember at all, although I suppose I must have spent some time there) into the Chancellor's official residence, No. 11 Downing Street. It was then a charming family house (not, as present needs dictate, invaded by offices and in part arranged as a flat for the Chancellor and his family). The main rooms looked out over No. 10's large garden, which the Prime Minister usually shared by mutual courtesy with his colleague in No. 11. I quite often played in the garden, and sometimes came across Mr. Baldwin, who was very benevolent: I would scramble up onto his knee while he was sitting reading the newspapers, and converse with him, until the poor man was liberated by Nana or the nurserymaid, Gladys, arriving on the scene.

Beyond the garden wall stretches Horse Guards Parade, affording the inhabitants of Downing Street the most splendid view of all the events which take place on that most spacious and splendid of parade grounds. A snapshot memory for me is of kneeling on a window seat one grey foggy morning, hearing sad music, and watching a horse-drawn gun carriage bearing a flag-covered coffin and escorted by troops proceed slowly across Horse Guards Parade and disappear under the archway. I was told it was Earl Haig (Commander-in-Chief Western Front in the First World War) being borne to his military funeral: that was January 1928, and I was five.

The Great War was still a brooding shadow less than a decade since its ending, and personal griefs lay very near the surface. Nana's brother Mark, a lieutenant, had been killed in action, aged nineteen, leading his men in August 1918. His photograph in uniform always stood on Nana's dressing table. Every 11 November while we lived in London she took me with her to stand with the great crowds that gathered near the Cenotaph to mark Armistice Day, the anniversary of the day the Armistice was signed in 1918, at the eleventh hour of the eleventh day of the eleventh month. Today the event is commemorated on Remembrance Sunday, the Sunday nearest to 11 November; then, the whole country stopped as the hour struck on the day itself. I remember the red London buses drawing to a halt, and people walking on pavements stopping in their tracks and standing motionless. I felt the solemnity and the heavy grief of the crowds, and although I cringed at the cannon announcing the two minutes' silence, I stood ramrod still. Then (as now) two minutes seemed an eon of time: looking up I saw grave, desolate faces, and the slow tears trickling down Nana's cheeks. Afterwards, when we got home, she would remove last year's poppy from the frame of Mark's photograph, and replace it with the new one.

During these years Nana and I spent the winter months in London, except for Christmas and New Year, when the whole family returned to Chartwell. My day and night nurseries at No. 11 were on the second floor, right over that famous front door: one day I was caught trying to pour water on the policeman on duty below—I can't remember whether I succeeded in doing so before I was whisked away and much scolded. My London life, like that of most well-found children at that time, involved a lot of getting in and out of leggings and good tailored coats; gloves were de rigueur whether it was cold or not. I went to Macpherson's gym near Sloane Square, where I wore a blue knitted jersey and knickers, and climbed and jumped and marched like anything. There was also much walking in St. James's Park, and feeding the ducks, which is fun at any age. In the Park was an open-air school, to which the children came, I was told, from very poor homes: there were no school meals then, and the government wives formed a roster for supplying and serving hot soup to the children at their break-time throughout the winter. Mummie took me with her when it was her turn, giving me my first experience of "do-goodery": the children looked very pale, and I felt embarrassed and useless.

For the rest of the year, Chartwell was always home base; and although a quiet fell on the house upstairs when my parents departed for London or on their travels, my delightful nursery life continued, punctuated by the excitement of their coming home again, perhaps with one or more of my siblings, heralding much coming and going of guests and general activity both in and out of doors. The "Big Ones" were all at various stages of their education during these No. 11 years, and mostly away at boarding schools or, in Diana's case, in Paris being "finished": I was suitably impressed in the year she came out (1928), when I watched her practicing her curtsey in the drawing room, with a sheet pinned to her shoulders for a train, and her three white feathers fixed rather haphazardly on the back of her head.

I was not dull or lonely during my parents' weekday absences (governed by the sittings of Parliament) or their holidays away from home. I had my animals to look after, my dolls and all my friends "downstairs" to call upon, and when I was old enough to go to the gardens and the garage yard on my own, I had my outdoor calls to make as well.

Nana in all matters ruled my existence. Always loving, and always there, she could also be quite stern; I wanted her approbation above all things, and looked to her for enlightenment on all matters. Her lieutenant was a charming and excellent nurserymaid called Gladys (or Addi-Addis to me), who had been in my parents' service as underhousemaid at Sussex Square since early 1921; in the reorganization of the nursery that autumn following Marigold's death she was appointed nurserymaid under the newly arrived Nana. She was a treasure, and stayed with us till 1927, when she left to take a job as a fully fledged nanny—but even after that, for several years she used to come back to look after me when Nana was on holiday, using up some of her own precious holiday to do so. I never lost touch with beloved Addi-Addis, and used to visit her right up to her death in the 1970s.

Domestic service often offered romantic opportunities. While Gladys was with us she met our very good-looking footman, Alfred Blackwell, who left us to take up gardening (he would eventually become Head Gardener at Bristol Zoo): he and Gladys were married in 1930. Round the same time another romance developed in our household which was of great interest to me. In 1928 a very nice young chauffeur, Sam Howes, came to us, starting at No. 11: about a year later, Olive, a charming and excellent parlour maid, joined the staff. Working both in London and at Chartwell, they were soon courting, and in 1932 Olive gave up her job to marry Sam. Together they set up house in one of the cottages in the stable yard at Chartwell, and Olive would often come back to help out up at the "big house." I had made great friends with Olive, and she would most hospitably often ask me in to tea, after which Sam would let me sit on his wonderful motorbike. Sam and Olive had no children, but Olive must have had a miscarriage in the early days of their marriage, for one day she told me she had "lost" her baby. I didn't actually know she had had a baby, and I did feel it was rather careless of her—but fortunately I sensed the subject was a delicate one and restrained myself from saying what I thought. Sam and Olive left in 1935: no doubt he was looking for better pay than could be found in private service, and as he was a clever engineer he found work with (I think) Rolls-Royce in the Midlands. After the war they emigrated to the United States, where again Sam's skills ensured him a career in engineering. After he retired he and Olive came to England quite often; they got in touch with our family again, and in the last years of my mother's life always came to see her on their visits. On these occasions I was overjoyed to see again such wonderful friends from my childhood days.

One very important person on the estate was of course the head gardener, Mr. Hill; he had succeeded Waterhouse, the Campbell-Colquhouns' gardener, and continued at Chartwell till his death from cancer in 1944. Mr. Hill and his extremely handsome wife had a daughter, Doris, who was two years older than I; we made firm friends and spent a lot of time playing together—indeed, she was my principal outdoors companion for a number of years. We lost touch with the coming of the war; she married one of the gardeners at Chartwell, and lived in Westerham: I'm happy to say we are now in contact again, and she has filled in gaps in my memory of the "old days."

I have already mentioned my visits to the secretaries, and their patient indulgence towards me. Mrs. Pearman, who came in 1929, and Grace Hamblin, who arrived in 1932 to help her with the ever-increasing load of literary work, reigned over the office in my childhood. After nine years in post Mrs. Pearman became seriously ill and had to retire; she died in 1941. Grace, who was only twenty-four when she came to help out, soon became a linchpin, beloved and trusted by us all. She lived with her parents (her father was the head gardener at a neighbouring property), and when I first knew her she worked entirely at Chartwell, though from the beginning of the war she came to London and worked as my mother's private secretary. I could not manage the required "Miss Hamblin" and called her "Hambone." When Grace died in 2002, in her ninety-fifth year, I realized I had known and loved her for seventy years.

I also had friends in Westerham, and Nana—who drove the runabout "nursery" car—used to take me to call on them. Mrs. Cosgrove kept the sweet shop on the Green and lived behind the shop in a very old cottage with extremely low ceilings: both Mr. Cosgrove and their daughter Mollie were large and tall, and I remember thinking they must have felt rather "squashed." There was great excitement and interest when, in the course of some redecorating, Mr. Cosgrove uncovered part of a very old plaster frieze; I was taken in behind the shop (a great privilege) to see it. Mrs. Cosgrove always let me have a sweet after we had made our purchases, taken from one of the long row of glass jars (no prepackaging then): pear drops were my favourites, and even now their smell evokes nostalgia.

Another visit would be to the baker's shop kept by the Boreham family on the corner of the Green with Vicarage Hill. In cold weather especially a most delicious smell wafted forth every time the shop door opened; inside, the aroma was even more concentrated—and if the door from the shop to the back was open, one could glimpse the great oven and trays full of buns or loaves being loaded in by white-clad bakers. I was allowed to choose something to take back for tea: dough-nuts were my favourite, and I always wished the globule of red jam in the middle might have been a little bigger. Mrs. Boreham looked rather like a cottage loaf herself, being rather short, with her apron tied tightly round her middle and her fine brown hair arranged in a bun on top of her head. Some thirty years later the Boreham family (the business being carried on by the sons) would make my wedding cake.

At the end of each of these busily and happily occupied days came an evening ritual—reading aloud. This was a treasured highlight of my routine, and my greatest punishment was to be deprived of this great treat. Starting after teatime, Nana would read to me; when bed-time arrived, we adjourned upstairs, and the reading continued while I undressed, folding my clothes carefully (Nana keeping one eye on the page, and one supervising this process); we then removed to the adjacent bathroom, where I took as long as possible to wash—tiresome interruptions to the narrative being occasioned by very necessary knee scrubbings. Swathed in a towel, I would try to spin more time out: "Oh, we *must* finish the chapter—*please.* . . ."

Nana seemed an inexhaustible reader, and throughout my nursery years I listened enthralled to her renderings of many books—some of them favourites with my grandchildren's generation still: all of Beatrix Potter, and the Christopher Robins; then *Black Beauty* (I remember sobbing into my face flannel over poor Ginger's story); *The Cuckoo Clock* and *The Tapestry Room* by Mrs. Molesworth; Lewis Carroll's *Alice's Adventures in Wonderland* and *Through the Looking-Glass;* Kenneth Grahame's *The Wind in the Willows* and Charles Kingsley's *The Water-Babies*—and, of course, J. M. Barrie's *Peter Pan.*

There were also some very Victorian religious stories, which most certainly have not stood the test of time: one I recall in particular was about an armour-clad soldier called Agathos (a fearful bore and prig) who was (of course) ever ready while slacker comrades slept; another was a real tearjerker called *Jessica's First Prayer,* in which the prototype of a Barnado orphan, who did not know about God, is rescued from her heathen background, and utters her first prayer (on her deathbed, of course).

But Nana knew when and how to move on: to *Little Women* and the *What Katy Did* series; and to tales of history and action—quite my most favourite being *The Little Duke* by Charlotte M. Yonge. Then there were Walter Scott's *Ivanhoe* and Stevenson's *Treasure Island* (Blind Pew terrified me).

Much better (and of more enduring influence) than Agathos was Bunyan's *Pilgrim's Progress;* and I see from faded inscriptions in my handsome green Centenary Edition of the works of Charles Dickens that Nana and Sarah gave me volumes as birthday and Christmas presents when I was nine or ten. My social conscience was further educated by Harriet Martineau's *The Peasant and the Prince,* and her namesake Harriet Beecher Stowe's *Uncle Tom's Cabin.* And still my first reaction on hearing Oscar Wilde's name is to remember and read again (to myself if no grandchild is at hand) his wonderfully beautiful collection of stories in *The Selfish Giant.*

My most favourite "magic" books were George MacDonald's *The Princess and the Goblin* and its sequel *The Princess and Curdie,* with the thrilling and beautiful "old" Princess, who conferred on Curdie the miner's son the gift of being able to divine by a mere handshake whether a person or one of the terrifying creatures by which he found himself surrounded was a human (and therefore capable of redemption) or irredeemably vile. I suppose these books could be regarded as the pre-cursors of the Narnia books of C. S. Lewis.

My introduction to poetry was Robert Louis Stevenson's enchant-ing *A Child's Garden of Verses*—and, of course, A. A. Milne's rhymes; but these horizons were rapidly broadened when, from the age of seven or so, I started lunching in the dining room. Here, along with the gen-eral company of family and guests, I would be spellbound by my father when he was in "reciting" vein. Eagerly I listened to his renderings of Macaulay's *Lays of Ancient Rome* and thrilled to the tale of how splendid Horatius held that bridge "in the brave days of old." Soon I knew all the verses of the "Battle Hymn of the Republic"—when we all joined in the "Glory, Glory Hallelujah"s like anything. At mealtimes, too, Rudyard Kipling, Rupert Brooke, and Byron dawned on me, and I received my first apprehensions of Shakespeare—all dredged up from my father's prodigious memory, stretching way back to his Harrow schooldays. And all these "classics" were interspersed with the music-hall songs enjoyed by Papa and his friends when they were gentlemen cadets at Sandhurst in the last years of Queen Victoria's reign. For my tenth birthday, Sarah gave me a lovely green leather-bound copy of *The Oxford Book of English Verse:* much faded now, it is still a treasured possession.

Another grown-up of importance to me in this child's world largely peopled by adults was Nana's mother, Lady Maude Whyte—my great-aunt Maude, known to me as Aunt Maudie. She lived at No. 56 Lans-downe Road, W11, in elegant but rather shabby gentility, looked after by a devoted old family retainer, Maggie, who lived in the basement and "did everything." This area of Notting Hill is now rather smart, much inhabited by actors (stage and screen) and members of the more intellectual professions, and used as the location for award-winning films; but then it was considered "very far out," a borderline area where impecunious gentlefolk, such as Aunt Maudie and her equally strapped-for-cash sister, my grandmother Lady Blanche Hozier (who lived not far away in W8), could just afford to live. My grandmother, indeed, was in the habit of cheerfully inviting her guests to visit her in "The Wild West."

When I see how delightful the grandmother-grandchild relationship can be, I have always been sorry that I never knew any of my grandparents: Lord and Lady Randolph died before I was born, as did my maternal grandfather, Sir Henry Hozier; and Granny Blanche lived the last years of her life in Dieppe, where she died in 1925. But Aunt Maudie, I now see, was a "grandmother" figure in my life. I sometimes went to stay with her, which was a great treat: I was rather in awe of her, but Maggie was very sweet to me in the kitchen, and gave me all sorts of goodies forbidden in the drawing room. I remember that throughout the house all the floorboards creaked, and that the streets outside were still illuminated by gas lamps, lit by hand each evening.

Although a badly off widow, Aunt Maudie also owned two seaside cottages at Buck's Mills in North Devon: her husband, Theodore Whyte, was a Devonshire man, and they had lived in nearby Bideford. I can only imagine the cottages must have been advantageously let at various times, but naturally these mundane economic considerations did not at this time concern me. Nana used to take Sarah and me to stay with Aunt Maudie at the smaller of the two houses, Buck's Cottage, which clung precariously to the cliff's edge just above a crashing waterfall. After days of rain I used to cower in my bed and listen to the ocean, and to the rumble of the boulders being swept down in the swollen torrent to the beach below, and wonder if I and my bed would be swept away too. The cottage had a wonderful old flagged floor (beneath which there was said to be a smugglers' cave), and although there was electricity we bathed in turn in a tin bathtub placed before the kitchen coal range—an arrangement both fairly primitive and totally delightful.

Buck's Cottage was at the top of the steep path which led down to the beach—which was a paradigm for all beaches: boulders and pebbles (smoothly rounded by endless poundings) gave way to coarse golden sand (perfect material for sand castles), punctuated by quite fierce black rocks with wonderful coral-lined pools full of anemones, mussels, darting tiny fish, and small "nippy" crabs, filled and emp-

tied (except at very low tide) three times in every twenty-four hours.
The beach sloped fairly gradually, but quite definitely—a great incen-
tive to becoming a proficient swimmer. There were thrilling, crashing
waves, but no treacherous currents that I can remember, until quite
far out—which was forbidden water to us smaller ones. Sitting in our
bathing towels, a bit shivery after swimming, munching our elevenses
or picnic tea (somehow even Nana could not prevent the sandwiches
being gritty with sand!)—we would gaze straight out to Lundy Island,
eighteen miles away, with its steep cliffs and rocky Shutter Point, fatal
to so many men-o'-war, Spanish and English alike—a tale familiar to
us from Charles Kingsley's *Westward Ho!,* for Nana had a special Buck's
reading "menu," which recounted the Armada legends that have gathered round that coastline. She also read me the romantic story of
Lorna Doone (I blenched at the appalling death even of the terrible
Carver Doone—the story's villain—being sucked relentlessly down
into the black depths of one of the quagmires on Exmoor). And although "The Smugglers' Leap" from *The Ingoldsby Legends* actually refers
to the Kent coast, it was during these blissful Devonshire holidays I
squirmed with excitement at the account of that ghostly pursuit of
the fleeing Smuggler Bill by the desperate and determined Exciseman
Gill. My father often recited from this treasure trove of poetic, narrative legends, the cynical yet infinitely moving "The Execution" and
"The Jackdaw of Rheims" being among his favourites. I incidentally
received my earliest lesson in English grammar from his quoting from
the latter poem: "heedless of grammar, they all cried, 'THAT'S HIM!'"

When the weather was wild and wet, we donned our macs and gum
boots and sallied forth, clambering up slippery paths to the "Berries"
(the rough common land stretching back inland from the perilously
unguarded cliffs' edge) for long walks. Sometimes the force of the gale
threw one, screaming excitedly, to the bilberry- and heather-covered
ground; below us the sea foamed and raged and the waves lashed our
beach. Returned home, dripping and soaking, we stripped and dried
in front of the kitchen stove, and never did cocoa taste better.

Sometimes my mother would visit us, and, there being no room in our cottage for another guest, she would stay at a local hotel up at Buck's Cross on the main road. It must have been quite simple really, but I equated it with the Ritz. Nana, Sarah, and I would collect her in the morning, and we would spend the days together. Sometimes she would take us to Hartland Abbey to lunch with friends of hers, the Stucleys. We always visited the nearby village of Clovelly, which is built up and down a steep cliff, with a precipitous cobbled high street leading to the little fishing harbour: no cars are allowed, and donkeys carry all and sundry up and down. It was then, and is still, always thronged with people in the holiday season. I loved the donkey rides, and the ice creams, and the "tourist trap" shops. Buck's Mills boasted no such amenities, which were indeed considered very common by our grown-ups (although the post office—a long walk up to the top of the village—sold ice creams as well as newspapers). One expedition I enjoyed less was luncheon at the Abbey, for this meant putting on socks and generally tidying up. Our hosts were very kind, but I languished under the longueurs of the conversation, which very properly was not devised for my amusement and seemed to be all about obscure relations of whom I had never heard. But worse was to come: in the afternoon my mother and any other grown-up guests headed for a famous local woodland walk near Clovelly, with wonderful vistas of the sea, known as "The Hobby Drive." I thought it was endless (it is in fact three miles long, which is quite a hike for a child); I used to become excruciatingly bored and always behaved badly—so much so that one year even a genuine blister was attributed to general bolshiness. How pleased I was to get back to dear Buck's, and my beach friends, and endless happy occupations!

FROM THE EARLY DAYS of his marriage to my mother Winston had always been most attentive to their nursery world, regularly reporting its news to Clementine when she was away; now, many years on, he seemed delighted to find nursery life revived and, despite ministerial and parliamentary affairs, seemed always to find time for the "Benjamin" as well as for the older ones. "Mary is flourishing," he wrote to my mother from Downing Street in March 1925, while she was away in Dieppe with her own, dying mother. "She comes and sits with me in the mornings & is sometimes most gracious [I was two and a half at this time]. Diana is just back from school & we are all planning to go and see Randolph [at Eton] this afternoon."

My father and I evidently enjoyed each other's company: "Mary is very gracious to me & spends ½ an hour each morning in my bed while I breakfast," he wrote in February 1926. "Some of her comments are made in the tone & style of a woman of thirty. She is a sweet." The following month he told Clementine, who was travelling in Italy, that I had breakfasted with him, while Diana and Sarah (sixteen and eleven respectively) and he had all dined together. Later in March, when the whole family were sending our birthday greetings to her for 1 April, Winston was evidently much amused that I had observed to his brother, Jack: "Mummie is bored with me so she has gone to Rome."

In October 1927 I was evidently beginning my "London season," and my father wrote to my mother: "Moppet and Maria [pronounced as in "fire"] have shifted their headquarters to London. I looked in on them on my way through and was very graciously received. In fact as I took my leave Maria said to Moppet, who was calling her, 'I must take my visitor downstairs,' which she accordingly did with a great air of ceremony." Mr. and Mrs. Baldwin were obviously most kindly disposed towards me; one day the Prime Minister came down to Chartwell and I was deputed to welcome him. Winston reported the event to Clementine: "Baldwin came to lunch & was greeted with much ceremony by Mary. How women admire power!" And a few weeks later my father had an amusing incident in our London life to report: "Yesterday she encountered Mrs B in the garden and was taken by her into the Cabinet room and introduced together with the pug to a number of people. I said to Moppet 'Was she dressed all right?' meaning, was she tidy? to which Mary replied 'Oh, yes, she (Mrs B) was wearing a nice grey *frock*'!"

During this same absence Winston wrote to Clementine, who was travelling in Italy with Diana, from Chartwell: "What a delightful postcard correspondence you carried on with Mary! She showed them all to me with gt pride. I am sorry she has shifted her Headquarters to London. I shall be alone here next week without the interruptions of her charming prattle & ceremonious entrances."

All these accounts seem to show me as a somewhat "quaint" little person and—except for trying to pour water on a policeman from my first-floor nursery—as, on the whole, a good child. However, I have to record an incident which reveals me as having been perfectly capable of behaving atrociously. In the summer of 1927 my mother commissioned the artist Neville Lewis to paint my portrait at Chartwell. In the book *Studio Encounters* he gave this account of our sittings:

> Mary was an attractive child of about six or seven years old [in mitigation I must point out I was in fact not quite five]. She was to sit the next morning, but when I was ready to start she decided that she was not going to sit and did not want a painting done. She was the most obstinate child I have ever met. Nothing her parents could say made any difference. She would not be painted. She had a very patient governess, who let Mary sit on her knee and read to her to keep her quiet. I pretended to be busy painting her doll, which was on a table next to her, but if she saw me looking at her she would say 'Don't look at me, you are only to paint the doll'. I did a reasonably good job, in spite of the trouble she gave me, and Mr. and Mrs. Churchill were pleased.

The portrait, which I have now, is a delightful picture of a proper crosspatch, with a red face, shiny nose, very blue eyes, and untidy blonde hair.

Jack Churchill's wife, Lady Gwendeline (always called Goonie) was also staying at Chartwell at the time, and she asked Mr. Lewis to paint their only daughter, Clarissa, who was two years older than I. I (justly) fared badly by comparison, Neville Lewis writing: "She

[Clarissa] really was a lovely child. She was a bit older than her cousin and was well behaved, and there was no trouble in getting her to sit still." I don't remember this shaming episode at all, but I well recall my mother telling me in later years how dreadfully naughty I was, and how mortified she and Nana had been by my behaviour.

IN MAY 1929 Parliament was dissolved, and there was a general election. My parents took a house in the constituency (the West Essex Epping Division, later renamed the Wanstead and Woodford Division of Essex) where my father had in 1924 won the seat which he would represent as a Conservative for the remaining forty years of his parliamentary life. Our house for the campaign was The Wood House in the grounds of Copt Hall, a large mansion that had been destroyed by fire: the overgrown ruins seemed very spooky to me. Nana and I were included in the electioneering party, and I remember we girls wore our father's election colours round our hats and drove round with our parents on their vote-raising drives. While Winston was safe at Epping, the Conservatives overall were roundly defeated, and Ramsay MacDonald formed his second Labour government. We therefore said goodbye to No. 11 Downing Street, which would hold many vivid memories for me in later years.

For the next ten years my life was essentially Chartwell-based, with visits to London only for day trips or short visits. For a few years after Winston's serious financial losses in the Great Wall Street Crash in October 1929, my parents either stayed at the Goring Hotel near Victoria Station or rented houses for the parliamentary sessions.

I was now nearly seven, and had received no formal education. Nana must, I suppose, have begun teaching me to read and write, and my mother had started to teach me French. Diana, who (in a model grown-up sisterly way) gave me some French lessons while our mother was away in the winter of 1928, wrote to her that she found she had taught me a "terrific lot already." Strangely enough, the only recollection I have of being slapped by my mother was related to reading a French book in bed with her: I must have worn out her patience, and she gave me a good cuff! Now, in the autumn of 1929, I started to attend a small school in Limpsfield, about four miles from Chartwell—Irwin House. Clementine wrote to Winston: "Mary has become a school-girl! Every morning, arrayed in a blue tunic, white shirt & scarlet girdle Moppet motors her to a little school where she is being taught to read & count." The headmistress was Miss Grace Raikes, a large, tall, and imposing lady with a beehive hairdo. (I wonder if it was a wig?) I started school with the strict instruction—which would certainly not be necessary now—that as I was naturally left-handed I was not to be forced to use my right hand, as was common practice at the time.

Someone who would become a great feature in our lives in school holidays now appeared on the scene—a charming, silver-haired, vivacious Frenchwoman, Madame Gabrielle L'Honoré. Soon after her arrival, Clementine wrote to Winston (who was on a lengthy Canadian-American tour): "Madame L'Honoré is the most tremendous success. She looks like Madame de Pompadour, takes away all Diana's young men from her, & would lure a deaf & dumb ourangoutang to speak French." For the next nine or ten years "Madame" came in the summer, and sometimes in the Christmas holidays too, to teach me French—and she made it all so much fun. Deft with her fingers, she made marvellous marionettes, and we constructed a theatre and presented plays written by ourselves; she was a mine of inventiveness and imagination. To the English books Nana had read to me were now added *Les Malheurs de Sophie, Sans Famille,* and *Les Misérables.*

Because Madame only came to us in holiday time, she was at pains to keep desk work to a minimum: the result was that my spoken French and comprehension were way ahead of my knowledge of grammar and my capacity to express myself in writing. At school I spoke French more fluently and with a much better accent than most of my classmates—and, indeed, of some of the mistresses, which did not increase my popularity; on the other hand, I lagged well behind the other pupils in written work. But Madame's methods gave me a taste for speaking and reading French, and as my parents were strong Francophiles I grew up with a deep attachment to France and its people. I loved listening to my father recount episodes in Gallic history—his great heroine was Joan of Arc. All this was to be an enrichment to me throughout my life.

I now settled down to the usual routine of term time and holidays. In the mornings I had to attend to my animals before breakfast, and when goats joined the menagerie I had to get up really early to feed and milk them and tether them out. Nana and I breakfasted in the dining room, which has lovely arcaded windows, and on some mornings the valley below the house, stretching away to Hever and Penshurst, was filled with swirling mist—sometimes one could not see down to our lakes. Nana used to say: "The sea's coming in! There's a tidal wave! You must escape at once!" The waiting school car was the rescue boat and only I could go: I had while she counted to ten to decide on two things or people I could take with me to safety. I cannot remember if my choice ever varied, but usual choices were my pug dog and my add-a-pearl necklace (I evidently had a prudent streak). On looking back, perhaps dear Nana may have felt a little sad that Mr. Pug and my jewels had priority over her.

For a time in the late afternoons, back from school without yet the slavery of homework, I had freedom to enjoy all my Chartwell occupations, and in spring and summer I soon disappeared into the garden, accompanied by the dogs, perhaps to find Doris Hill, or to visit whatever great projects were in progress. While my father was constructing the redbrick walls which now surround the kitchen garden, he had the delightful idea of building a little one-room cottage in the line of the wall for Sarah and me: it was meant for us both, but Sarah, who had started at boarding school in 1927, outgrew its pleasures fairly soon, and this charming dwelling became known as the Marycot.

My father reported the important occasion of my first public engagement to my mother while she was away on a round of visits with Diana:

Mary's house is growing and I hope to have a treat for you when you come . . . Mary has taken the greatest interest in the work and laid the foundation stone with great ceremony. She was presented with a bouquet by the Prof. [Professor Lindemann] and then manifested a great desire to make a speech. We all had to stand for five minutes while she remained in deep thought, her lips frequently moving over the sentences. In the end she said she regarded it as a great honour to have been called upon to lay this foundation stone and that she hoped she would spend many happy hours in the house when it was finished. (Loud cheers.)

Incidentally, this occasion was also recorded in a picture painted by my father from a snapshot the Prof took of the occasion: it hangs in the studio at Chartwell now.

The Marycot was the source of endless delight and occupation for me and my friends. It had a real small coal range, a dresser, kitchen table, and chairs; china had been specially chosen and there were all the utensils required for baking. Under Nana's tuition I learned to make drop scones and (very rocky) rock cakes, and I am afraid "cottage" teas were inflicted on long-suffering friends and relations. Furnishing the Marycot, and providing extra accessories, gave wonderful opportunities for very welcome presents: Nana particularly outdid herself in imagination and generosity. Just before my seventh birthday, my mother wrote to Winston, who was in America:

Moppet who always thinks of the most enchanting gifts is having a Dove Cot made for her—It will be erected (the night before) near Mary's cottage & she will find in it a pair of white fantail pigeons—I am green with envy as it is much nicer (as usual) than my present which is a tiny brass chandelier with 4 arms to hang from the ceiling of the cottage. You are giving her a lovely swing which (also in the night) will be put up outside the red brick wall. The swing will unhook & a trapeze can be substituted.

NANA WAS A DEVOUT ANGLICAN, and prayers at bedtime were a ritual—always related to the daily happenings of my life, with earnest petitions for the needs of animals and humans alike. My parents were not churchgoers (except for rites of passage), and I do not recall very early experiences of going to church. Chartwell geographically lies in the parish of Crockham Hill, but inasmuch as parochial matters impinged on our family's life we regarded beautiful Norman St. Mary's, Westerham, as "our" church (no doubt my parents were dunned for good causes in both parishes). But in 1930 a very remarkable priest, Melville Williams, aged forty, with his charming, selfless wife, Mary, and their large and still growing family, came to be priest-in-charge at St. Andrew's, a modern church (the present building dating from 1895) in Limpsfield, the village a few miles from Chartwell where I attended school. Melville Williams had fought in the Great War, and then served in India, reaching the rank of captain; he had entered Holy Orders after retiring from the army. A dedicated priest, a brilliant communicator, and a dynamic personality, he soon made waves throughout and beyond the scattered community which was his charge. Nana heard about the lively children's service he held on Sunday afternoons, to which children from far and wide soon flocked. For five years of his time at St. Andrew's, "Father Bill," as he was unstuffily (for those days) known, was to have a profound influence on me, for which I have ever been grateful. Through his children's service we were all grounded in the fundamentals of catechismic knowledge; there was the minimum of "tiny tottery," and we were gradually grafted on to the main worship of the church by attending Sung Eucharist (whose central importance he strongly stressed over Mattins, which most then regarded as the "normal service"). Soon the Mattins congregation consisted of only the more elderly and hidebound parishioners. Mr. Williams had a great feel for language and—reflecting his Welsh background—for choral music and congregational singing.

And of course, at that time the language of the liturgy was that of the 1662 Book of Common Prayer. I was rooted and grounded in that, and have so much of it still by heart—as I have hymns, learned through constant repetition: the simple Victorian verses that have come down the generations, the wonderful rhythms and cadences of Wesley, the poetry and mysticism of George Herbert, and so many others marking the stages of the Christian year and religious experience, as do the collects, with their matchless symmetry—the supreme exemplars, surely, of "Thought for the Day." By sheer accident, governed by the year of one's birth, for Anglicans of my generation our religious education and early churchgoing were steeped in the old Prayer Book and King James Bible, while for younger generations these have become the texts of history or literature lessons. Now we must accept the amiable banality of the successive newer forms of worship, where the search to supply "something for everyone" has resulted in reams of unmemorable language, and a Book of Common Worship which is almost impossible to find one's way about. (Forget about travelling with it—or, a consideration which was certainly present for many of my generation, going into battle with it!)

A great feature of St. Andrew's church life became the yearly Nativity play, written, produced, and directed by Mr. Williams. Performed for several successive nights, this ambitious project engaged the enthusiasm and involvement of our congregation, and many people (some of whom rarely crossed the threshold of any church) were drafted to help with specialized skills in carpentry, stage lighting, costumes, and so on. A fruitful recruiting ground for helpers was the bar at the Carpenters' Arms, the popular pub in Limpsfield Chart (a hamlet southeast of the main village); aunts, cousins, and grandmothers of the performers were eager assistants.

The scenes of the Nativity were depicted on a large stage covering the whole area of the choir, and were introduced by a mother reading the Christmas story to her children at bedtime. During the three or four years this play was performed the younger cast members were promoted from the listening children or shepherd boys on the hill to more prominent roles, according to the rate of individual growth and talent. Thus I progressed from the smallest child to the older, rather bossy one—who was always putting the others in their place—and then to the innkeeper's daughter. Mr. Williams was, I think, the sole arbiter of casting, and some of the "lead parts" revealed unexpected talent in normally quite unremarkable members of the congregation: I remember a thrilling, rather fierce Gabriel, a horrendously frightening Herod, and a wonderfully pompous High Priest, Zachariah (who usually read the Old Testament lessons at Mattins, had a double-barrelled name, and didn't have to act at all). The part of the Blessed Virgin Mary was taken by a different girl every year, and in 1935, the last year the play was performed, I was chosen for the role: Nana coached me for hours, as I had to recite the entire "Magnificat"—the "'Marseillaise' of the Church," Mr. Williams said.

It was during these "St. Andrew's years" that I made some life-lasting friends. I got to know the Williams children very well: when they came to Limpsfield they were five strong, soon to become six with the arrival of Janet; the seventh and youngest, Veronica, born after Mr. Williams had moved to another parish, was to become my god-daughter. In this wonderfully lively family group I naturally gravitated to those round my own age, my immediate contemporaries being Nancy and David—I was generally more at ease with girls than boys, who rather alarmed me, and to the gaggle of Williams brothers I think I must have seemed a rather odd, prissy little creature. It was very salutary for me, brought up virtually as an only child, to experience the rough-and-tumble of parsonage family life. Mary Williams was very sweet to me, and allowed me to help her in the kitchen, where I became quite good at making jellies and large quantities of Bird's Custard.

At this time also Mrs. Saunders and her two daughters, Betty and Eve, who also went regularly to St. Andrew's, came into my life. Margaret Saunders was a rich widow whose largeish house and garden gave on to the golf course at Limpsfield Chart; Betty and I were the same age, and Eve was four years younger. Betty was dark-haired, plain, and partly disabled down her right side from a paralysis sustained at the time of her birth; but she was plucky and tenacious, and managed to keep up with her sister and me pretty well, though the sheer effort of doing so made her seem somewhat dour. Eve—in striking (and painful) contrast—was a pretty, blonde, blue-eyed, fairylike figure, with an easygoing, fun-loving disposition. The girls and I became great friends, and I was often asked to Ballards Mead, with or without Nana. Although she was kindness itself, Mrs. S. somewhat alarmed me: she had very shiny round glasses and a rather loud voice, and seemed to fill whatever room she was in. She genuinely loved music, and participated enthusiastically in singing in church (always having a large hymnbook with the tunes in it, which greatly impressed me); but her voice had a very strange "wobble" to it, which was quite embarrassing if one was in the pew in front of her. She was immensely hospitable, and her house always seemed full of people—including a stream of nice young overseas servicemen and -women whom she had to stay under the auspices of a hospitality organization. A few years on, Eve would marry one of them: a charming, good-looking officer of the Royal Canadian Navy who swept her off to Canada soon after the war.

I had a great deal of fun with Betty and Eve, the Williamses, and other local children of our age-group. Usually organized by Mrs. S. and Nana between them, we had picnics and skating expeditions to the ice rink at Purley, as well as much larking round in the Ballards Mead garden. I particularly remember how "our" grown-ups devised our participation in the parade of floats in Oxted to celebrate the Silver Jubilee of King George V and Queen Mary in May 1935. Our theme was "Fruits of the Empire," and some creative genius built a large wooden construction representing a "tin" of canned fruits which was borne on the Saunderses' car, out of which our group, disguised individually (with varying degrees of success) as fruits from the Empire, were seen to be emerging: it was all great fun, and I think we won a prize. A great personal Jubilee treat for me was being taken by Papa and Mummie to Westminster Hall to witness the King and Queen receiving Loyal Addresses from both Houses of Parliament on 9 May: I was rising thirteen, and it was my first "state" occasion.

It was thanks to the Saunders family that I had my first taste of Scotland; they often took a house in some remote and beautiful part of the Highlands, and invited several friends to stay, including Nana and me. There we children all ran wild in the heather, climbing the mountain, and (predictably) one day losing ourselves in an impenetrable mist: on being found, needless to say, we were all much scolded by the panicked grown-ups. I remember picnics on the wonderful empty beaches near Ardnamurchan Point, and swimming in the crashing breakers—cold; very cold; but not nearly so icy as the dark and rather sinister depths of Loch Awe.

In the early years of her marriage to Winston, and as their nursery increased, Clementine always wanted—and tried—to spend seaside and holiday time with the babies; but as she became increasingly involved in her husband's political life, this became harder to arrange. There was a tug-of-love: Winston loved his children, but he always wanted her with him; much though she loved us, her priority was quite clear—then and always.

By the time I came along, after the agony of beloved Marigold's death, nursery life had been reconstructed with the blessed advent of Nana. But now the three elder children had their pressing claims, and again letters between Winston and Clementine are full of these: Randolph's first reports from Eton; Diana's French family; Sarah's worrying "glands." Inevitably, knowing that I was in Nana's safekeeping—and that, as we have seen, Winston was very good at holding the fort with the stay-at-home child—Clementine concentrated on the bigger ones, especially, of course, in their school holidays. I never even thought about it at the time, but looking back it must have seemed quite strange to outsiders that nearly all my "away" holidays—to Devonshire, to Scotland, and later to France—were with Nana, whose role over the years developed seamlessly from nanny to duenna.

I found a revealing sentence in one of Clementine's letters to a former secretary, Margery Street (Streetie), who had come to us in that year of grief and loss—1921—and had stayed for twelve years before leaving in 1933 to go out to Australia to nurse a desperately ill sister. Clementine missed her very much, and they corresponded regularly thereafter: my mother's letters are full of news about our family and household which Streetie had got to know so well. In September 1934 she wrote from Chartwell with all the news, and, telling Streetie what great delight her birthday telegram had caused me, continued: "She and Nana have just returned from a fortnight spent in Brittany with the Grant Forbes. You know they live quite close at Squerryes & have also a villa near Dinard. Before that they [Mary and Nana] were for the same length of time in Argyllshire with Mrs Saunders (another neighbour) so I have been quite deserted." The pattern of these holiday travels with Nana repeated itself for several summers, and although they freed Clementine to make plans with Winston or the older girls, with long hindsight I see that those Scottish and French jaunts were factors in Clementine's slowly—and at first subconsciously—growing perception that she was increasingly playing an almost peripheral role in my life.

I loved my parents unquestioningly, and my mother I held in considerable awe: I thought her very beautiful, sought to please her, and greatly feared her displeasure. My relationship with Nana was quite different—much more natural and workaday—and I turned to her for everything.

But for a long time I was unconscious of these nuances in our family relationships, and the stars and planets in my child's universe rolled on their appointed courses without collision.

CHAPTER 3

Sisters and Cousins

———

MY CHILDHOOD'S HEROINE, AND MY GREATEST FRIEND, WAS Sarah. Both Diana and Randolph were too far distant from me in age—being thirteen and eleven years my elder—to be part of my scheme of things; while they were (mostly) very nice to me (although I was always rather alarmed by Randolph), and I was gratified if they paid attention to me, they inhabited a different world, higher up the slopes of Mount Olympus—the world of grown-ups. Although Sarah was eight years older than I, until she went to boarding school when she was twelve or so she was part of our nursery world, and under the tutelage of Nana; even after that, in the holidays for quite a time she moved easily between drawing room, dining room, and nursery—and indeed, may have found the cosiness of the nursery a welcome refuge from some of the formalities of adult life. I quite simply adored her: she was my great confidante, and the sympathetic and wise recipient of any complaints or puzzlements I had from time to time about the grown-ups in whose complex universe we both moved.

Our favourite game in the winter and spring holidays was "fox hunting." Both of us were taught to ride at local riding schools, but hunting did not really come our way as children; however, our fertile imaginations transported us to the grandest hunting countries. The rather battered sofa in the nursery at Chartwell had wide upholstered arms, which provided Sarah and me with excellent mounts. Sarah was "Lady Helen," superbly mounted on her thoroughbred sofa arm, beautiful and immaculate in her riding habit, with top hat and veil surmounting her perfectly coiled chignon—the cynosure of all eyes in the hunting field. Her constant companion, whom she treated with condescension and occasional irritation, was myself—"Mrs. Podgy": egregiously named, badly turned out, her wispy bun forever escaping from under her bowler hat, Mrs. Podgy (who rode astride) was mounted on a common, coblike sofa arm, consistent with her lower social and financial status. Lady Helen and Mrs. Podgy made a somewhat ill-assorted pair, and Mrs. P. at times had difficulty in keeping up with Lady Helen, as she galloped ahead when the hounds were in full cry, sailing over fences and hedges: however, Mrs. Podgy could be extremely useful should her elegant friend happen to drop her whip, or decide not to jump a five-barred gate and prefer it to be opened for her. Happy hours were thus spent by us in the "hunting field": Randolph, writing to his mother, waxed positively lyrical about the beauty of Chartwell one springtime, adding: "The weather is very mild—no sun but quite warm. Mary & Sarah however insist on staying in the nursery with all the windows shut."

In term time, a great treat for me was to be deputed, with Nana, to visit Sarah at her school, North Foreland Lodge at Broadstairs on the Kentish coast, for "exeat" weekends, if our mother could not do so herself. I remember some bitterly cold winter visits: Broadstairs must be one of the coldest places in England! Nana and I would stay at a very cosy bed-and-breakfast called the Dutch Tea Rooms and visit Sarah, or take her out, according to the planned programme. As I myself was a day girl throughout my school career (apart from one term as a weekly boarder), Sarah's boarding-school life was of great interest to me, and of course I loved meeting her special friends, several of whom would come to stay at Chartwell in the holidays.

I have a clear memory of a notable event I was allowed to share with Sarah. In 1930 Amy Johnson, the pioneer aviator, made history by becoming the first woman to fly solo from England to Australia. The entire country had followed in the press, and through radio broadcasting (then in its infancy), the various stages of her marathon—and, at that time, extremely hazardous—flight, with bated breath: she was the heroine of the hour, and a song had been written in her honour: "Amy, wonderful Amy . . . ," the words of which we all knew by heart and sang incessantly. A wonderful welcome was prepared for her on her arrival back in this country at Croydon Airport: I don't know whose idea it was, but Nana took me and Sarah to join the crowds waiting for her. It was a very long wait, and we were quite a long way from where she actually descended from the aircraft which had brought her home—but we cheered ourselves hoarse, and thought it all well worth it.

In 1931, rising seventeen, Sarah left North Foreland Lodge and that autumn went to a fashionable finishing school in Paris, kept by three remarkable Frenchwomen, les Mesdemoiselles Ozanne. By now, of course, our days in the hunting field were long since over, and the thrills and spills of the chase had been superseded by hours of listening to the gramophone: Sarah (whose stage ambitions were just awakening) would moon round singing and improvising dances, while I wound up the gramophone, and supplied her audience and corps de ballet. We quite often got shouted at from above by Papa as we tended to have the volume turned up to maximum. Sarah's increasingly grown-up wardrobe was a source of wonder and admiration to me, and, of course, a good deal of dressing up went on: she was wonderfully tolerant of this—as she was of my fiddling round with the clutter of makeup on her dressing table. The "Lady Helen" and "Mrs. Podgy" of our hunting days had by now been reincarnated as "Miss Michaila," the famous dancer and actress, and her faithful (if only fairly competent) secretary, "Miss Smith."

But although Sarah was as sweet and affectionate to me as ever, the difference in our ages, and the fact that she had now definitely joined the grown-ups, made a gulf too wide to bridge in terms of shared amusements or way of life, and quite naturally she and Diana, five years her elder, became and remained bosom friends, sharing their more mature confidences, plans, hopes, and disappointments. In the run-up to Sarah's official debut in 1933, Chartwell visitors came to include girls and young men with whom she had made friends on weekend visits and dances, and with whom she would share the delights, vicissitudes, and longueurs of the then essential rite of passage of "coming out" (an expression which, like the adjective *gay*, has changed its connotation since those days).

I found these new-style visitors a fascinating development, and took a keen interest especially in Sarah's beaux, among whom I had my especial favourites. I used to make myself popular on the tennis court by ball-boying, being especially obliging if any of my favourites was among the players. One of these was Harry Llewellyn: from Wales, he was a true countryman, an accomplished horseman and keen rider to hounds; he tried to get Sarah to enjoy hunting, but although as "Lady Helen" she had led our nursery field she never took to the real thing. Later, after the war, Harry and his wonderful show jumper Foxhunter would become world-famous. It was he who gave Sarah her beautiful chocolate-brown spaniel called Trouble—very aptly named, as it turned out.

A local friend was William Sidney, the heir to nearby Penshurst Place and the barony of De L'Isle and Dudley. He seemed very nice and mild—"Sweet William," they all called him. Often when he arrived to see Sarah, she would not be ready (punctuality was never one of her attributes), and she would dispatch me downstairs to entertain him: many years later he would remind me that I used to play the gramophone records for him to while away the time until Sarah appeared. Bill's mildness belied the qualities which earned him the Victoria Cross on the beaches of Anzio in 1944.

But the "star" among Sarah's boyfriends as far as I was concerned was Dick Sheepshanks. In a letter to Streetie in November 1933 my mother described all Sarah's principal young men, and about him she wrote:

Mr Dick Sheepshanks nephew of the Sheepshanks who was Randolph's Tutor [Housemaster] at Eton. Small dark intel-

ligent grubby bolshy impertinent. A marvellous dancer both
ball-room & acrobatic & 'patter' dancing [tap dancing]. Very
good at games (tennis which pleases me) especially cricket. This
one Sarah's favourite & I think he is rather dangerous. He looks
unscrupulous but Sarah says he isn't. He is employed by Reu-
ter's News agency.

Dick was a bit older than Sarah's other friends, dark, rather cynical-
looking, and—I thought—utterly fascinating. He was very nice to me,
and though I was only twelve I fell hopelessly in love with him. He
demonstrated his left-wing tendencies by refusing to change for dinner; as Sarah recounted:

This was ignored the first time, but the insistence did not go
unremarked by my father.
    'Young man,' he said to Dick. 'What do you do?'
    'I'm at Reuters, sir.'
    The glare softened. 'Good. What department are you in?'
    'Obituaries, sir,' he replied, and the family contorted them-
selves not to laugh.
    After a moment's silence, my father said, 'Have you got a lot
on me?'
    Dick replied, 'Pages and pages, sir.' They became firm friends.[1]

In 1937, during the Spanish Civil War, on which he was reporting
on the Republican side, Dick was killed by flying shrapnel while travelling in an open jeep with three press colleagues. When I heard the
news (I was fifteen) I wept bitterly.

After her "season," for which she had never had much relish, Sarah
embarked on a two-year course in modern dancing at the De Vos
School of Dancing, from where she auditioned for and was accepted
by the famous impresario C. B. Cochran to be one of his "Young Ladies" for his current show, the revue *Follow the Sun,* which opened in
Manchester just before Christmas 1935. The male star of the show

was Vic Oliver; quite soon he and Sarah were in love, and early in the new year they informed Winston and Clementine that they intended to be married. Her parents, not surprisingly, were strongly opposed to the match—Vic, born Victor von Samek, was of Austrian-Jewish extraction, eighteen years older than Sarah, and not yet divorced from his Austrian wife. Their visit to Chartwell was not a success. Sarah confided her love for Vic, and their wish to be married, to me—who, of course, thought it very romantic. I liked Vic at once: then and later he was charming to me, paid me a lot of attention, and gave me very grown-up presents.

Winston and Clementine pressed for a delay, insisting that Sarah must have time to think. Vic went back to America to pursue his theatrical engagements and Sarah, having promised her parents that she would take no sudden action, endured unhappy months of separation, during which the situation introduced an element of strain into her normally loving and easy relationship with her parents. One point Winston stressed dramatically to her was that, quite apart from his and Clementine's dislike of Vic, he had not at that point acquired American citizenship; if he were to remain an Austrian national, Winston told her, "in three or four years you may be married to the enemy and I shall not be able to protect you." Sarah gave him her solemn promise that she would not marry Vic until he had become an American citizen.[2]

At length, realizing that her parents' opposition to the marriage was absolute, and that Vic had no prospect of coming back to England in the foreseeable future, Sarah decided to go to America and join him. He had sent her a ticket, and Sarah quickly made secret preparations. She did, however, tell me of her plans, because the ship, the *Bremen,* on which she had booked her voyage, sailed on 15 September—my fourteenth birthday; she trusted me completely, and was deeply concerned at the thought of my shock and dismay when I heard the news (particularly as it would be on my "special day"). I was charged by her to tell our parents that she loved them dearly, and deeply regretted that she had felt compelled to take this course of action. I felt immensely proud that Sarah should confide in me and entrust me with a task (although, it gradually dawned on me, not a very enviable one) in what I regarded as a highly romantic situation, in which I was completely on her side.

Sarah broke the news to her parents in a letter delivered by hand on the morning of the fifteenth: it so happened that Winston was away in France, so Clementine had to face this grievous shock alone. I can clearly remember the events of this day. Sarah had also sent me a letter; and, despite her hectic rush, she had remembered my birthday and sent me presents—a beautiful glass Madonna and child (I have it still) and some rare stamps for my collection. In her letter she wrote:

My darling Mary, Please forgive me for deserting you on your birthday. Please understand—I wish it were any other day. Many many happy returns—and don't let anyone spoil your birthday. You have been sweet and kind to me—without you some days would have been unbearable . . . In haste, my love to Miss Smith—so capable and patient.

Sarah—Miss Michaila.

When I was summoned to my mother's room, I went with considerable foreboding. I found her in a distraught state, with Nana at her side. The scene is vividly fixed in my memory because—although I had on occasion seen my mother very angry or indignant—I had never seen her cry: now she was sobbing uncontrollably, with the fateful letter in her hand, and it shook me to the core. She told me that Sarah had gone to America despite all her promises, and then—seeing me dumbfounded but silent (and my face showing no surprise)—she asked: "Did you know?" I have to confess I mumbled in shamefaced acquiescence—and, judging that the message Sarah had enjoined me to deliver might not be well received, I failed at this juncture to deliver it. Whatever my mother's feelings about my evident complicity, she never rebuked me. By the afternoon an outward semblance of calm had been restored, and the grown-ups unselfishly devoted themselves to giving me the (as always) lovely birthday party they had planned.

Nearly fifty years later, after Sarah's death, I would find among her papers a very long letter I had written her describing this scene:

CHARTWELL
26TH OCTOBER 1936

My darling Sarah,
There's so much to tell you that I hardly know where to begin!
First of all, thank you so much for the lovely Madonna and the stamps, it was so sweet of you to remember my birthday in the midst of all your worries . . . On my birthday at about eleven, Mummie sent for me; I wondered what it could be; there was no doubt once I got inside the room; I not only smelt one rat, but fifty thousands! And as for cats, why they were slipping out of bags in all directions! Mummie was prancing round, her hair in a turban, her bath towelling dressing gown on, and her face covered with grease! I felt so sorry for her because, she didn't in the least understand how you could want to marry Vic, or how you could run away, she was completely bewildered, and I don't think I've ever seen her so broken down with grief. I was so happy to think that you were at last happy; it was sweet of you to say that I comforted you, I felt I couldn't do much but it was so nice to know that I'd helped . . .

My present memory of that scene (reassuringly) accords with the account of it I wrote at the time—in all but one respect: now I find it painful to acknowledge the flippant and unsympathetic tone of parts of the description I gave to Sarah of my mother's distress. Sarah's long-drawn-out struggle with our parents over her wish to marry Vic, in which I took her part with passionate partisanship, had—I now understand—resulted in my first experience of divided loyalty, and this—combined with normal teenage bolshiness—resulted in my lack of understanding of my parents' (and particularly of my mother's) point of view. Looking back now with the benefit of hindsight, and of the close and loving relationship I was to develop with my mother, I realize I later came to forget these adolescent tensions.

Of course, the whole story of Sarah's dramatic departure "leaked," and was splashed across the newspapers both here and in America, causing Winston and Clementine further mortification. Randolph was dispatched across the Atlantic to try to remonstrate further with her, and American lawyers were enlisted to investigate Vic's marital and nationality status. Despite my loyalty to Sarah, I was painfully impressed by this first object lesson in how children can cause intense distress—even when they love them—to their parents.

Sarah got a dancing role in the same show as Vic, and despite the rigours of touring wrote all her news to me. Replying to her on 2 November 1936, I wrote: "I've just received your letter—Whoopee! How sweet of you to write to me. If you go on keeping on about how lovely New York is, I shall not stay behind to replace those 'that failed,' but fail myself, and come out to you and the Hot Dogs!"

In a later instalment of the same long letter (4 November) I continued:

I'm so happy to think you're at long last going to be married. I should very much like to send you something, but . . . it might get lost so easily, so I think I'll wait now till you come home. When are you likely to? I think you would be received favourably round Christmas; we are all staying here [Chartwell] . . . and it would be so nice if you brought Vic, and if no one else would talk to him, I and my animals would receive him and help him not to feel lonely. Please come home soon! I do miss you so much . . . I don't like staying behind and running messages and telling cooks please will they go to Mrs—, and playing croquet, & having my hair brushed & washed out of my head—where 'others have failed!' So buck up & return 'Sweet dove(s) return' to the bosom of your bigoted family, there to be bored! I don't think I've got much else to say except that I love you & hope you'll be happy with all my heart.

> *With tender love to you both.*
> *Mary. Miss Smith*

Sarah and Vic were married that Christmas Eve in City Hall, New York, their witnesses being his lawyer and a cleaning lady. Vic had by that time become an American citizen—so Sarah had kept her promise to her father. In the New Year they returned to England, where they lived in London, and both pursued their stage careers. Sarah was, of course, received with warmth and love by her parents—and both she and Vic with rapture by me. The attitude of the family as a whole was very much to make the best of it, and that bygones should be bygones. Vic was an agreeable family member, and he developed a pleasant relationship with Clementine; but Winston never got to like him.

With Sarah's departure for America and her marriage, the "nursery" days of our relationship were over; but the love and understanding forged between us in those early years would last, despite our very different characters and the very different courses our lives would take, throughout our lifetimes.

IN 1934, WHEN I was twelve, I left Irwin House and moved up the road to the Manor House School, next to the church in Limpsfield. This was my mother's second choice. She wanted me to go to St. Paul's School in London, but I flunked the entrance exam: I felt much humiliated, and realized I had disappointed her.

The Manor House was primarily a girls' boarding school: about two hundred strong, it also admitted a contingent of about twenty day girls, of whom I was one. The headmistress—Miss Katharine Gribble—was an unusual person. She was exactly of the generation which had lost husbands, lovers, and sweethearts in the Great

War, and I suspect she was a schoolmistress by default. Although she was a brilliant French scholar and a gifted teacher, and highly cultivated in music and literature, I do not think she was a university graduate. She was nearly very beautiful, with piercing blue eyes and silvery hair, and her very feminine appearance and style of dressing was most un-headmistressy: she wore long, romantic dresses (in the style made fashionable years later by Laura Ashley), with immaculate ruffles at wrist and throat, and her manner of address was like a rushing torrent—mostly in French, in which tongue one was meant to respond: thanks to Madame L'Honoré, I scored rather well here. Although there was a "Mademoiselle," Miss Gribble herself taught French throughout the school, and there was a French-speaking table in the dining hall, to which captives were committed by rotation. Miss Gribble was the only teacher who ever managed to instil in me some rudiments of French grammar: some of her axioms stick even now in my memory and come to my rescue: *"Les fleurs que j'ai mise sur la table hier sont mortes aujourd'hui."* Goodness, how sad!—and a frequent occurrence, I have found—but a rule unforgettably learned. Miss Gribble would at times make dramatic gestures or interjections in the normal routine: one such at the end of prayers left the assembled school and staff agape. Instead of ending with the usual "Grace," she closed her books and, staring fixedly at us all, declaimed: "For God's sake—let us not live to be useless!"—and marched out of the Assembly Hall.

Like most headmistresses with pronounced personalities, La Gribble aroused violent extremes of like or dislike among her pupils. The younger ones were astonished or abashed by her excessive enthusiasms; the older ones, embarrassed by her manner, either were dumbstruck or, if among the braver (or bolshier?) sixth formers, adopted a non-receptive, verging-on-the-hostile attitude which later on, in my army days, I learned to recognize as that most effective and disconcerting of weapons known as "dumb insolence."

I was to be at the Manor House for nearly five years and was fairly happy there, despite being very bad at lacrosse and netball (I was better at games in the summer term, as I swam well and was a goodish tennis player). I longed to be popular—which I certainly was not. Having lived up to this time almost exclusively in the company of grown-ups, I tended to prefer talking to the older girls and the mistresses, which was neither practicable nor likely to endear me to my contemporaries and classmates. At academic work I was a plodder, though I mostly liked learning—except for loathsome maths. Overall, I think I would have been quite unhappy if it had not been for three loyal and companionable friends: Jean Edwards, Rose Jackson, and Pat Tickell. All four of us are widowed now, and still in touch from time to time.

During term time I had a busy life, as I explained in a long letter to Sarah started on 26 October 1936 (after she had gone to America), which I wrote in instalments over nearly a fortnight: "I must stop here till tomorrow, it is 6.15 [a.m.] & I must go and do my goats, canaries and dogs before going to school! Au revoir!" Nine days later I continued: "I'm sorry this letter is written in short instalments, but you see I have so little time to do anything, as I don't arrive home till 6.45, then supper at 7.30 & bed . . . so all my letter writing is done before I get up in the morning, today I am writing at twenty minutes to six!"

At weekends, and in the school or parliamentary holidays—unless my parents were away—Chartwell throbbed with life. The most frequent "stayers" were my uncles and aunts with their children: usually they came family by family, diluted with other guests, but at Christmas they were all squeezed in at the same time or spread over the New Year. The family fell into two groupings as follows: Uncle Jack, my father's only sibling, younger than he by five years, Aunt Goonie and their children, Johnny, Peregrine, and Clarissa; and Aunt Nellie, my mother's younger sister, Uncle Bertram Romilly and their two boys, Giles and Esmond—totally inappropriately known as "the Lambs."

The "Jacks" were closer as a group to Winston and Clementine and their older children, both in ages and because during the First World War the two families had combined households and nurseries both in London and at Lullenden. Johnny and Peregrine were close contemporaries of Diana, Randolph, and Sarah (indeed, Peregrine and Sarah, only eighteen months apart in age, were bosom companions). By now the days of the frolics in the tree house, from which I had so much minded being excluded as a small child, were long past, and all these older ones had moved on to different enthusiasms and more grown-up enjoyments.

Clarissa was only two years older than I, but our personalities were very different—she was a reserved child, and seemed to have been created "grown up" all in one fell swoop; I must have seemed odd to her with my more extrovert nature and with my animals and family of dolls, so we were not great companions for one another. Aunt Goonie doted on her lovely flaxen-haired, blue-eyed only daughter, and showered her with fulsome affection and solicitude: although I was somewhat embarrassed by this (as probably Clarissa was too), I remember being considerably shocked by her icy indifference to her mother's displays of affection.

Aunt Goonie's personality—kind, but remote—and her subtle, elusive style of beauty were not easily appreciated by a child. Uncle Jack, on the other hand, was a great favourite of us all: he was genial and easygoing, and he had a particular talent that was a universal delight— he could play a wide repertoire of tunes by striking his nails against his front teeth! His rendering of the national anthem was particularly splendid.

The two Hozier sisters were very different in both character and temperament. Nellie was much easier-going and less highly strung than Clementine. Large and amiable, she was a chain-smoker, and her clothes always seemed dusty with ash. She invariably carried a large and capacious handbag: "I could leave for Peru today," she would say as she rummaged in its depths. However, from the time of her marriage to Colonel Bertram Romilly of the Scots Guards in 1915, her life had been dogged by difficulties. The Romillys were badly off financially—an unfortunate circumstance not improved by Nellie's being a compulsive gambler (like her mother). Uncle Bertram had suffered a severe head wound in the war, and although his brain was unaffected he was particularly sensitive to noise and stress; in consequence he made a very ineffectual father to his lively sons, born two years apart. Nellie always tried to protect him from childish uproars, and the upbringing of the boys largely devolved on her: it was unfortunate in these circumstances that she was suffocatingly over-maternal, over-indulged them, and was wont (in front of them) to inform her friends and relations and their contemporaries how beautiful and brilliant they were.

It was not until many years later that I learned from Sarah's autobiography that the Romilly boys were most unpopular with their Churchill cousins:

> We Churchills had a definite antipathy towards them, and this was to grow through the years until we were all properly grown up and affection was restored. The early antipathy was made stronger by the fact that their mother would insist on calling them, right into their teens, 'My darling angelic boys, Gy-gy and Ese-wee', when they both had respectable names like Giles and Esmond—and a very fair share of brains.[3]

Protecting her fragile husband, Nellie would stand loyally by her sons (especially Esmond) through a series of adolescent peccadilloes. Later, Giles would be a prisoner of war in the grim fortress prison of Colditz, and in 1941 Esmond, a navigating officer in the Canadian air force, would be lost (missing, presumed killed on active service) over the North Sea. Still, despite trials and tragedy, Nellie would remain debonair, gallant, and undaunted, and with her winning charm and gregarious nature, throughout her life she made a host of friends. Winston was very fond of her—"la Nellinita," he would call her—and despite some sisterly tiffs, Clementine and Nellie were devoted to each other. The Romilly family often stayed at Chartwell.

Not used to boys, I was wary of Giles and Esmond—but anyway, being six and four years older than I, they were in the group of "Big Ones," so I did not have a great deal to do with them. Inasmuch as I did, I greatly preferred Esmond to his elder brother: Esmond was brusque and noisy (and of course treated me with disdain), but was usually quite kind, in a rough sort of a way, and with his freckly face, snub nose, and fair hair he was infinitely preferable in my eyes to Giles, who had smooth, dark looks and was very standoffish and supercilious. I usually kept out of the way of both of them, but in the Easter holidays when I was about eight Esmond decided that I should learn to ride a bicycle: so one morning he took me down to the tennis court to teach me. He was an impatient instructor, and his method consisted of vigorous shoves accompanied by yells of: "Pedal! You idiot—pedal!" I was panic-stricken, and fell off several times—but I did learn to ride a bicycle. I never got a kind word, but I adored him despite his tyrannical ways.

Both boys were sent to school at Wellington, and in their midteens first Giles, and then Esmond, became communists; then, in 1934, Esmond ran away from school amid a blaze of publicity. In the run-up to all this, he drew attention to his political beliefs while staying at Chartwell by sporting a black Homburg hat and refusing to wear a black tie for dinner (the latter sartorial gesture seems to have been an accepted way in upper-class circles at that time of expressing left-wing revolt). Unfortunately this bold act fell rather flat, as his uncle Winston failed to notice his nephew's incorrect attire.

Round this time, when I was about eleven, I became a victim of Esmond's political convictions. We were both in quarantine for some childish affliction (German measles, I think) that required us to be isolated: we were therefore forced into each other's company, much to Esmond's disgust. To while away the time he tried to teach me to play cards, which proved a dismal failure—so we turned to conversation. Esmond lay on the bed, and, lighting a cigarette—which I thought very wicked and daring—proceeded to test out my religious belief.

"I don't believe in God," he said. "It's absolute tosh!"

"Well, I do," I said.

"Anyway, I bet I can make you deny Jesus Christ in sixty seconds flat," Esmond taunted.

I said: "No, you couldn't."

Esmond got up and drew a washbasin full of cold water, frogmarched me to it, and held my head down. After two dousings I of course denied my Saviour.

NOTHING GLOWS SO CLEARLY in my memory of my childhood and teenage years as the Chartwell Christmases. My excitement and anticipation mounted during the preceding weeks, particularly as just outside the day-nursery door was a poky closet that was usually of no significance but, as Christmas approached, became tantalizingly known as the "Genie's Cupboard," and was strictly out of bounds: here my mother and Nana spent a good deal of time in secret conclave, accompanied by much rustling of paper. Then I used to watch the gardeners bringing in the Christmas tree, and transforming the house with ivy, holly, and laurel branches: although modern decorations are very glamorous with their glittering effects and twinkling lights, I can still remember how beautiful was the effect of the different textures of the entwined leaves, and the gradations of the lustrous greens. A great bunch of mistletoe was hung strategically in the front hall, and a large and beautiful Della Robbia plaque of the Christ child in swaddling clothes gazed pensively down upon us.

Then there was the excitement of the arrivals—aunts and uncles and cousins of all ages, whom I was deputed to conduct to their quarters. The only "outsiders" that I can remember were our two regular "bachelors," Professor Lindemann (the Prof) and Eddie Marsh (more of these two in the next chapter), whom my parents regularly rescued from cheerless Christmastimes.

When we were all assembled on Christmas Eve, the double doors between the drawing room and the library would be flung open to reveal the lighted Christmas tree, radiating a delicious piny, waxy smell from the white candles, painstakingly lit with tapers by Nana and a responsible helper: it was a beautiful sight. Predictably, one year—it was 1932—the tree caught fire, and was ablaze in mere seconds. Esmond, aged fourteen, wrote this graphic account in his diary:

The Christmas tree caught fire in the afternoon, which I thought rather exciting. Aunt Clemmie and Mummy lost control of themselves (the former just screamed out: 'Shout fire!', while the latter rushed about the room, alternately shouting and doing silly things like opening windows. I must say I expected her to be more useful in that sort of situation.) Cousin Moppet [Nana] was absolutely in her element. She, of course, got the fire extinguisher and put out the fire. I think she slightly enjoyed the comparison between her and Mummy, Randolph (who did nothing) and Aunt Clemmie. But I think she also slightly despised them. I thought I myself was rather clever. I stood there at first, thinking what a marvellous blaze it was, slightly lost my head, and thought of getting out of the front door. However, I then saw Cousin Moppet rush in with a fire extinguisher, followed by Mary who was sobbing hysterically, with a large basin of water. This I seized from her in a masterly fashion and poured it over the blaze, which was now completely under the control of Cousin Moppet. I at least impressed Mummy. Questioned by her this morning as to the part I played, I replied that I had rushed out to get water, and what's more I think I believed it when I said it.*

The Christmas party usually seems to have prolonged itself over the New Year. Amusements and activities were not hard to come by: in the year of the "Great Snow"—1927–28—the lane below Chartwell was so deep in drifts that a tunnel had to be bored through to allow traffic to pass; there was skating on the big lake, the older children made a wonderful igloo, and my father created a splendid life-size snowman.

* In the account I gave of this incident in the biography I wrote of my mother, *Clementine Churchill,* first published in 1979 and revised and updated in 2002, I wrote that Randolph had fetched the fire extinguisher and put out the fire: evidently my memory played me false, and I am glad to have found a truer eyewitness account in Kevin Ingram's *Rebel: The Short Life of Esmond Romilly.*

Amateur theatricals were a special feature in 1933: the dining room made a good theatre with its dividing curtains, and my mother wrote a lively account of it all to Streetie.

We all acted at Christmas—even me! You will hardly believe that. We (Sarah, Mary & myself) acted a short play by Gertrude Jennings called 'Mother of Pearl' . . . I took the part of a dirty old tramp & I enjoyed it enormously . . . Mr. Gurnell the Chemist came & made us all up. Then there was a thriller called 'The Hand in the Dark' in which Mrs Romilly, Sarah & Esmond performed. They wrote it themselves & it was really quite gruesome.

We gave 3 performances 3 days running & you can imagine the disorder of the house. Nana prompted & produced & was very severe! Mr Pug [Winston] was too sweet. He said it was all lovely & that I was so tragic I made him cry!

CHAPTER 4

Growing Up with Grown-ups

APART FROM OUR CLOSE RELATIONS, THE MOST FREQUENT "OUT-side" guest at Chartwell during my youth was Professor Lindemann (later Viscount Cherwell), known to us all as "the Prof": he had been my father's friend since the early twenties, and up to the outbreak of war in 1939 his signature appears in the Chartwell visitors' book 112 times. The son of a French-Alsatian father and an American mother, he was brought up in England, though educated also in Germany and France. He was a brilliant scientist, and for nearly forty years was Winston's close friend and his mentor on all scientific matters: during the twenties and thirties he was Professor of Experimental Philosophy (Physics) at Oxford University and head of the Clarendon Laboratory there. All these distinctions of course were way beyond my understanding or interest—I only knew him as a prominent figure in Chartwell life and the great friend of both my parents (my mother particularly enjoying his company, as he was a first-class tennis player). The older children also liked him very much, and he was extremely helpful and hospitable to Randolph during the latter's time at Oxford. But for me he was just a remote, though benevolent, presence. However, there was one side of this curious person which riveted both Sarah and myself: the Prof was a strict vegetarian, and my mother took immense pains to see he was provided with delicious special dishes. He said he liked eggs, but Sarah and I used to observe with astonishment how he would meticulously remove the yolks, consuming only the whites.

The next most frequent nonfamily visitor was Eddie Marsh (later Sir Edward). A former civil servant, he had been private secretary to my father throughout his ministerial career before the war, and had become a close personal friend of both Winston and Clementine. He was immensely erudite—a classical scholar, and a patron of the arts and literature—and was Winston's literary mentor, consulted on all my father's books. To a child he seemed too extraordinary for words, with his bushy eyebrows and slate-squeak voice.

Other "regulars" were two of my mother's first cousins on her mother's side, Sylvia Henley and her younger sister Venetia Montagu.* During my mother's difficult childhood (her parents were separated and were on very bad terms) she had stayed a great deal with her Stanley cousins, and her nearest contemporaries among their large family, Sylvia and Venetia, were to remain lifelong friends. Both widowed by the 1930s, they were women of exceptional intelligence and culture, possessing highly developed critical faculties and having inherited the forthrightness which was—and is!—a Stanley characteristic. Winston had always liked them, and found them stimulating company; I was much in awe of them. Cousin Venetia's only daughter, Judy, was two years younger than I, and although later on we were to become the greatest of friends, we did not take to each other as children.

Another woman friend of my parents who was much part of the Chartwell scene in the thirties was Horatia Seymour. When Clementine had made her debut, Horatia, who was a few years older and, like Clementine, both beautiful and badly off, had initiated a friendship that would last their lifetimes; when Clementine married Winston, Horatia was one of her bridesmaids. Winston greatly enjoyed her company, for she was both clever and—a lifelong Liberal herself—au courant with the political events of the day. Despite her great beauty, Horatia never married, but she was always in demand as a guest in elegant social

* Daughters of the fourth Baron Stanley of Alderley (later fourth Baron Sheffield).

and political circles. In 1931 she took the lease of Wellstreet Cottage, a charming small house along the road from Chartwell, in the construction of which Winston himself took a considerable part: its first inmates were Winston and Clementine themselves (plus Nana and myself), who took refuge there when the "big house" was shut up for the winter months to effect a major economy in the wake of the Wall Street Crash in 1929, in which Winston suffered great financial loss. However, by 1931 this draconian economy had been abandoned, and they were delighted to find an excellent tenant for Wellstreet in their great friend Horatia Seymour, who made a most agreeable neighbour.

"Miss Seymour" (as she was to me) became a great feature of my life: she was exceptionally kind to me, and used to ask me to tea without Nana, which I thought very grown-up. A very good pianist, she introduced me to some of the treasures of music: Bach's "Jesu, Joy of Man's Desiring" I first heard played by her, and it became a lifelong joy for me. She may well have thought (and rightly) that while the English language, spoken and written, was well represented in my education, music was notably lacking. Having said that, she also helped to broaden my literary knowledge. Although Nana read so many books to me—and of course, by now I was reading a good deal for myself—it was Horatia Seymour who introduced me to Jane Austen, reading aloud to me *Pride and Prejudice.* Hers was a wonderfully enriching friendship for a growing girl, and, happily for me, it was one that would carry over into adulthood.

OF COURSE, I ALSO GOT to know all the local "regulars." Desmond Morton, who lived down in the valley near Edenbridge, came and went frequently, and would be closeted with Papa: as head of the Industrial Intelligence Centre, he was throughout the thirties a regular source of valuable information to Winston about German industry and the covert manufacture of armaments. To this, of course, I was oblivious, but what I did know from the grown-ups was that in the Great War he had been shot through the heart and miraculously survived; that the bullet was still lodged in his heart; and that, if it were to move, he would drop dead. As well as the long sessions with my father, Major Morton played a lot of vigorous tennis with my mother, and I have to confess that this knowledge added (for both Sarah and myself) a certain apprehension or piquancy to watching them play. (I must add that Sir Desmond, as he later became, after a long and distinguished career, died in his bed.)

As Chartwell was only an hour's drive from London, to the five or six houseguests would very often be added several more for luncheon: Duff and Diana Cooper, John and Hazel Lavery, Lord and Lady Camrose, and Max Beaverbrook were among these. To accommodate greater numbers, Nana and I and any child guest would have our own *katzen tisch* (cats' table), and if luncheon was very prolonged, we children were allowed to slip away; but if one was at the "big table," one had to stick it out. This was not very hard if Papa was in reciting vein, or a row blew up over politics—especially if the argument was with Duff Cooper, the veins on whose forehead would stand out in a most terrifying way! I later learned that this feature, well known to his friends, was described as "veiners."

Lady Colefax, one of the few London hostesses who was anti-appeasement, and in general politically *bien pensant* according to the Churchill coterie, also greatly intrigued me, as I heard her referred to by my parents as a tremendous "lion hunter." Oh, how I longed to hear her no doubt thrilling tales, rather than her political views! But on the one occasion when a gap occurred in the general conversation and I tried to seize my chance to ask her if she'd shot any lions lately, I found myself suddenly, literally, almost smothered by my sisters—and urgently sent on an errand.

My father's love for, and great preoccupation with, painting, which had begun in the dark days of the Dardanelles crisis in the First World War, led to some of my parents' warmest and most rewarding friendships. His first mentors had been John and Hazel Lavery (he a celebrated portrait painter, she a considerable artist herself): they were neighbours in London, and had descended on Hoe Farm, the house my parents had taken for the summer of 1915, summoned by Clementine to help and advise when Winston first was gripped by the idea of painting. Starting him off on what was to prove a lifetime passion, the Laverys were indeed his "painting godparents." A little while later, when Winston was serving on the Western Front, during his periods of leave at home he would spend hours in John Lavery's studio. That was several years before I was born, but in the twenties and thirties the Laverys were regular visitors to Chartwell; Sir John and Winston would disappear to the studio, leaving Hazel Lavery and Clementine to talk. My mother always emphasized to me what a great beauty Lady Lavery was—and now, from my present perspective, I see from photographs and portraits that she was indeed outstandingly beautiful: of American-Irish extraction, she was a passionate Irish Nationalist, and when independent Eire printed its own first banknotes her striking profile represented the newly fledged nation. All this was explained to me by Mummie, who was very fond of Hazel, but as a child I thought her very odd—wrinkled and wild-looking, with very crudely coloured red hair. Tinting in those faraway days was primitive, and "dyed" hair (the euphemistic contemporary terms of *highlighting* and *lowlighting* not having been coined) was not owned up to but mentioned only in hushed tones.

The next major influence on Winston's painting was W. R. Sickert, who, then at the height of his fame, came into my father's life in 1927, when Winston was Chancellor of the Exchequer. Mr. Sickert had been a friend of Lady Blanche and her children (Clementine was about fifteen at the time) when they lived for a short while in Dieppe, where he was a longtime resident, but Clementine and this friend of her girlhood had not met for twenty years when he and Winston were introduced. The two men took to each other at once, and my father had some long teaching sessions at No. 11; Mr. Sickert also came down to Chartwell several times. I'm sorry not to recall meeting this great painter, who was also an eccentric and fascinating personality: I was only five or six at the time, and had not as yet been promoted to the dining room for luncheon.

The French painter Paul Maze was, for a time, a frequent visitor to Chartwell: he and Winston had met in the war, but it was not until the midthirties that they became close friends. Not only was Maze a stimulating "companion of the brush," whose advice and ebullient companionship Winston much enjoyed, but—as an ardent Anglophile and follower of political affairs—he saw in Winston the great champion of Anglo-French cooperation, and as the thirties wore on he shared Churchill's sombre view of the darkening international scene. Paul was, I thought, a very jolly (if rather noisy) guest, and particularly kind to me, giving me at Christmastime in 1933, when I was eleven, a very beautiful charcoal drawing of the Thames near Tower Bridge. (I didn't really appreciate this extremely generous present then, I'm afraid.) Although I did not sense it at the time, my mother did not care for Paul— I think the dislike was probably mutual—and found his frequently recurring visits tiresome, and so eventually they ceased. However, Paul and Winston maintained their friendship through the ensuing years.

But the painter-friend of my parents who became a great feature in all our lives during the thirties was William Nicholson. He started coming down to Chartwell in 1933—the year of my parents' Silver Wedding—when a group of their friends commissioned him to paint a conversation piece. Nicholson by then was a highly esteemed artist and at the height of his repute as a portrait painter. Of enormous and idiosyncratic charm, he soon became a favourite with all the Churchill family. Sittings for the picture were a pleasure, not a tribulation, although we all thought it quite curious that he chose to paint Winston and Clementine having breakfast in the dining room *à deux,* for in the course of their long married life our parents had rarely breakfasted together—indeed, my father specifically attributed the happiness of their union in part to this fact! But this use of artistic licence resulted in a delightful painting, and the artist caught his sitters' characteristic attitudes and likenesses. For me—then as now—the picture captures all the charm of the Chartwell dining room: it shows a sunny day, with the door into the garden open; through it has strolled one of my numerous bantams looking for crumbs; the newspapers are spread on the table, and on them is lying Tango, the adored and indulged marmalade cat.

Sittings over for the day, William would occupy himself in a variety of ways. He painted many lovely pictures at Chartwell, of the harvest fields, or the black swans; sometimes he and Winston would sit side by side painting the same view—for example, a sunlit scene by the swimming pool (today, their versions of this subject hang side by side in the studio). From my Scottish holiday in the summer of 1934, I wrote:

> *Darling Papa,*
> *We have just arrived in the 'Western Highlands'. I wish you and*
> *Mr. Nicholson would come up here and paint, as the scenery is very*
> *beautiful and wild.*

My mother, apart from being captivated as we all were by Mr. Nicholson, warmly welcomed his influence on Winston's painting, chiefly in the "softening" of his palette.

When not occupied in painting, "S'William" (as we called him after he had been knighted in 1936) would quite often come to the nursery, where we would play a lovely game he had invented: he would cover a piece of paper with oval and rounded shapes—tier upon tier of them—to represent a football crowd, and then we all had to draw in the features and the expressions. He would also draw my pug dog, and he never tired of sketching the beautiful Tango: I have several of these drawings still. And, as I have earlier recounted, my family of ill-assorted dolls were all drawn for me by this charming, eccentric man.

S'William was as much fun as a companion out of doors as indoors, his skill as an expert boomerang thrower (I do not know in what circumstances he acquired this outlandish skill) adding excitement and an element of apprehension to any country walk in his company. Indoors once more, we would all admire (and unsuccessfully try to emulate) his skill with *le bilboquet* (cup-and-ball). He was sweet and indulgent to me, and on several occasions invited Nana and me to luncheon with him in his enchanting small house, 11 Apple Tree Yard, St. James's. This was a wonderful treat, with its unvarying menu of two grilled herrings each and mustard sauce.

A regular transatlantic summer visitor in the thirties was the American financier and elder statesman Bernard Baruch, who had started life as an office boy and made a fortune by speculation. He was a near contemporary of Winston, and the two men had met in 1918 when Winston was Minister of Munitions and Baruch a commissioner on the American War Industries Board; they had become great friends, and remained so thereafter. Bernie Baruch was immensely tall—certainly the tallest person I had ever seen—with white hair and piercing eyes: he was extremely benevolent to me, but I was in great awe of him. I told my mother that I was sure Jehovah looked exactly like him; Mummie repeated this to Mr. Baruch, who was not at all displeased.

As well as the regular "stayers" and "lunchers" there were some very thrilling "shooting stars." On a visit to Hollywood in 1929, Winston had met and greatly taken to Charlie Chaplin; so when the latter was in England two years later, he was invited to Chartwell. His first visit was in February 1931, when Clementine was away in America with Randolph, who was on a lecture tour. Winston wrote her this account of Charlie's visit:

> Last night we had Charlie Chaplin to dinner. Jack [Churchill] and Johnnie [his son] came from London and slept the night. Bracken and Boothby motored down for dinner. Mary stayed up by special arrangement and seemed absolutely thrilled by Charlie. He has been wonderfully received in this country and treated with far more honour than any Royalty. He made himself most agreeable, and with much good nature performed various droll tricks . . . Diana also came to dinner looking very pretty, and got on very well with the great man.

Among the "various droll tricks," as Winston described them, was a brilliant impersonation of Napoleon, using a coat and hat snatched from the coat cupboard. Charlie was over in England for the premiere of his film *City Lights,* which in due course I was taken to see. Later that year, in September, Charlie came to Chartwell again, when a very good photograph was taken: sadly for me, I was not included in the lineup—however, my pug dog squeezed in!

One guest who made an indelible impression on me was Colonel Lawrence—Lawrence of Arabia, who came to Chartwell three times in the thirties. He and Winston had first met and seen a great deal of each other in Cairo, when Winston was Colonial Secretary and the whole shape and future of the Middle East was under discussion. This extraordinary scholar-hero, who had organized the Arab army in its revolt against the Turks in 1916, and had ridden with them into Damascus, had later written the account of his exploits in his celebrated book *The Seven Pillars of Wisdom*. Winston admired and liked him, as did Clementine, and they had all become friends: but Lawrence was not an easy colleague—and, as Winston once remarked, he had a strong propensity for "backing into the limelight." In 1922 Lawrence had joined the RAF as an aircraftman, under the name of Ross; in 1927 he changed his name by deed poll to Shaw.

My parents had of course told us children about Aircraftman Shaw's true identity, and about his amazing adventures in the desert, and we knew he was a hero. He would arrive, dressed in his air force uniform, with a great roar on his motorcycle (which would—alas—prove to be fatal), and I always tried to be round to greet him; I liked him very much, and noticed his piercing blue eyes and intense manner. On one occasion when he was staying, my father told me to come down to the drawing room in my dressing gown before dinner, as there was a surprise for me. And indeed there was—for sitting there was my friend, attired in the robes of a Prince of Arabia!

I have a clear memory of a summer's morning, very early—I had been down to the stables looking after my goats; as I was returning to the house, I discovered my "friend" strolling on the lawn. So I joined him, and together we walked up and down, making footprints in the dew-drenched grass. I wish I could remember what he said: I'm sure I prattled away about my animals.

My parents evidently had guessed at Lawrence's lonely life, and had invited him to spend the Christmas of 1933 with us all: he wrote a charming letter to my mother on 17 December, regretting that he could not accept her invitation because he was moving into his cottage, Clouds Hill:

Dear Mrs. Churchill,

That was a very kindly idea of yours, but this Christmas is reserved for a most important occasion in my life. In it I inaugurate my cottage.

Perhaps that does not sound important enough to you, so I will explain. Years and years of living in suitcases and barracks eventually gave me the feeling that I wanted a home—and close by the Tank Corps camp in which I then lived (1923) there stood a ruined cottage in a clump of rhododendrums [sic] on the heath. Egdon Heath, Hardy called the district.

It is a heather and copse upland, between Dorchester and Poole. So I bought the ruin . . . and with the proceeds of my Arabian gold dagger I floored and roofed it. The walls were sound. For the ten years since I have been patching it, and buying equipment for it, and collecting books and gramophone records for its furnishing. I have put in water and a bath (no drain!) armchairs (no bed) a table . . . There is no paint or paper or plaster, no brass or copper, no cooking place, no grates, no pots or pans. Sancta simplicitas in stainless steel, very labour saving. No gardening: just wild bushes and heath and trees . . . The intention this Christmas, as I began by saying, is to inaugurate the cottage. I have camped in it, now and then, for odd nights: but this time I have three consecutive days and nights of freedom. I am going to sit in the finished cottage, and see if it is good.

. . . So you see, I'm quite exclusively booked for Christmas, upon a vital experiment. That does not lessen your kindness in asking me to Chartwell. Chartwell is a nice name, but my cottage is called Clouds Hill. Good, don't you think, for an airman's retirement?

I hope you and Winston are well: and that he is thinking more of Marlborough II than of the House of Commons. I grudge the time he spends on those dull parties. Governing is one thing: politics another, surely.

High time this letter ended. I hope to come to your door, suddenly, one
day—and find you in!

Yours ever,
T. E. Shaw

True to his word, Aircraftman Shaw paid Chartwell another visit
quite soon, on 25–26 February 1934: this is the last time his signature
appears in the visitors' book. The following letter was his "thank-you."
It would seem he had left in a hurry on account of bad weather conditions (very important if you are on a motorbike!).

13 BIRMINGHAM STREET,
SOUTHAMPTON.
[UNDATED: BUT SOON AFTER MON. 26 FEBRUARY 1934]

Dear Mrs Churchill
This is really to say 'Goodbye' to Mary: I missed her at the last moment, as I
came down from disturbing Winston out of a wisdom sleep.
  Please tell her I'm sorry about it, and also because there hasn't been any
rain out here. The merry little snowstorm that faced me for half an hour on
Monday somehow missed Dorsetshire . . .
  If I take a course of swimming lessons meanwhile, will I qualify to visit
you once more in the summer? Or would ability to stoke a boiler do instead?*
Chartwell's inhabitants are as exciting as mixed drinks and much better in
taste. Also I got my 'Crises' inscribed.†

Yours sincerely,
T. E. Shaw

---

* Clearly a reference to the huge boiler Winston had installed to heat the new swimming pool, completed in the summer of 1933.
† His volumes of WSC's *The World Crisis,* my father's history of the First World War,
published between 1923 and 1927.

T. E. Shaw left the RAF in 1935. In May that year, returning home, he had an accident near Clouds Hill and was thrown from his motorbike: he died from his injuries a few days later, on 19 May, aged only forty-six. I had whooping cough that spring; Nana and I went down to Buck's Mills in May for me to recuperate, and it was there that I heard the news—first of the accident, and then of the death of my fabulous friend. I was deeply shocked, and I remember poring over the details in the newspapers.

The only other grown-up whose death had touched me closely up to now had been that of my great-aunt Maude—Nana's mother— who had died after rather a long illness (cancer, I think) in 1933, aged seventy-four. Nana had gone home to the "creaky" house in Lansdowne Road to help nurse her, and for a term I became a weekly boarder at Irwin House.

Although I was a little frightened of her, I loved Aunt Maudie dearly, and she was a great feature of my childhood. I knew she was very ill, and I had been gently, but quite realistically, prepared by Nana, who wrote to me regularly; but it was Sarah who told me that she had died, and walked me round and round the kitchen garden while I cried. In a letter to Nana the same day Maudie died—3 April—I wrote: "I am trying not to cry because it is not sad for Maudie, for her it is glorious happiness; she has gone to her perfect rest." Two years later, I found this Christian acceptance harder to apply to my "Prince of Arabia."

One afternoon when I was about fifteen, my father took me with him when he went to visit the great Ll.G.—Lloyd George—who lived at Churt in Surrey (his house was named Bron-y-de, Welsh for "slope of the south"), an easy drive from Chartwell. I remember he received us in a very comfortable summerhouse at the top of the garden. I was of course thrilled to see my father's great colleague and chief, for whom he nurtured glowing admiration and affection, and about whom I had quite frequently heard my parents speak. My mother, who had been his ardent supporter in the years of the great radical Liberal reforms of Mr. Asquith's government before the Great War—and while acknowledging Ll.G.'s magnetic charm (particularly towards women)—

had always had a reserve in her feelings for the "Welsh wizard," and she had an inconvenient memory for his slyness which, if she warmed to the topic, she roundly called "treachery."

I was strongly and immediately struck by the great man's white locks, his animation, and his celebrated Celtic charm. Over the tea-cups he and my father plunged instantly into political talk, while I occupied myself contentedly with the scones and delicious honey from "home" bees. But presently—perhaps sensing I was not paying much attention to the topics under discussion—Mr. Lloyd George kindly involved me in the conversation, telling me how, while sitting quietly one morning, he had seen a fox pass quite close to the summerhouse. I surely must have regaled him in return with a lively account of animal life at Chartwell—wild and tame—including stressing the size of the splendid golden orfe in the water-garden pool, which were my father's pride and joy: Papa would have certainly corroborated my enthusiastic appraisal of their magnificence.

Later that summer Ll.G. paid a return call on my parents at Chart-well: sadly for me, I missed seeing him as I was away in France, staying with the Forbes family in Brittany. But I heard all about his visit, and from Les Essarts, St. Briac, I wrote to Mr. Lloyd George on 20 September 1937:

> *Mummie in one of her letters told me that you had been over to Chartwell, and had brought me some lovely green gages; thank you so very much; I am most disappointed to have missed you, and also the green gages. I hope, however that you will come and visit us very often at Chartwell, when I am there.*
>
> *I am having great fun out here, fishing, riding, swimming and tennis.*
>
> > *With very much love, and many thanks*
> > *from, Mary*
>
> *p.s. Now that you have been to Chartwell, I hope you realise how big our fish really are!*

CHAPTER 5

Family Affairs

D URING THESE YEARS, I HAD AT VARIOUS TIMES BEEN CONSCIOUS
of tension between my mother and Nana, though early on it had to
be very obvious for me to notice it—protective wishful thinking, I
suppose. To their credit, it was extremely rare for them to air their
differences in front of me, but sometimes Nana would return to our
quarters after being with Mummie with clear signs on her face that
she had been crying. At these moments I was overcome by embarrassment rather than sympathy—the sight of a grown-up crying being
positively offensive to me—and I think it was not until I was fifteen
or sixteen that I actually asked Nana the reason for her distress, or
that she herself (despite her professional sense of loyalty) volunteered
the reason for it, which was invariably a scene of reproaches by my
mother, starting from some trivial matter to do with plans involving
me, my manners, or my clothes (buttons off cardigans, or crumpled
dresses—Nana being admittedly quite negligent in these matters) and
progressing to a wider field of complaints probably involving household matters, during the course of which Clementine waxed hysterical, and was not open to reason or argument. These unedifying scenes
always culminated in Nana leaving the room, utterly defeated, in
floods of tears. I, of course, was on Nana's side—but to little avail; I
merely seethed inwardly, and hugged Nana.

The situation between Clementine and Nana was not the normal employer-employee relationship on account of their close family connection; moreover, during the 1930s Nana came to play an important role in the household apart from looking after me whenever Clementine was away from home for any long period of time, writing long newsy letters to her, not only about my doings and sayings (in considerable detail), but also covering domestic and family minutiae that might have been left out of Winston's regular letters, which gave a broad overall report but also included news from beyond the Chartwell world. Particularly during Clementine's four-month cruise as Walter Moyne's* guest on his yacht the *Rosaura* during the winter and spring of 1934–35, when she travelled to the farthest reaches of the Pacific, Nana was a vital link with family and home affairs.

Despite the occasional stormy scenes, Clementine was truly fond of Nana, and knew full well how much she depended upon and owed to her; she also increasingly understood that (with good reason) I turned first to Nana in almost any circumstance. By the time I was in my midteens, my mother and I already had a shared pleasure in tennis; she herself played a good deal with me, and during the thirties a most charming and excellent tennis coach, Miss Dorothy Cathcart-Jones, came regularly in the spring and summer holidays to give me lessons, and to play enjoyable "coaching" games with Mummie and myself, and any of the elder ones who were around. Many years later my mother told me that it was round this time that she began to cast about for some means of developing a closer relationship with me without entering into open competition with Nana. Some of her friends had taken up skiing (then much less highly developed than nowadays as a family holiday sport), and she decided that this would provide an ideal way in which she and I could share a holiday abroad together, in circumstances which would be fun for us both. I was of course thrilled with the idea, and felt very grown-up to be going away with Mummie on my own (although with a very faint shadow of apprehension at the prospect of such prolonged and unusual intimacy).

* The politician Walter Guinness (1880–1944), created first Baron Moyne in 1932.

Our first skiing expedition was to Zurs-am-Arlberg in Austria, in the Christmas holidays of 1936. There we joined up with Aunt Goonie and Clarissa (now fifteen), and Cousin Venetia Montagu and her daughter Judy (aged twelve). We stayed on this occasion at the Zurserhof, the rather grand hotel which lay at the extreme edge of the village. The holiday was an enormous success, and Mummie wrote lively letters to Papa describing our somewhat erratic progress in the art of skiing. When I had to return for the new school term, my mother sent me home with her maid Jefferies, and she herself stayed on for a week or so with Tor-Tor (Mary Marlborough's sister) for company, to continue grappling with this new activity which had really enthused her. In retrospect I see it was very plucky of Mummie and Cousin Venetia—then in their fifties—to tackle this highly energetic and demanding sport.

The following year we went again to Zurs, this time staying in a more modest hotel (which was also much more fun): the Flexen, situated in the heart of the village, and owned and run by a charming family, the Skardarsys (a younger generation of whom would still be in charge over forty years later, when I would in turn bring my children there). Our party this year was again Cousin Venetia and Judy, plus Clarissa.

Our third and last skiing holiday was at the end of the same year, this time at Lenzerheide in Switzerland; Mummie and I went out in time for Christmas, leaving Papa to go to Blenheim. My stay in Lenzerheide was made particularly jolly, on and off the slopes, by the presence of a large number of the Grant Forbes family. The highlight of our skiing expeditions was reached when Mummie took me and six of the Forbes family on a day trip to Davos, from where, after ascending a further 3,000 feet, and eating a large luncheon, we all—with varying degrees of skill and speed—descended one of the Parsenn runs (about 14 kilometres). It was in Zurs, in the early New Year, that we heard of the tragic news of Dick Sheepshanks's death. Mummie said, "Sarah will be very upset"; I went out into the freezing dark, and sat and sobbed my heart out in a snowdrift for this love of my youth.

Clementine's strategy worked: for it was during these three lovely holiday times that I started to begin to get to know my mother—and, most important, to enjoy her company. During the long après-ski evenings, I would go to her room and, wrapped in dressing gowns and with well-greased faces, we would enjoy long sessions of talk or reading aloud. I greatly enjoyed it when Mummie regaled me with accounts of her childhood and youth: I loved to hear about Kitty, her elder sister, whom she adored, and the twins (Bill and Nellie), and about her fascinating, unpredictable mother, Lady Blanche Hozier, and terrifying old Lady Airlie, her grandmother. Clementine had had an insecure childhood: after her parents' separation when she was about six years old, Lady Blanche and her four children led a somewhat peripatetic existence—always short of money—and the occasional unwelcome visits of their father, Sir Henry Hozier, cast a shadow of anxiety over their lives. Kitty, her mother's unashamedly avowed favourite, tragically died of typhoid just before her seventeenth birthday: Clementine was heartbroken.

And of course I was riveted to hear about how my mother made her debut, under the wing of a rich and benevolent older relation: from looking at old photographs I realized how exceptionally beautiful she had been as a girl. I wanted full details of her beaux, and was particularly impressed by Sidney Peel's long and faithful courtship (he sent her white violets every day). And then—at last—Mr. Winston Churchill arrived upon the scene!

A particular pleasure of our après-ski evenings was the long reading-aloud sessions. We concentrated at first, I remember, chiefly on poetry; some of it was holiday reading set by my school, but my mother greatly extended our explorations. We would take it in turns to choose and read from anthologies or collected works. Thus I discovered Keats's Odes, and his "Eve of St. Agnes"; Shelley's "Witch of Atlas"; Milton's "Ode on the Morning of Christ's Nativity"—and so many more treasures. Presently my mother veered away from poetry to prose. Her preference was for memoirs, histories, and biographies; she also enjoyed classical novels, and long books of several volumes never daunted her (I'm afraid I never was able to emulate her in this), and in addition read a lot of French books. She pointed me to many authors and books I very much doubt I should have discovered for myself—such as Ernest Renan's *Vie de Jésus,* and the long and curious *Tale of Genji,* translated from Japanese by Arthur Waley, to mention only two.

But the development of a closer relationship between my mother and myself was not always equable: there were tempestuous passages between us from time to time. I sometimes found her difficult to understand and extremely demanding; I dreaded her displeasure, and the emotional, electric storms that could brew up. I myself must have often irritated her—I was, after all, in my "terrible teens" (more elegantly described by the French as *l'âge ingrat*)—and must have been at times excessively tiresome, graceless, and, I fear, a dreadful prig. This last unattractive attribute, I think, was in part the reverse of the shining coin of high moral standards inculcated in me by Nana.

My relationship with my father was altogether much easier—it just seemed to happen. Of course, he did not have to deal with the "small print" of my life or wrestle with my shortcomings in the same way as my mother; nor was there any tussle of authority or conflict of loyalty—in Clementine's absence, all "nursery" matters were referred to Nana. My father could be quite solicitous: "Shouldn't the child be wearing a vest, Moppet? It's really quite chilly still. . . ."

There were, of course, "no-go" areas: his study and bedroom were generally out of bounds, unless I was sent as a messenger: "Fetch your father—tell him it's lunchtime." These missions were often unsuccessful, as I was not good at breaking up evidently important conversations, and frequently I myself became preoccupied with treasury tags or trying to use the "klop" (WSC-speak for a paper-hole punch). No noise (whistling particularly was abhorred) outside Papa's study was permitted, and a thunderous roar of rebuke and reproach would result from any infraction of this not unreasonable rule: nor were interruptions to his painting welcomed. But when touring the grounds and gardens, inspecting the livestock, or occupied with the current project, my father welcomed company and "henchfolk." In my teens I loved these outdoor occupations just as much as I had as a small child; and his love of birds and animals, domestic or wild, was a great bond between us. My letters to him reflect our shared interests:

Dear Papa,

Thank you very much for your lovely long letter. [Sadly I do not have it.] I am sorry I have not written sooner but I thought I would wait till I could tell some news about Chartwell. Well, Chartwell is looking much the same as it did [when you] went away. Two of my baby bantams died while I was away, so now I have only got five baby bantams. Yesterday I went and bathed with a friend, and we played in the afternoon . . .

Well I really must stop now, tender love to all.

MARIA

X X X X X   X X X X X X

PS One of the baby Canadian geese had to be killed, because Arnold [farm bailiff] says [the] white swans are mateing [sic] and have fought the Canadian geese.

A year later my father wrote to me before setting off on his long "sightseeing" tour in Europe:

My darling Mary,

I was very glad indeed to get your letter and to know that you are happy in Scotland under a shining sun. Mummie and I and Sarah are starting on Saturday for Brussels, the capital of Belgium, whence we can see three of the

*great battlefields of John, Duke of Marlborough, Ramillies, Oudenarde and
Malplaquet. It will be very interesting because Colonel Pakenham-Walsh
is going to explain on the ground to us exactly how it all happened. We
are travelling there from Dover to Calais, and then Professor Lindemann
motors us in his car through some of the battlefields of the Great War to our
destination.*

*After that I am going to motor all across Europe from Brussels to the
Danube in Bavaria along the line your great ancestor marched with a small
English army and conquered all our foes as he met them. Give my love to
Moppett and write often.*

> *Your loving father,*
> *Winston S. Churchill*

Later during that holiday Winston was taken ill with typhoid fever,
and spent some time in a nursing home in Salzburg. Although my letter to him starts with concern over his illness, I naturally assumed he
would want a Chartwell update:

> CHARTWELL,
> WESTERHAM, KENT
> SEPT:12TH [1932]

Darling Papa,
I am so sorry to hear you are ill, I do hope you will be better.

*At the present nothing very much is happening, except that Arnold is
filling up the lovely woodshed with wood,* and that I am riding Judy, Nana's
poney [sic] about in the grounds.*

*One of the heifers is going to calve in two or three days, it will be so lovely
to have a little calf.*

---

* A large new woodshed had recently been completed: the brick columns and piers were
largely WSC's own handiwork.

*I am so very very very sorry that you and Sarah and Mummy cannot be
here for my birthday, it won't be half as nice without you.*

Well I really must stop now, tender love to all

MARIA

XXXXX   XXXXXX

From our skiing holiday in early 1937 I wrote my father a long letter, describing mountain scenery, a bit of social life, and details I was
sure would intrigue him about a mountain hare!

HOTEL FLEXEN

ZURS-AM-ARLBERG

AUSTRIA

11TH JANUARY 1937.

My Darling Papa,

*I hope you and everyone at Chartwell are quite well. I am having a simply
marvellous time. Yesterday Mummie and I went for a whole day's expedition
to a lonely lake in the mountains called the Zursersee . . . while Mummie
and I were toiling painfully up the mountain [no ski lifts then!] we were
overtaken by a good looking young man, who Mummie told me was Prince
Starhemberg,* he stopped and talked to us for a few minutes.*

*We saw yesterday also the tracks of a snow hare. In the summer they
are a discreet brown, but in the Winter they discard their quiet 'smoking
suits' and don a coat of pure white; when they want to have a meal they dig
through as much as six feet of snow, to find the grass. They find it very easy to
go fast up hill because of their long legs, but they are very slow coming down
because their legs get in the way. I think it would be such fun to have a hare at
Chartwell.*

* Ernst Rüdiger, Prince von Starhemberg (1899–1956), Austrian nationalist and conservative politician. From 1934 to 1936 he was leader of a right-wing grouping of parties
known as the Fatherland Front and became the country's Acting Chancellor, though by
1937 he had been ousted from power.

Last week I went to a Tyrolean Ball, it was great fun and very rowdy. I did not retire to bed till nearly midnight.

Please give my love to all my animals, also remember me kindly to Friendly.

With tender love from
MARIA

Friendly was one of my bottle-fed lambs who remained as a pet: he proved to be singularly unattractive as an adult—and far from "friendly" in disposition. We were all delighted when eventually he was banished, having nearly knocked my father over.

Reviewing my letters to my parents all these years later, I see that in writing to each of them I covered a different spectrum of news and views: to my mother I reported my now developing social life in greater detail than when I wrote to Papa and, when staying in other people's houses, I usually gave her details of the menus. Playing around in her bedroom in my childish years while she was conducting her daily conference with the cook had impressed upon me unconsciously what great importance she attached to having good food, and the detailed trouble she took to achieve it.

Through the winter of 1934–35 when my mother was away on her long voyage, I wrote her very newsy letters, covering my daily life in great detail, and including a lively account of the stay-at-homes' Christmas. In the previous summer my father's contemporary and great friend Sunny Marlborough (who had been so kind to me when I was ten and given me Jasper, the Blenheim spaniel), had died, aged only sixty-three, and had been succeeded by his son John (Bert) as tenth Duke. Bert was in his late thirties, and he and his wife Mary (Cadogan) continued in a younger generation the kindness and hospitality of his father; they had invited the Chartwell cousins to Blenheim Palace for the first Christmas of their "new reign."

I was enormously excited at the prospect of staying away (without Nana) with Papa and the "Big Ones," and wrote daily hour-by-hour accounts of our visit. Sarah had been made responsible for shepherding me and our maid, May, from Chartwell by train to Oxford, and we met up with the rest of our party—Papa, Diana, the Jack Churchills, and the Prof—at Blenheim, where a large party of guests was assembling. My generation of Spencer-Churchill cousins consisted of Sarah, then aged round thirteen; Caroline (my near contemporary at elevenish); Sunny, then the only son, who was nearly eight; and five-year-old Rosy. "The children are all sweet and I like them very much," I wrote to Mummie on the evening of the twenty-third, just after we had arrived. I reported that the

luncheon menu was

> 1) <u>*Curried eggs on toast & ham*</u>
> 2) *Beef or Pheasant*
> 3) *Crepes Suzettes. Plain pancakes.* <u>*Mince Pies.*</u>
> 4) *Cheese, coffee, fruit, Wine.*

The things that I had are underlined.

After lunch I changed into my kilt, & went and bicycled. About 4.15 we came in and changed for tea, I put my white silk on* . . . then we had supper [presumably in the schoolroom].

The Menu consisted of—

> 1) <u>*Minced chicken with a creamy sauce & mashed potato*</u>
> 2) <u>*Fruit salad & cream*</u>
> 3) *Fruit.*

Then I went to bed.

On Christmas Eve I hunted in the morning, but, as I told Mummie,

---

* When I see how much changing went on, I'm not surprised we had brought May with us!

. . . I came home in time for lunch.

> MENU
> <u>Oeufs en Cocottes Parisiennes.</u> Roast Chicken. Cutlets.
> <u>Canary Pudding & Jam</u>
> Ground rice.

After luncheon we went & rode our bicycles.

In the garden there is a most beautiful waterfall [Capability Brown's Grand Cascade] I do wish you were here it's such fun!

In the afternoon Clarissa & Peregrine arrived & we had a cinema.

In the evening one of the maids fainted. Then we had supper.

> MENU.
> *Fish & Chips & Lemon*
> *Orange Mould.*

Then we hung up our stockings & went to bed.

I of course weighed in with a full account of Christmas Day, which started for me when I woke at "4.40 a.m.! & opened my stocking." I then descended on Sarah's room, where I found my parents' presents—a clock and a pearl for my add-a-pearl necklace. A long inventory then followed of the presents with which family, "Cousin Mary," and "the cousins" had showered me. That night all ages were allowed to stay up for dinner with the grown-ups: "after tea we all rested. Then I got dressed for dinner, not one of us were [*sic*] late. The table decorations were lovely, after dinner we all danced till 11 p.m.!" I remember this quite well—my cousin Blandford (Bert, the Duke) danced with me and, tiring of fox-trotting, I threw some cartwheels, somewhat hampered in my style by my first long dress.

Boxing Day was of course given over to sport: "After breakfast we took various forms of exercise. Cousin Blandford went shooting, but

Papa (who by the way didn't want to shoot) complained of indigestion, & stayed in bed!"

I would also spend the next Christmas at Blenheim. That year it was Winston who was the "wanderer": he had planned a long "working holiday" to grapple with volume three of his major work *Marlborough: His Life and Times,* combining this with finding winter sunshine and scenes to paint. Clementine had been with him during the first part of his travels in Spain in early December, but she returned home for Christmas, which she and I spent at Blenheim. It was a brief visit, as she and I were on the eve of our first skiing expedition, but a very enjoyable one: during those two Christmases at Blenheim, I established links with my cousins—especially with Caroline—which would last our lifetimes.

Winston, meanwhile, was not very happy in Tangier, for although he had congenial male political company (Lord Rothermere and Mr. Lloyd George), the weather was odious and he missed Clementine and a family Christmas. However, it was on this trip that, searching for sunshine, he found it in Marrakech, which was to become a favourite holiday place for him thereafter.

Diana and Randolph continued through my teenage years to be remote figures. Randolph went (somewhat briefly) to Oxford, which he left to go to America on a lecture tour; thereafter politics and journalism chiefly occupied him. His spasmodic visits to Chartwell became always associated in my mind with shouting, banging doors, and rows: I tended to keep out of the way.

Diana was entirely benevolent towards me, but was chiefly London-based, although coming down to Chartwell for weekends. She quite often made country-house visits with her mother, and she went with both Winston and Clementine to America for the winter months of 1931–32—that disastrous visit when Winston was knocked down by a car on Fifth Avenue and quite badly injured. I was of course thrilled when Diana became engaged to John Bailey in the autumn of 1932: I thought him very good-looking, and I enjoyed the general brouhaha of the wedding plans. I was one of her bridesmaids on 12 December at St. Margaret's, Westminster, where our parents had been married. Our dresses were really ravishing—white tulle over silver lamé—though I remember the camellias in my wreath pressed painfully into my head.

I was deeply upset and shocked just over two years later, when, early in the New Year of 1935, Nana told me Diana and John were going to be divorced. I had seen them only as a romantic and glamorous couple—and my religious feelings were also strongly assaulted: marriage was "till death us do part." Clementine was away just then on her *Rosaura* voyage, and it was Nana, as well as Winston, who kept her in touch with the divorce proceedings. Although Nana herself must have been greatly upset by the situation, she loyally went to court with Diana when her case was heard. Proceedings were conducted according to the usual contemporary hypocritical formula of fake adultery, with the man "behaving like a gentleman" and supplying the incriminating evidence with a paid prostitute: the grounds of "irretrievable breakdown" of a marriage were not heard of then. Naturally at the time I did not know or understand any of this.

From my early teens I began catching up with some of my older cousins (although of course the actual difference in age between us was the same). Peregrine was kindly disposed, but always rather silent; he was Sarah's boon companion and it was only much later in my life that I got to know and appreciate him. But Johnny, his elder brother, was the greatest fun: the exact contemporary of Diana, and therefore thirteen years older than I, he was an artist, and in 1933 and 1934 he spent much time at Chartwell, where his uncle had commissioned him to decorate with frescoes (in which genre he specialized) the walls in the loggia depicting the triumphant campaigns of John, first Duke of Marlborough. During his visits I came to enjoy his company very much: he was almost an acrobat, and I was amazed and delighted by his handsprings and somersaults, which he obligingly performed at my request. He was also very jolly and played the piano very well; I seem to remember he was particularly fond of the Meistersingers. In 1934 he married a most beautiful girl, Angela Culme-Seymour. The following year, in August, they both came to stay at Chartwell, with their sweet baby of a few months—Cornelia Sarah.* I thought them the most romantic couple, and I think I had my first perception of erotic passion from them: swimming in the beautifully translucent pool, I was showing off my aquatic prowess and approached Johnny and Angela underwater when I saw them kissing passionately—her long black hair was loose, and bubbles arose from their embrace. I was at once puzzled and entranced. The ravishing Angela, however, fell under a cloud of deep disapproval among Johnny's relations and friends when, the following spring, while she and her husband were living in Spain, she bolted off with a lover, abandoning not only Johnny but their year-old baby.

Much later she recorded her impressions of the Chartwell world:

> He [WSC] loved his cat, who was given the most delicate titbits and lashings of cream. I sat next to Clemmie sometimes, and she was very good at taking notes whenever she thought Winston needed to be reminded of something or have something done ... She was very kind and friendly ... I liked Sarah who was learning to dance the first time we went there, but now was under a cloud having married a comedian called Vic Oliver.† Mary seemed to be an extraordinarily self-possessed girl, always smiling, or anyway looking happy.[1]

And then, on my mother's side, there was the Stanley/Ogilvy cousinage. Sylvia Henley and her three daughters (all older than I), and her younger sister, Venetia Montagu, and her daughter Judy, were intimates, and have already featured in these pages. My mother's Scottish Ogilvy kin were, in my generation, the now famous Mitford tribe of six sisters and one brother—Nancy, Pamela, Tom, Diana, Unity (Bo-Bo), Jessica (Decca), and Deborah (Debo), all born between

---

* Later she would always be called Sally. She is now Lady Ashburton.
† Angela in fact "bolted" in the summer just before Sarah went to America to marry Vic.

1904 and 1920. Nearest in age to me, though still a year or two older, were Decca and Debo; Unity, born in 1914, was Sarah's exact contemporary. Their parents, Lord and Lady Redesdale—Cousin David and Cousin Sydney to me (although later known to a worldwide audience as Muv and Farve)—were in the 1920s on pleasant, but not very close, terms with Winston and Clementine. The Mitfords lived largely in the country near Oxford, but they had a London house, 26 Rutland Gate, from where Cousin Sydney launched her daughters upon the social world. Tom and Diana were the same ages as our Diana and Randolph (who was at Eton with Tom), Pamela only a little older, and the five of them were close friends—indeed, Randolph was deeply in love with Diana, who, with Tom, often stayed at Chartwell. When Diana Mitford married Bryan Guinness in January 1929, our Diana was one of her bridesmaids.

I remember once lunching with my mother at Rutland Gate and being somewhat bewildered by the sheer numbers of Mitfords of all ages, all of whom seemed to speak at once! It was sad for me that I was not destined to "discover" my matching-in-age Mitford cousins Decca and Debo until over forty years later: from the early thirties our families became distanced by the loudly proclaimed political views of Unity and Decca, who declared themselves respectively to be ardent supporters of fascism and communism. Diana fell in love with Sir Oswald Mosley (Tom), who had founded the British Union of Fascists, and in 1933 she left Bryan Guinness and, living in a house of her own, openly pursued her love affair with Mosley—a situation which shocked her own parents as well as society at large. That same year Diana and Unity went to the first of the Nuremberg rallies, where their ardour for the Führer was predictably fanned, and they gave numerous interviews to the press, though it was not until February 1935 that Unity, now twenty-one and living as a student in Munich, actually met Hitler. She quickly established a friendly relationship with the Nazi leader, and she and Diana became part of his accepted circle. Back at home, Lord and Lady Redesdale were "absolutely horrified" by their daughters' association with, and acceptance of hospitality from, "people we regard as a murderous gang of pests." Both their parents went out on several occasions to Munich, but were quite unable to moderate Unity's outbursts and embarrassing behaviour. On one occasion, Unity introduced her mother to Hitler: she was much disappointed that Sydney Redesdale was not overcome as she had been by his charisma, and "does not feel his goodness, and wonderfulness radiating out like we do."[2]

The Redesdales' mortification was of course exacerbated by the constant publicity which their daughters' conduct (especially Unity's) attracted; but although Winston and Clementine must have felt genuine sympathy for their situation, inevitably the families saw less and less of each other—the more particularly since from 1933 Winston was growing increasingly hostile to Hitler, the Nazis, and all their works. But up to 1935 Tom Mitford's name still appears several times in the Chartwell visitors' book—and Diana, who had always been a favourite, was invited to luncheon with my parents in the late summer of 1936: it was the first time she had been to their house since her divorce, and since she had been living openly with Tom Mosley and had adopted his political views. Diana had just returned from Germany, where she and Unity had attended the Olympic Games in Berlin as Hitler's personal guests, and Winston evidently wanted to ask her about Hitler: Diana tried to persuade him that it would be a good idea for the two men to meet—she thought they would get on well together—but Winston would not entertain the idea.[3]

The following year it was Decca's turn to seize the headlines, when she eloped to France with Esmond Romilly: she was nineteen and he eighteen. They had met towards the end of January 1937 at the house in Wiltshire of a mutual cousin, Dorothy Allhusen. In July 1936 the Spanish Civil War had broken out, and within a few weeks Esmond had joined the International Brigade: that December he had taken part in the Battle of Boadilla del Monte, and was also sending home dispatches to the News Chronicle. The conditions were appalling, and in early January he had been invalided home with dysentery. Released from hospital a few weeks later, Esmond went to stay with Mrs. All-husen, where Decca was also a guest.

Decca had for some time been following her rebellious cousin's career (much of it gleaned from overheard nannies' gossip) with keen interest and admiration—particularly his running away from Wellington; being herself a communist, her sympathies were naturally with the Loyalists, and she was thrilled by Esmond's involvement in the war in Spain. That weekend the cousins fell in love, and shortly afterwards they eloped together. Their intention was to get married at once, but they soon discovered that, both being minors, they could not be married without parental consent. Unabashed, they headed for Bayonne (on the French-Spanish frontier), where they waited to obtain Decca's Spanish visa.

The ensuing brouhaha was followed ecstatically by the press (for whom the combination of rebellion, romance, politics, and the peerage was irresistible): and it was, of course, the subject of much family concern and comment. Although I hardly knew Decca, I was very fond of Esmond, despite his teasing and tormenting, and so I followed the saga avidly in the press (hunting through the columns of the several newspapers which were daily on offer at Chartwell) and through the grown-ups' generally disapproving conversation: and although I was primly shocked by "the young people's" conduct, secretly I did think it tremendously dashing and romantic. I had earlier been thrilled by Esmond's joining the International Brigade—although thinking it was wrong-headed politically, as of course I was influenced by "home opinions." My father, who had always been opposed to communism, was more sympathetic to General Franco and the Falange, but he was repelled by the accounts of the brutalities committed by both sides, and was quite sure that both Britain and France should maintain the strictest neutrality. "Neither of these Spanish factions expresses our conception of civilisation," he wrote. He thought, moreover, that the Spanish war took the public eye off the principal threat for the future; and he fully appreciated as the war progressed that the participation of German and Italian airpower had sinister implications beyond the horror of the bombing of Guernica in April 1937, which so profoundly shocked public opinion in the Western democracies, and gave the first inkling of what air attack held in store for civilian populations.

Hoping to stop the marriage, Decca's parents caused her to be made a ward of court: but eventually Sydney Redesdale, who had herself visited the runaway pair in Bayonne (where they had returned after a short time in Spain full of adventures and discomfort), became convinced that nothing would persuade Decca to change her mind, and the Redesdales withdrew their official objection. Esmond and Decca were married in a civil ceremony in May, at which both Sydney and Nellie Romilly were present. To my naïve understanding, it seemed that all was well that ended well.

CHAPTER 6

A Bright Life and
a Darkening Horizon

B Y THE TIME I WAS RISING THIRTEEN IN 1935 I WAS TAKING AN increasing (if spasmodic) interest in the large issues which dominated Chartwell talk, dominated more and more by the rise of Hitler and the threat posed by a rearming Germany. The controversy about self-government for India had passed well over my head, although I remember on the school run sitting on bundles of pamphlets with emotive titles such as *India: The Jewel in the Crown*. However, the Indian question was the principal theme of the by-election in the Liverpool constituency of Wavertree (a Tory-held seat) which took place at the beginning of February 1935.

Randolph, at twenty-three, was determined to blaze his own trail both as a journalist (at which he was very successful) and as a politician. An aggressive supporter of his father's views, constantly drawing public attention to Winston's continuing exclusion from the government, he now presented himself at Wavertree as an "Independent anti-India-Bill Conservative"—despite there already being an official Conservative candidate. Winston, although strongly opposed to the government's policy of granting self-rule to India, was embarrassed by Randolph's action, but out of loyalty spoke at his eve-of-poll meeting. The result of the election was entirely predictable: the Tory vote was split by his intervention, and the socialist candidate was the victor.

Naturally, the government and Conservative mandarins alike were furious with both the Churchills—*père et fils.*

During these winter months Clementine was away on her Far Eastern cruise, but Winston kept her informed about every detail of the Wavertree saga. On 31 January 1935 he wrote to her: "The whole family with the exception of Mary [it was term time] have gone up to Liverpool for the election, including Moppet. Mary is parked at the Fox's* where she is quite happy, but I am going to make her come back here for the Sunday."

Although I was disappointed to miss the fun up north, I followed the campaign with my father keenly, and was thrilled by Randolph's bold fight. But soon I too had the chance to watch and help in an election campaign much nearer home, for in March there was another by-election, this time in Norwood, south London. Again the main topic of controversy was the India Bill, which was passing through committee stage debates in the House of Commons. This time Randolph did not stand himself, but threw his noisy support behind the Independent Conservative candidate. Winston thoroughly disapproved of this further foray of Randolph's, and did not lend him any support: in fact the two had a blazing row over the matter. However, it was of course suspected in party circles that he had his father's approval.

In both these political skirmishes I felt totally engaged. The finer points of the Indian argument were lost on me, but I was full of sisterly admiration for Randolph's spirited interventions, and heartily supported his hostile campaign against the government and the Conservative party caucus, about whose defects and machinations I heard a great deal of talk at home. Indeed, I would hear a great deal more in the same vein as the thirties rolled on, for although I was growing up politically in a Conservative environment, my mother had strong Liberal leanings harking back to my father's radical days in the early years of their marriage. I learned to distrust the National government of the day and the grandees of the Conservative party (in particular Mr.

* The Fox family were very nice neighbours who lived near Westerham.

Baldwin),* and I came to have a consistently suspicious view of Conservative Central Office and all its works. These attitudes, absorbed at a most impressionable time of my life, have basically remained with me, although battened down during my years as a Conservative politician's wife.

At the time of the Norwood by-election Clementine was still on her travels, and again Winston kept her in touch with election news:

> The Norwood by election, of which I wrote to you in my last letter, has absorbed all the children except Mary, ... [school again] ... Randolph's party consists of half a dozen of his Wavertree friends ... together with Diana (whose principal occupation now is fighting by elections), Sarah (half-time with dancing) and Moppet (indefatigable).

Eight days later he wrote again:

> Randolph has been here for the week-end and all is well between us ... Mary has been roped in to the electioneering and was addressing envelopes with all the rest of our progeny and Moppet last Saturday afternoon. You never saw such a political household ...

The Norwood election resulted this time in the complete rout of the Independent Conservative (who lost his deposit), and the official candidate, Duncan Sandys, won with a satisfactory majority over the socialist.

A romantic coda to this not very edifying contest was that, although they did not meet during the campaign, Diana observed Duncan Sandys from across the hustings: a little while later they met—and on 16 September they were married.

---

* Stanley Baldwin (1867–1947), Lord President of the Council 1931–35 and Prime Minister (for the third time) 1935–37. In 1937 he was created first Earl Baldwin of Bewdley.

IN MAY 1935 CLEMENTINE arrived home from her journeyings, which had lasted over four months and had taken her to the ends of the earth. Great was our joy—and Winston's most of all: he had missed her so much. She arrived home just in time for the celebrations surrounding the Silver Jubilee of King George and Queen Mary. A memorable treat for me was accompanying my parents to Westminster Hall on 9 May to witness the King and Queen receiving loyal addresses from both Houses of Parliament—my first "state occasion"! Going alone with either my father or mother—perhaps especially with my father—to some special event was always a great privilege, and these events have always stood out vividly in my mind over the years. I clearly remember when I was nine being taken by Papa to see Noël Coward's *Cavalcade,* which opened in London in September 1931. It was a wonderful play—the first example of an "upstairs-downstairs" saga—and with his unerring touch Coward struck a chord with the public in this year of political and economic crisis, which saw the formation of a National government under Ramsay MacDonald in August. People flocked to see the play; my mother's diary records that she had tickets booked for three performances during that winter. I felt tremendously grown-up being taken to the theatre *à deux* with my father. After the play we dined at the Savoy Grill on cutlets and ice cream, and were visited at our table by Duff and Diana Cooper (whom I knew already as they were regular visitors to Chartwell) and "Bendor," the Duke of Westminster.

Winston loved circuses, and he and Clementine would regularly be invited by the Mills brothers to the large luncheon which preceded the opening of the Bertram Mills Circus season at Olympia. I too came to be included in the invitation, so that would make another lovely treat for me just before Christmas; when my mother was away, my father would take me on my own.

Altogether I had a lovely life, based at Chartwell, with my animals and my local friends, riding (at local riding schools), tennis and swimming, and my skiing expeditions. My mother thought I should learn to play golf, and in the winter term of 1937 I had a course of lessons from the professional at the Limpsfield Golf Club: however, as I failed to get off the first tee in twelve sessions, it was decided by common consent of my mother, the "pro," and myself that my athletic prowess did not lie in this field.

In my letters to my mother in the New Year of 1935, while she was on her Far Eastern cruise, I relived my social and sporting life— and rereading them now makes me quite breathless! In the first three weeks of January I had been to four evening parties (some ending after midnight), paid a visit to London (staying in the flat in Morpeth Mansions, near Westminster Cathedral, which my parents had bought at the beginning of the decade), and seen two plays, *Toad of Toad Hall* and the pantomime at Drury Lane, *Cinderella*—what hardy perennials these have proved! I was becoming quite clothes-conscious, writing to Mama on 4 January: "Tomorrow I go to a party 8–12.30! I shall wear my blue ¾ length frock, because I wore my long white one last year at their party." I later reported triumphantly: "Before supper there was dancing, and I was in every single dance!" Many daylight hours were filled with Pony Club rallies, lectures, and meets. A P.S. to one letter reads: "The last week of the holidays I have been going to the Stables at 8 every morning to learn all about Stable work." (Little seems to have changed in over half a century, judging from my grandchildren's holiday activities—except I'm sure present-day teenage parties are more sophisticated.)

Nana at this time was inaugurating some financial training for me: "Now comes the great News! I have started my ALLOWANCE!!!!!!!" I wrote to my mother on 4 January 1935.

Nana keeps the keys of a cash box, in which is my ?'s allowance, I draw cheques for the amount I want, and she cashs [sic] them, Nana also has a pass-book, her name is
Whyte's Bank LTD

3 Nursery Villas
Nursery S.I.
My Auditors, who cheque [*sic*] my accounts once a month are
Tally & Hambone Ltd (Miss Tallents & Miss Hamblin)
[the secretaries at Chartwell]
Office House,
Back Square (Stairs)
N.I.

Perhaps prompted by this new formality in my financial arrangements, I seem to have become quite commercially conscious about now. I had embarked on breeding budgerigars—inspired and organized, I imagine, by Nana. My flock inhabited a range of aviaries at the top of the orchard; the birds were azure blue and brilliant green, and fortunately they were not near the house, for they made a fearful din; but they were certainly very pretty, and formed part of the after-luncheon Chartwell tour. There must have been about a hundred of them, carefully segregated. Feeding and cleaning them took quite a slice of my time, as did the organization of their mating, nesting, and breeding arrangements. Whatever commercial sense lurked in my makeup (and I have to say it never at any later time demonstrated its presence) was aroused by my budgerigars, and someone suggested to me that I might turn an honest penny by selling breeding pairs. Launching into business, I had a smart letterhead devised—The Happy Zoo—and a formal receipt stamp. I fear I must have importuned guests: I certainly have a receipted bill sent back to me years later by Lady Gladwyn (Cynthia Jebb). She and Lord Gladwyn had lunched at Chartwell, and departed with a pair of budgies in a box: she kindly said she remembered that the birds gave entire satisfaction. I also evidently traded with members of my family. Writing to Winston, who was in the South of France, in September 1936 after a visit to his constituency, Clementine recounted: "The next day I went over to Woodford & opened a Fête . . . I took over one of Mary's budgerigars in a lovely green cage as a present for Sir James Hawkey's little grand-daughter.* That was a great success."

I don't think there were many takers for my goats, although I gave one or two kids away to "good homes." The original two acquired from gypsies by my father, plus their progeny, made a mini-herd of about ten, and they involved me, it would appear from the following letter, in a practical form of barter. Mr. Kay, who lived at Bessels Green about six miles from Chartwell, was a conductor on the Green Line bus which served the Westerham–Bessels Green–Sevenoaks route; in his spare time he bred goats, and was the owner of a very handsome (and very stinky) billy goat. I do not know how I first made contact with Mr. Kay—I think it was through one of the gardeners at Chartwell—but I certainly remember riding on his bus in order to discuss my goats' matrimonial affairs: as a result his billy goat would from time to time pay a courtly visit to my nanny goats with entirely satisfactory results. Forty-five years later, dear Mr. Kay sent my husband a letter of mine written in the spring of 1939 (as the world was teetering towards Armageddon), saying he thought I would like to see it: needless to say, I was enchanted to have that happy, carefree time recalled so whimsically. On my "official" writing paper I had written:

THE HAPPY ZOO,

CHARTWELL,

WESTERHAM, KENT.

APRIL 4TH 1939

Dear Mr Kay,

I must apologise for not writing to you sooner about my now large family of goats; but what with their arrival and school and the crisis† and one thing and another I have had very little time.

The goat family is at present:

---

* Sir James Hawkey was for many years Winston's constituency chairman.
† Hitler's annexation on 15 March of the territory still remaining to Czechoslovakia after the Munich Agreement of September 1938.

> *Mary—triplets—2 nannies & 1 billy*
> *Milly—twins—2 nannies*
> *Molly—twins—1 nanny & 1 billy.*
>
> They are all very pretty kids, and seem strong and healthy . . . I am
> especially pleased that there are only two billies, because I do not want to keep
> any of them. I understand from Mr. Jackson that you would like to have any
> billies, and I should be delighted for you to have them if you still want them.
>
> I hope that you have had as much success as I have had; please come over
> sometime and see my farm; perhaps we could arrange a day?
>
> I feel I must thank you again for all the help you gave me in the autumn,
> I should never have been able to have found a billy without your assistance.
>
> *Yours sincerely,*
> *Mary Churchill*

But while my life was filled with all these innocent occupations
and amusements, and life at home seemed so ample and carefree—as
indeed it was for me—Clementine's prediction that Chartwell would
prove too great a burden financially had only too soon started to ful-
fil itself. In 1925—within a year of their having moved in—my parents were discussing the idea of letting the house for a few months
every year. This plan proved impractical, but in the winter after the
Wall Street Crash of 1929, when Winston sustained a great financial loss, Chartwell was run down to a low ebb: the only room left
open in the "big house" was Winston's study (so that he could work
at weekends), and my parents, Nana, and I squeezed into Wellstreet
Cottage, the small house Winston had recently built overlooking the
kitchen garden. Originally intended for a married butler, the cottage
became a timely retreat for us in this lean period: I thought it great
fun and very cosy. And one winter—probably 1931, when Winston,
Clementine, and Diana were all in the United States for over three
months, and Sarah, Nana, and I were on our own for the Christmas
holidays at Chartwell—to save on heating and servants the ground-
floor rooms were shut up and swathed in dust sheets, while the dining

room downstairs divided nicely into a most comfortable sitting-room-cum-dining-room, which made an excellent winter arrangement with so few of us at home.

Various other changes were made at various times in (largely unsuccessful) attempts to economize: Inches, our very nice butler, departed in the spring of 1937, my mother explaining in her reference for him that the reason for his leaving was that they were getting a parlour maid instead (who would, of course, be paid less). That year must have been a bad one financially: writing to Clementine (who was in St. Moritz skiing) on 2 February 1937, Winston had reported:

> I think we had a very cheap month here. The wine has been very strictly controlled and little drunk. We get our fuel in for the central heating in five ton batches . . . The last lot lasted three weeks instead of a fortnight, although the weather has been raw and generally damnable. The telephones showed a marked reduction . . .

Selling Chartwell was very much in their minds: a possible buyer was "nibbling," the estate agent reported. Winston continued:

> . . . If I could see £25,000 I should close with it. If we do not get a good price we can quite well carry on for a year or two more. But no good offer should be refused, having regard for the fact that our children are almost all flown, and my life is probably in its closing decade . . .

How strangely that last sentence reads with hindsight!

I was, of course, oblivious to the details and stress of these economic worries—but I came to know that Chartwell might have to be sold, and I minded very much. I used to take my goats for long walks up into the woods from where I could look back across the lake to the house—and where I sat down on a log and cried bitterly. For me Chartwell was the Garden of Eden: I was intensely aware of natural beauty and, like my father, never tired of gazing out over the panoramic view of the Weald of Kent from our hilltop, with its changing lights and shadows; or of the beauty of the orchard at Chartwell with the daffodils in the early mornings when I and my animals were the only ones about, and the dew was on the grass. These were intense and joyous experiences for me.

Throughout these years I read a lot. The *What Katy Did* books which I enjoyed in my early teens were succeeded by Baroness Orczy's thrilling tale of the Scarlet Pimpernel—and of course I swooned with love for Leslie Howard in the title role of the film. Nana had read to me Charles Dickens's *A Tale of Two Cities* at a much earlier age, and I had sobbed at Sydney Carton's noble sacrifice on the guillotine for love. I read with avidity Margaret Irwin's historical novels *The Winter Queen, Royal Flush,* and *The Stranger Prince;* I also read some serious nonfiction, including a life of the prison reformer Elizabeth Fry.

But undoubtedly the book which made the deepest impression on me at this time was *Testament of Youth* by Vera Brittain, published in 1933 and given to me when I was fourteen or fifteen by one of the mistresses at the Manor House (who was, incidentally, a Quaker). I have just read this wonderful book again—and it has moved me as much as it did over seventy years ago. It is not only gripping as the autobiography of a young woman from a sheltered middle-class background who left a hard-won place at Somerville College, Oxford, to become a VAD nurse, in which role she encountered at close quarters the horrific casualties of trench warfare and sustained bitter personal bereavements; it is also an elegy for a whole generation of young men who were swept away, the loss of whose talents and energies was an invisible but very real impoverishment of our national life in the postwar decades. Vera Brittain became a convinced pacifist, and was a prolific writer and lecturer, strongly supporting the League of Nations in its earliest years; at first a Liberal, she later joined the Labour party.

Testament of Youth made me question for the first time the politics I heard expounded at home—although I cannot recall that I was very brave in voicing my doubts about rearmament! Nonetheless, it made me think harder about the issues of the day and try to test (if only to myself) opinions I had hitherto automatically accepted as right. But the "home" arguments struck a natural chord with me—and I heard powerful protagonists!

Some public events still stand out in my childhood memories with snapshot clarity. I have told how Sarah and I had been taken by Nana to watch Amy Johnson's return home at Croydon in 1930 from her heroic solo flight to Australia: early that October the papers were full of lurid pictures of the wreckage of the airship R-101 which crashed into the ground near Beauvais in France on an experimental flight from Britain to India, killing all but seven of the fifty-four passengers and crew. I remember "shock horror" talk among the grown-ups: the possibilities of commercial air travel were still on the drawing board or at an exploratory stage.

Another event which had me glued to the papers and illustrated weekly magazines was the tragic death of beautiful Queen Astrid of the Belgians in summer 1935. Her husband, King Leopold III, was driving and rounding a bend by Lake Lucerne in Switzerland when the car left the road and rolled down the hillside. The Queen died at the scene of the accident; the King was only slightly hurt. The tragic saga went on for days, with heart-rending pictures in the press of their young children, of the Queen's lying-in-state with a partially bandaged face, and of the bereft, heartbroken, and guilt-laden King following her coffin at the funeral.

A great landmark on our car journeyings between Chartwell and London was the Crystal Palace: removed from its original site in Hyde Park, where it had housed the Great Exhibition in 1851, and rebuilt, it dominated the hill near Penge in southeast London. Nowadays we have real "glass palaces," but then Paxton's great construction of panes of glass and massive round corner towers seemed very remarkable and imposing. On the night of 30 November–1 December 1936 the Crystal Palace caught fire and, save for the towers, was utterly demolished.*

---

* The towers were taken down in 1941 as they were thought to be guiding landmarks for German bombers.

I remember being woken up and going downstairs to join the rest of the family and household, who were gathered on the lawn, gazing in disbelief at the great glow in the sky to the north. I think perhaps this event had the same effect on me as the sinking of the *Titanic* had on an earlier generation: the unthinkable could happen.

Of the great royal crisis of the 1930s—the abdication of King Edward VIII—somewhat surprisingly, considering how closely my father was involved in it all, I have no particular recollection. My parents were for the most part in London during the crucial days, and, although she held very strong views on the subject, I don't recall my mother talking to me about it at the time—partly, I think, because I was not meant to know about "mistresses," divorce proceedings, and all that sort of carry-on!

NINETEEN THIRTY-EIGHT would be an important year for me personally, for I was to sit my School Certificate (somewhere between today's GCSEs and A levels). At school I worked very hard, but at home was still immersed in the life of my beloved Chartwell. In the week the examination started I wrote to my mother, who was at Cauterets-les-Bains in France, doing a spartan cure after a bout of blood poisoning. After sympathetic enquiries about her health I embarked on an account of life at home:

> I am writing this at *6.15 a.m.* as I was awake and felt energetic. This afternoon I begin the Certificate with Biology. The examinations spread over about 8 days. Yesterday Papa and I walked round all the lakes, and in the round one below the pool there are about 1,000 little golden orfe! Isn't it exciting? They are no bigger than this, and pale goldy yellow in colour with here & there a touch of red. They look so sweet swimming about in the weeds. Papa is very much excited, as indeed we all are, and he says their existence is due to the horrible common tenches, pike etc, which would prey on them, having been killed.

These must have been the spawn of the enormous golden orfe which were (despite considerable hazards from herons and even fish thieves) becoming a major feature at Chartwell. I then reported on important garden news I knew she would want to hear: "Mummie darling, the foxgloves [white and ravishing] and the blue poppies are lovely, and the rose garden in a blaze of colour . . . How I wish you were here to see all this." After more school and home news, I ended "Please think of me throughout this week 'specially hard'!" And I added a rather touching P.S.: "I shall try my very hardest in this exam; because I would like to get the Certificate and give it to you in token for my gratefulness for the wonderful life and education you and Papa have given me, and for which I can never hope to repay you. msc."

Much to my own family's surprise I did very well in my exam: as my mother recounted vaingloriously to her friend Streetie in Australia:

> [Mary] is my comfort & my glory. She is as tall as me & is going to be very handsome. She passed her School Certificate brilliantly winning 'credit', 'goods' & 'Distinctions' in every subject except Geometry which however she 'passed'—As a reward I have given her a chestnut mare called Patsy which she rides all the hours she is not at school. She is now in the VIth Form. Next Autumn [1939] she is going as a Day girl to Queen's College [Harley Street, London] to do Domestic Subjects for one year after which she will (we hope) have a diploma—She is so sweet and loving to me—She has been hunting with the local pack & I have been out with her on a hired horse several times.

After news about the rest of the family, Clementine added: "According to this 'programme'! Mary will not be presented [at Court] till the Spring of 1941 when she will be 18½."

These letters show how much better the relationship between my mother and myself had become: the "skiing holidays strategy" had attained its main objective!

In the same letter Clementine wrote: "Life here is very wearing. One crisis after another. If after all we have to fight think of all the ground lost by our repeated retreats & loss of face." Nevertheless, despite her consciousness of the grave situation politically, it is interesting to see that she was making plans quite a way ahead: in the event, while I did go to Queen's College for two terms, in 1941 I would be enlisting in the army, not being presented at Court!

From about 1937 I started to follow public events in Britain and Europe—which were now succeeding each other at an alarming rate—in earnest and with keen interest. The *Anschluss* of 11 March 1938, when German formations crossed the Austrian frontier, and Hitler entered Vienna incorporating Austria into the Reich, shocked Europe and the world, but was unhappily accepted as a fait accompli by the League of Nations, and also by Britain and France, which had already acquiesced in the German reoccupation of the Rhineland in 1936 through vacillation and lack of unity of purpose. In February 1938 in the House of Commons, Churchill had warned that Czechoslovakia might be threatened with the same fate as that which hung over Austria, and on 14 March, again in Parliament, he told members that it was now economically and militarily exposed.

I had become keenly interested in the "Czech question" ever since Shiela Grant Duff had visited my parents at Chartwell in the summer of 1937. A distant cousin of my mother's—whom, however, she had hitherto never met—and always interested in the political issues of the day, Shiela had become a journalist on leaving university, at first working for the *Chicago Daily News* in Paris, under whose editor, Edgar Mowrer—himself expelled from Germany in 1933—she became keenly aware of the menace presented by Hitler. Between 1935 and 1938, now in her twenties, she was a frequent visitor to Czechoslovakia, where she made many politically active friends, among the most significant of whom were Hubert Ripka, the diplomatic correspondent of a prominent Czech newspaper and himself a close friend and collaborator of President Beneš; Tomáš Masaryk, the founder President of Czechoslovakia; and his son Jan Masaryk, who was ambassador in London during these years. Through her reports in the *Observer* newspaper, Shiela tried to alert its readers to the plight of the Czechs under the ever-increasing pressure of German expansionism, taking advantage of the ethnic problem posed by the Sudeten Germans, and to the threat this situation must inevitably represent to peace in Europe. Desperate at the British government's and public's indifference and inertia, at Ripka's instigation Shiela wrote to Winston Churchill, describing the increasingly acute tension between Germany and Czechoslovakia, and begging him to exert all his influence to make our government adopt a firm and unfaltering stance: "The crisis has never been so great," she wrote, "and I am convinced that only a stand on our part can overcome it. Czechoslovakia is, for the moment, almost entirely dependent on us."[1] On receiving this letter, Winston and Clementine at once invited my mother's brilliant and impassioned cousin to luncheon at Chartwell. The occasion was a great success all round: Shiela had excellent talks with my father, and my mother and I also took to her immediately—indeed, I presented her with one of my goats!

During the next fourteen months Shiela came several times to Chartwell, bringing with her Dr. Ripka and Edgar Mowrer; on several occasions Jan Masaryk was also invited. (It has to be admitted that my genuine concern for the Czech people was intensified by the latter, who was very good-looking and full of charm!) Later also came Edvard Beneš, after he had resigned the presidency and left his country in the wake of the post-Munich debacle. Present myself at many of these occasions, I became gripped by the week-by-week unfolding of the Czech crisis, up to its culmination in the Munich Agreement at the end of September 1938, in which Britain and France agreed to the dismembering of Czechoslovakia.

During the weeks leading up to what Winston Churchill and his colleagues regarded as a shameful "solution" to the threats posed by Hitler, war seemed a real likelihood—trenches were dug in the London parks, and gas masks were distributed. Then, after his third meeting with Hitler, at Munich, the Prime Minister returned home on

30 September, waving a piece of paper bearing his signature and that of Hitler, and declaring he brought "peace with honour . . . peace for our time." Only too soon it would prove to be neither.

Neville Chamberlain was hailed as the saviour of his country and European peace by the vast majority of people in Britain: but those who, like Churchill and his colleagues, saw the Munich Agreement as utterly shameful, and the mere deferring of the now inevitable challenge to Hitler's power, continued to express vociferously, in the press and in Parliament, their opposition to the continuing policy of appeasement.

In his war memoirs my father wrote of the passions which raged in Britain about the Munich Agreement.

It is not easy in these latter days, when we have all passed through years of intense moral and physical stress and exertion, to portray for another generation the passions which raged in Britain about the Munich Agreement. Among the Conservatives, families and friends in intimate contact were divided to a degree the like of which I have never seen. Men and women, long bound together by party ties, social amenities and family connections, glared upon one another in scorn and anger.[2]

On one occasion at Chartwell about this time, Admiral Sir Roger Keyes* and his wife had been luncheon guests: "Munich" had inevitably been a topic of discussion, and Eva Keyes had shown herself to be supportive of Mr. Chamberlain. I remember that my mother set upon her with fury, reducing the poor lady to tears.

At school too I sensed tension among both the staff and the girls—the latter reflecting clearly the opinions of their parents. Miss Gribble—no doubting where her sympathies lay—led us in prayer and thanksgiving for Mr. Chamberlain: I was outraged, and declared

* Roger Keyes (1872–1945), later Lord Keyes of Zeebrugge; MP for Portsmouth 1934–43; Director of Combined Operations 1940–41; First World War naval hero and friend of WSC.

that it would have been more appropriate had we prayed for the poor Czechs whose trust we had betrayed so shamefully: my emotional outburst was not received well by my peers.

World events apart, the summer and autumn of 1938 were happy months for me: after we received my School Certificate results I basked in the sunshine of parental approval, and I started my last year at the Manor House in an aura of success. As sixth formers, my companions and I had a most stimulating curriculum, created for each of us from our chosen subjects and taught by some remarkably able mistresses with strong personalities. There were many expeditions to London for plays, concerts, and exhibitions. We also enjoyed our first taste of elitism: a special "un-classy-roomy" place for our work in a cottage in the grounds, necessitating voluminous, deliciously warm green cloaks for the walk there, and a special room near the main dining hall where our tea was brought to us by some wretched third former (as a punishment for being late or idle); we could walk up the street to the Limpsfield village shop without seeking prior permission. These were some of the headier fruits of seniority which came our way (along with, of course, some tedious monitoring duties) in our last lap of school life.

My reward from my parents for my academic prowess was, as my mother had told Streetie, a lovely chestnut mare, Patsy, who was my pride and joy. She resided at livery at Scamperdale Farm near Edenbridge (about three miles from Chartwell), the establishment of Mr. Sam Marsh, a celebrated personality in the equestrian world who had retired from competing to run a riding school and stables, and who was a much-sought-after master of equitation. Many and happy were the hours I spent with Patsy at Scamperdale Farm, and going to gymkhanas and hunting as often as possible.

That winter my mother went for another cruise as the guest of Lord Moyne in *Rosaura*—this time to the West Indies. My father and I kept each other company at Chartwell; there was an exceedingly cold spell just before Christmas, which made progress on Orchard Cottage (the small house he was building at the bottom of the orchard, intended as a possible retreat in any crisis) very difficult, and Winston complained to Clementine: "There is a sharp cold spell: the temperature is bloody: Snow covers the scene: the mortar freezes: I envelope myself in sweaters, & thick clothes & gloves." We went together for our annual treat to Bertram Mills Circus at Olympia, and to the hospitable Marlboroughs for another glowing Blenheim Christmas.

In January Winston also sought the sunshine, and stayed with Maxine Elliott at the Château de l'Horizon near Golfe-Juan. The weather at home was odious, and I reported to him: "Chartwell still stands intact despite rain, frost and gales, and the woodwork in the cottage [Orchard] seems to be getting on well. The parrot [a singularly disagreeable African Grey] is in the highest spirits, and has bitten me once since you went away."

Clementine came back earlier than planned from her cruise. Political tensions invaded even sophisticated company under blue skies, and having suddenly decided "East—West—Home is best," taking typically instant action she booked herself on a homebound ship from Barbados and arrived back in early February. Naturally we were all delighted, and, acquiring a hireling, she joined me and Patsy for several days' hunting at the end of the season.

On 14–15 March 1939, Hitler completed his destruction of Czechoslovakia by annexing such territory as had remained independent after Munich: German troops marched into Prague and assumed total control of the state. The Protectorate of Czechia was proclaimed, and Czechoslovakia ceased to exist. Even to those who cherished no illusions, the suddenness of this latest outrage came as a shock. A few days after these searing events, on Sunday, 19 March, Shiela Grant Duff and Dr. Ripka came to luncheon at Chartwell: it may be imagined how like a tragic postmortem that meeting was.

During these increasingly fraught months, Winston would often recite a verse he had gleaned as a schoolboy of eight or nine from a volume of *Punch* cartoons he had seen at Brighton. The poem had been inspired by a recent railway accident caused by the train driver falling asleep:

Who is in charge of the clattering train?
For the carriages sway and the couplings strain,
And the pace is fast, and the points are near,
And sleep had deadened the driver's ear.
And the signals flash through the night in vain
For DEATH is in charge of the clattering train.

I was always gripped by it, and I think, almost more than anything else, it gave me a sense of the real and increasingly imminent danger we faced as a country.

Nineteen thirty-nine is the first year for which I have a more or less continuous diary. It is largely dominated by detailed accounts of my riding activities—instruction and work in the stables at Scamperdale (Mr. Marsh featuring very largely), and hunting days, described in detail. My various "crushes" with their somewhat hysterical ups and downs are also recounted, demonstrating the apparently inescapable syndrome of myself fancying those who did not fancy me. The Grant Forbes family and the Saunders and Scamperdale circles provided me with most of my social life. There is a good deal of religious introspection—and there are quite frequent, if spasmodic, references to the succession of crises which marked the ineluctable course towards war. On 24 March I wrote: "Rumania has signed a trade agreement with German [sic]. Things look very, very grave. Yet people do not seem so worried as at last crisis."

On Good Friday, 7 April, Italy invaded and annexed Albania. I had gone to a three-hour service at St. Andrew's, and afterwards the Saunders family, some other friends, Nana, and I all went primrosing and picnicking in woods nearby: "on returning home from such a peaceful, beautiful day—after such carefree joy we hear Italy has attacked Albania. Is all the world as I know it breaking up? Must all the world go mad again? Must Christ hang in vain—O God lighten our darkness!" On Easter Sunday I recorded a fulfilling church service and a luncheon at Chartwell, and noted: "Outlook gloomy. Situation very serious."

On looking back, the late spring and early summer of 1939 seem to stand out with an almost three-dimensional clarity. We were on a countdown—and more and more people were beginning to realize it. There were increasingly strong calls for Churchill to be included in the government; men were joining the Auxiliary Air Force and the Territorial Army. In early June the country was gripped and anguished by the loss of the submarine *Thetis* during trials: ninety-nine men—all but four of those aboard—perished from carbon-dioxide poisoning when a tragic error led to the bow end of the submarine becoming flooded and plunging to the seabed.

My diary is full of my last term at school. For the half-term holiday my mother took me to Paris—my first visit; Iris Forbes (who was at the Ozannes' finishing school, where Sarah had been) joined us. My mother had planned an absolute feast of delight and interest. We stayed at the Hôtel Prince de Galles, from where we made visits to Versailles, the Louvre, Notre Dame—my diary could not contain the ecstasy. We also saw several plays: *Cyrano de Bergerac,* with the décor by Christian Bérard; *Ondine* by Jean Giraudoux. At some point during this otherwise idyllic weekend I received a monumental reprimand from my mother on the subjects of ingratitude and bad manners—which, according to my diary, I felt I deserved.

During the summer, Chartwell life was full of guests coming and going; there was swimming, tennis, and croquet. My menagerie had been joined by a pair of enchanting fox cubs—Charles James and Victoria: they were never really "tame," but they were much admired and cosseted, and romped happily with our dogs in the garden. At Blenheim there was a great ball for Sarah Spencer-Churchill's "coming out." I, of course, was too young to attend, but I revelled in the accounts I heard from my family. In July my parents gave a dinner party before a ball given by the Astors at Hever Castle. My cousin Clarissa came to stay, and I remember how exquisitely beautiful she looked with her corn-coloured hair and willowy figure. I was awestruck too by the difference two years' seniority made; she seemed very unapproachable, and I could scarcely believe I had ever once played "Bears" or hide-and-seek with her. I rather wistfully wrote in my diary on 18 July: "I long to be able to go to these balls and parties—I only hope I shall enjoy them as much as I expect to."

The last weeks of my last term at Manor House spun by in a rush of swimming, sports, and tennis tournaments (I reached the finals of the singles before being severely walloped); and I took the leading part in the end-of-term play. I had various heart-to-heart talks about "life" from various members of the teaching staff, and Miss Gribble as she kissed me said she had been "glad of my presence in the school." I said tearful farewells to my dearest friends, Rose and Jean.

Fiona (my closest friend, and nearest in age to me of the Forbes family) came to stay for a fortnight, and Nana and I were to go to Les Essarts later on. In the interval my great and "grown-up" treat was to go with my parents to stay with Consuelo and Jacques Balsan at their beautiful house near Dreux, Château St. Georges Motel. My father had gone on ahead of us to visit the Maginot Line at the invitation of the French government; we left on 16 August, travelling by train ferry, and staying in Paris as before at the Prince de Galles. The next day the morning was devoted to shopping, and my mother bought me the most enchanting evening dress at the Trois Quartiers—spotted organdie with red cherry bows. My father arrived back from his tour and told us, as I recorded in my diary on 17 August, that "the spirit among the French soldiers is wonderful." While my mother rested, he took me off to see the tomb of Napoleon at Les Invalides: we stood looking down in silence on the final resting place of his great hero. Late that afternoon we drove down to St. Georges Motel.

Consuelo Balsan, born Vanderbilt, had been married to Winston's cousin, contemporary, and great friend Sunny, ninth Duke of Marlborough. After eleven years, and having provided him with two sons, she left him and Blenheim for good in 1906: they were divorced in 1920, and the following year she married Jacques Balsan, a lieutenant colonel in the French air force. Despite the bitterness between the Marlboroughs, Winston and Clementine kept up their friendship with Consuelo, and after her marriage to Jacques Balsan, with whom she was lastingly happy, were often their guests at St. Georges Motel in Normandy and at Eze on the Riviera.

St. Georges Motel—where we would spend the last days of holiday in peacetime—is a most beautiful seventeenth-century château, built in rose-pink brick: it greatly appealed to my father that King Henri IV (of Navarre) had slept the night there before the Battle of Ivry in 1590. Consuelo's exquisite taste and lovely possessions had made it as remarkable inside as out; here she and her husband led a cultivated and highly civilized way of life, offering warm hospitality to their many friends. Consuelo was also most public-spirited, and between them the Balsans were bywords for good works and generosity wherever they lived.

This August of 1939 the large house party gathered at the château was a mixture of French and other continental guests with some English friends. The weather was glorious, the scene pleasant and peaceful: Winston was happily absorbed painting the house and its beautiful *pièce d'eau,* and nearly every day his friend and painting companion Paul Maze came over from his family home nearby on the estate at the Moulin de Montreuil to keep him company. For the rest of us there were tennis and swimming, expeditions to nearby places of interest—and *fraises des bois,* whose delights I discovered for the first time. But over all our enjoyment hung a menacing cloud of uncertainty. My mother and I visited Chartres Cathedral: as we stood—drenched in the cool blueness of those glorious windows—I thought of the words of "Fare Well" by Walter de la Mare: "Look thy last on all things lovely, / Every hour."

These days passed most pleasantly; but, agreeable and civilized though the company was, all was not harmony, for one or two of the guests were hostile to my father's political views, and to Britain. Paul Maze remembered how, while he was talking to my father, one of the English guests shouted down from the stairs: "Don't listen to him. He is a warmonger."[3]

The news was becoming increasingly grave, and Winston decided he must return to England: so, less than a week after his arrival, on

23 August, he left St. Georges Motel and flew home. That same day Germany and Russia had signed a pact of mutual nonaggression: now Hitler, his eastern front thus made safe, could turn on Poland. Chamberlain had warned that in this eventuality Britain would stand by its guarantee given to Poland a few months earlier.

The next day, full of forebodings, my mother and I also packed up and bade our farewells. The holidays were over. As we passed through Paris on that glorious summer's evening to take the night ferry home, the Gare du Nord was teeming with soldiers: the French army was mobilizing.

ON ARRIVING IN LONDON on 25 August we found Diana waiting at the station barrier for us, with the news that her children, Julian (aged three) and Edwina (a baby of eighteen months), with their nanny, had been sent down to Chartwell, and that Duncan, a Territorial Army officer, had been called up. We too went straight to Chartwell, driving down through the night. War preparations were now going ahead in earnest, locally and nationally, though many people were still clinging to the hope that some miraculous last-minute happening might stave off—yet again—the awesome reckoning. I was enchanted to be reunited with my dogs and goats, the fox cubs, and the beautiful Patsy, and for the moment kept out of the way of the general flap and commotion.

The signatures in the Chartwell visitors' book (and the final ones until 1946) for what would be the last weekend of peace (26–28 August) were those of the Prof (an habitué indeed: it was the 112th time he had signed the book since 1925!) and General Sir Edmund Ironside, the Chief of the Imperial Staff, invited by Winston, with whom he had been in touch a good deal in recent times, to learn about Winston's latest contacts with the French generals and his tour of the Maginot Line. I was immensely impressed with Sir Edmund, exclaiming to my diary: "What a giant!" (It was his huge stature that earned him his army nickname of "Tiny Ironside.") Other visitors that weekend (but not "stayers") were Bob Boothby, Diana and Duncan, local neighbours Desmond Morton and Horatia Seymour—and Randolph, who had brought Noël Coward for dinner on the Sunday evening. I recorded in my diary for 27 August: "N.C. was charming, and sang and played many of his songs, 'Stately Homes of England'; 'Mad Dogs and Englishmen' and the 'Bitter Sweet Waltz.'" This must have been a charming interlude as we tottered on the brink.

During the next few days the official plans for the evacuation of mothers and children from London began to take effect, and house-holders in "safe" areas were being informed of the numbers of evacu-ees they would be expected to accommodate. Friday, 1 September, was a busy and fateful day, as my diary makes plain:

Up early moving furniture, making beds and generally turn-ing things upside down in order to be ready for the evacuated children. Rumour, confirmed by the Polish embassy came through at about 9 a.m. that Germany had marched on Poland and that bombing is proceeding. May God bless and strengthen the Poles & prosper their cause against tyranny. Went down on bicycle to Crockham Hill schools [which were being used as the evacuation centre] to act as a messenger . . . Blackout begins from tonight. Papa left for London before lunch, having been summoned by the P.M. & this evening he told us he has been asked to join a War Cabinet of 7 . . . God guide him in this great work.

Saturday the second was spent in helping to sew blackout curtains while awaiting the arrival of the expected evacuees: they eventually pitched up, and by the evening the Chartwell "ration" of two moth-ers with seven children between the ages of three months and seven years old had been installed in my old day nursery and kitchen and in bedrooms on the top floor. I had to grapple with all this as "Nana was out buying macintosh sheeting (!) & Mummie was in London. . . ." I'm not surprised that my last diary entry for that day was: "I retired to bed somewhat flattened!!" Like so many of that first wave of evacuees, our mothers and their children drifted back to London and their own homes after about three weeks, preferring the risk of bombing to the intolerable boredom of country life.

On Sunday, 3 September, my parents were both in London in the flat at Morpeth Mansions: in the country we learned that Britain's ultimatum to Germany would expire at eleven that morning. I had made plans to ride at Scamperdale with friends, and we were in the stable yard there when Sam Marsh came out, told us the Prime Minister would be broadcasting shortly, and invited us to come into his sitting room to hear him. At 11:15 came the brief statement by Mr. Chamberlain that, since no reply had been received to Britain's ultimatum, "consequently, this country is at war with Germany."

"Standing in the sitting room at Scamperdale and looking out at the blue summer sky, just as blue and gay as ever with white clouds floating slowly by, I found it impossible to believe that war has come," I wrote in my diary later that day. There must have been about five or six of us there—the "regulars"—all, of course, subdued and moved by the announcement. Sam Marsh abruptly sent us all to get saddled up—and he then led us in a gallop all round the farm, jumping the (normally sacrosanct) hunter trials fences. It was such a lovely, bright, breezy day, and this gesture of sheer theatre was the perfect touch— releasing tension and emotions. But I believe for us all it marked quite dramatically the end of our world as we had known it.

CHAPTER 7

Clearing the Decks

———

I RECALL THE NEXT FEW WEEKS AS ONES OF FEVERED ACTIVITY and commotion as we geared up our home front for whatever might befall. On that very first night of the war, 3 September, a German U-boat torpedoed the liner *Athenia* en route from Glasgow to Montreal, with heavy loss of life: the news shocked us and came as a grim harbinger of what we might expect. We witnessed helplessly from afar the agony of Poland as the Germans moved in, occupying Warsaw on 28 September. Meanwhile the British Expeditionary Force was dispatched across the Channel; petrol rationing began; the civilian population was issued with gas masks; and we were experiencing our first weeks of what would be over five years of blackout.

On 1 September, with war a virtual certainty, Mr. Chamberlain had asked Winston to join the small War Cabinet he was forming. Two days later, after the Prime Minister's broadcast, the House of Commons met briefly; afterwards he invited Winston to become First Lord of the Admiralty. It was the appointment he most desired, and he did not delay, reporting to the Admiralty that very evening. My mother must have telephoned me the news, and I wrote at once to my father:

CHARTWELL,

WESTERHAM, KENT.

3RD SEPTEMBER 1939

My Darling Papa,
I felt I must just write to tell you how proud and glad I am that you are in
the Cabinet.

　　Don't get too tired, and remember that you always have your very loving
daughter,

Mary

During these early days of the war I divided my energies between helping with the major task of sewing blackout curtains and doing four-hour shifts as a telephonist at the Ambulance Headquarters in Westerham, to-ing and fro-ing on my bicycle. I also had my own programme of wartime preparations. It was planned, to my delight, that I should live in London with my parents and continue my education at Queen's College, Harley Street; this meant that I had to dispose of my menagerie—a not inconsiderable task! The dogs and the cat could stay with Nana and the children in the cottage, but homes had to be found speedily for my goats and budgerigars, and the fox cubs had to be prepared to take up their life in the wild. I remember they scampered away happily when I released them in woodland quite far from the house, but I was anxious as they had had no training from a vixen mother in the ways of fending for themselves: for some little while I put out food for them. But it was pleasing for me in those last weeks at Chartwell, when I walked our dogs at night, sometimes to see two shadowy forms appearing as if from nowhere, to gambol again with their friends and erstwhile companions.

A painful parting was from my beloved Patsy. It would have been too expensive keeping her at livery just for weekends—which I completely accepted; but I sobbed to my diary, while acknowledging that I must keep a sense of proportion as the civilized world crashed round our ears. Happily for me, her new owner kept her stabled at Scamperdale, and most kindly allowed me to go on riding her. I even had some lovely last mornings of cub hunting. Goodbyes also had to be said to my local friends of all ages: husbands, sons, brothers, and fiancés were rejoining Territorial units or volunteering, while those left behind, the womenfolk, the old, and the very young, were throwing themselves into war work on the home front.

Meanwhile in London, Winston and Clementine prepared to move once more into Admiralty House, nearly a quarter of a century after they had left it. Long since converted into offices, or apartments for government ministers, in 1939 this grand and beautiful house, between Whitehall and Horse Guards Parade, was still available for the use of the First Lord. When the Churchills had lived there in 1913–15, for reasons of personal economy they had used only the upper floors of the house, shutting up the splendid reception rooms on the ground floor: now the exigencies of another war again made it sensible that they should inhabit only part of it, and Clementine, in consultation with the Office of Works, set about planning and furnishing living quarters for us on the top two floors. They worked together so speedily that we were able to move in towards the end of September. My mother, with a combination of "government issue" and our own furniture, and with many of our own pictures, had in a few weeks contrived to make the nursery and staff floors into a charming family apartment. We had lovely views over Horse Guards Parade and St. James's Park—and, importantly, there was a communicating door with the Admiralty itself, enabling Winston to be instantly accessible to his staff and reached with any urgent news. I was enchanted with my large bed-sitter on the attic floor—it had, I remember, an old-fashioned gas fire which "popped" in rather an alarming way.

I started as soon as possible at Queen's College, Harley Street, joining a part-time course in my favourite subjects—English literature, history, and French. I also enrolled with the Red Cross in one of their workrooms making dressings and bandages: this was a severe test of my patriotism, as all the other volunteers were years older than I, my natural aptitude with needle and thread is zero, and I found mastering herringbone stitch for the many-tailed bandages a task as difficult as it was tedious. I much preferred my shifts at a forces' canteen at Victoria Station (except when one of my superiors took the unsporting view that I talked too much to the customers, and planted me firmly behind the steaming tea and coffee urns, from where I emerged rather crossly, and with my hairdo predictably ruined).

Diana joined the WRNS (Women's Royal Naval Service) at the end of September, and as her husband, Duncan, a Territorial officer, was serving in the London area, she was posted as an officer to do welfare work at the WRNS headquarters: she looked ravishing in her tricorn hat and black stockings!

Sarah and Vic were living in Westminster in a glamorous (to my admiring eyes) flat, and were energetically pursuing their acting careers. However, they were not too busy to arrange a lovely family luncheon to celebrate my seventeenth birthday on 15 September.

Randolph, who had joined his father's old regiment, the 4th Hussars, provided the chief family excitement of the season when he became engaged to Lord and Lady Digby's red-haired daughter Pamela after a rushed and hectic courtship. Since his regiment might be sent overseas at any moment, their engagement was likewise a short one. I was naturally much excited by all this, and curious about my future sister-in-law, who was only a little older than I, but whom I would watch develop rapidly from a fairly dowdy country girl with freckles into a glamorous figure. For the moment, however, I was deeply preoccupied with my wedding outfit—a cast-off, cut-down fur coat of my mother's, with a really pretty hat made from the leftovers. Randolph and Pamela were married at St. John's Smith Square on 4 October; since the Digbys did not have a London house, Winston and Clementine gave the wedding reception at Admiralty House, where the splendid state rooms were opened up for the occasion.

When war was declared we had all braced ourselves for sudden and terrible events to descend upon us, and the ensuing months of almost uncanny lack of activity as far as enemy action was concerned, both on land and in the air, became known as the "phoney war" or the "twilight war." While energetic preparations continued, particularly in air-raid precautions and military training, life in many aspects continued much as before, although getting used to the blackout was a challenge for everybody.

For my part I was unashamedly happy and excited by what I regarded as my first taste of "grown-up" life—the visible badges of which were a telephone in my room and a latchkey. Being up to now a country bumpkin, and on my spasmodic visits to London having invariably been accompanied by Nana, finding my way round by bus and underground between Queen's College, my music lessons, modern-dancing classes, and my war work seemed quite an adventure—and, until I got the hang of it, very time-consuming. Sometime during this winter, also, I learned to drive and passed my test: Minis did not exist then, and I drove my mother's rather bulky Austin—when her own needs and petrol coupons permitted.

Being continuously with my parents in a relatively small house was also a new aspect of my life. My relationship with my mother seemed easier, for we were both very busy. As always, organizing our domestic life round Winston's needs and wishes was Clementine's priority: part of this was making the newly finished Orchard Cottage habitable, pretty, and comfortable for weekends, and during this winter and early spring we spent some happy times there. Winston's big study at Chartwell was kept open as he was still spending some time trying to finish his *A History of the English-Speaking Peoples**—and, of course, the red boxes arrived regularly with Admiralty business. But apart from these domestic concerns, Clementine straightaway involved herself in naval welfare activities. She helped raise funds for comforts for the crew of minesweepers and other coastal craft; in consequence there were always bundles of the thick fleecy wool, used to knit jerseys, lying about in our sitting room, ready to be pressed on visiting friends along

---

* Inevitably this soon had to be shelved, and it was not completed till after the war.

with needles and instructions. (I'm afraid I evaded being conscripted into this excellent work, my battles with herringbone stitch at the Red Cross workrooms being quite enough for my inadequate skills.)

From the first days there was a continuous stream of people for luncheon or dinner. The guests were mostly my father's political or naval colleagues, and I helped my mother with the entertaining, deputizing for her if she had an outside engagement. Our private social life was confined to family members and one or two very close friends, such as the Prof or Cousin Sylvia Henley, because for Winston mealtimes were merely a necessary and agreeable continuation of working hours, when he could get to know colleagues better, or pursue some line of thought or strategy. The shadow of secrecy therefore hung over conversation: the servants had to be "vetted," and the presence of outsiders or "fringe" friends inhibited the talk which was so vital to Winston. I don't remember my mother lecturing me about this aspect of our life; she assumed that I understood, which I did—as did other members of our family: we prided ourselves on being "padlock." Undoubtedly one heard things that were not for repetition: occasionally my father would say rather fiercely: "That's secret . . ." and then more mildly (if one looked a little hurt): ". . . I only label it!"

But while this period on other fronts earned its tag of the "twilight war," at sea hostilities had begun in earnest within hours of the declaration of war. First came the sinking of the *Athenia;* and in mid-September we sustained our first loss of a capital ship, the aircraft carrier *Courageous,* sunk by a U-boat in the Bristol Channel. The convoy system was only in its formative stages, and losses of merchantmen became a daily occurrence. A horrendous shock was the torpedoing by a U-boat on 14 October of the battleship *Royal Oak* while she lay in supposed safety in Scapa Flow, with the loss of eight hundred officers and men. Winston, with his vivid imagination and intimate knowledge of the Royal Navy, felt losses such as these deeply and personally.

A new and sinister danger developed when the Germans started laying deadly magnetic mines in coastal approaches and estuaries. For several nerve-racking weeks we had no countermeasures to set against these weapons, and by mid-November they had accounted for losses of 60,000 tons of British shipping in the North Sea. This problem caused my father and his Admiralty colleagues deep anxiety: he took the closest interest when some unexploded mines were found stranded in the mud at low tide near Shoeburyness, and followed minutely the tense first examination of these lethal objects by a few skilled and extremely cool and brave naval personnel. As a result of their investigations the secret of this deadly weapon was discovered, and effective protection for ships was speedily devised.

I was naturally passionately interested in anything pertaining to the navy: I often saw how deeply my father felt the losses of ships and men, and sometimes heard him discussing their significance from the strategic angle, and I remember the tensions surrounding the drama of the magnetic mines. Of course I did not know the whole story, but I learned enough to gauge how serious a threat they posed, and I was allowed to know the tale of skill and bravery that solved the mystery.

It was, of course, grippingly fascinating for me to be "in" on so much of all this. I was quite used from Chartwell life to being present when public events and politics were being discussed; I had become emotionally overexcited by the Munich crisis, and I had my own oversimplified lists of political goodies and baddies. Now, though, the whole emphasis was changed, and (although I did not analyze it in these terms at the time) I was seeing my father in a different context: I was seeing him at work. I met his Admiralty colleagues and learned their roles—from the Sea Lords with their multiple gold braid bands of seniority and rows of service medals, orders, and decorations, to the much younger and less-braided duty officers who might appear, unbidden, at any moment, with instant access to my father: bearers of news, sometimes good, often bad, which he might or might not communicate to those of us with him. Sometimes, with barely an apology to his guests, he would leave the room with the officer, table napkin in hand, and go through that locked door to where the war at sea was being conducted: sometimes he would return before the meal was finished and, picking up the thread of conversation as best he might while his plate (carefully kept warm) was placed before him, excuse himself with the (obvious) explanation and apology for the necessity of urgent business—and one knew better than to enquire further. But sometimes we might be told of some unfolding action at sea: then one would have a secret thrill when listening to the news a few hours, or perhaps even some days, later, and feeling one had been "in" on it.

Winston always had an admiration and liking for the young and brave, and while he was at the Admiralty he relished meeting those whose duty lay at the "sharp end." He personally interviewed the courageous and skilful team who first investigated the opportunely stranded magnetic mines, and ensured their gallantry was properly recognized: a few weeks later they were decorated by the King. The exploits of our submarines, and the special strains and dangers their crews endured in the claustrophobic conditions many fathoms down, gripped my father's interest and imagination. One particular young submariner, Lieutenant Commander Edward Bickford, visited him quite often. He was commanding officer of HMS *Salmon,* which had distinguished itself by torpedoing two German cruisers, an achievement for which he was awarded the DSO; my father respected his knowledge of submarine warfare as well as his bravery. Commander Bickford came several times to lunch or dine with us all; he was handsome, clever, and debonair, and we liked him very much. After a while we noticed with anxiety that he looked increasingly tired and drawn: the arduous winter patrolling was taking its toll. In late February 1940, Winston urged that the *Salmon* should go to Devonport as a "practice" submarine, and that Bickford should go for a spell to the Plans Division of the Admiralty: but when Winston saw him, he earnestly demanded not to be taken from active duty. His request was granted, and he returned to sea a short while after he was married in May 1940. At the end of July we were shocked and saddened to learn that the *Salmon* had been lost with all hands off Norway: she was thought to have struck a mine. Although I really knew him only very slightly, I took the news very hard. Edward Bickford was, I suppose, one of the first people I had met to be killed in the war; we had felt involved with his destiny, and I had been gripped by his glamour and gallantry. On 22 July I wept to my diary:

> It is practically certain he and his crew & their *Salmon* are lost. God rest their souls in peace. I feel so sorry for his poor newlywed wife. poor girl. I must say he was one of the best looking men I have ever seen—& such vitality & charm. I find it difficult to realise that he no longer exists—& that somewhere his dead body is being dashed & *mouldered* [*sic*] by the cold sea waves . . .

ALTHOUGH WINSTON AND Neville Chamberlain had been ministerial colleagues in Stanley Baldwin's government, they had never been close, and of course during Chamberlain's term as Prime Minister and his espousal of "appeasement" their relationship became increasingly acerbic; but with the war (and although Churchill's inclusion in his government was virtually forced upon Chamberlain), both men genuinely put aside past animosities, and in furtherance of general harmony my parents invited Mr. and Mrs. Chamberlain to dine with them at Admiralty House. I was included in the small dinner party, for which my mother expended herself in making the rooms pretty and the food delicious. All went extremely agreeably; in fact my father was gripped by the account the Prime Minister gave him of his early life of considerable hardship in trying to grow sisal on a small Caribbean island in which his formidable father, the great Joseph Chamberlain, had invested high hopes and a considerable amount of money: despite his son's heroic efforts over six years the project was a total failure. My father recalled in his war memoirs that "this was really the only intimate social conversation that I can remember with Neville Chamberlain amid all the business we did together over nearly twenty years."[1]

Anne Chamberlain presented a strong contrast, both in appearance and in manner, to her laconic, angular, almost scarecrow-effect husband: she was amply made and rather beautiful, in an "English rose" way, and she had a charmingly vague manner, occasionally asking some odd questions (disrespectfully described as "cuckoo" in my diary), which made one think she hadn't been following the general drift of conversation—perhaps she hadn't!

During the course of dinner an officer appeared three times, on each occasion announcing that a U-boat had been sunk. My father recorded that "nothing like this had ever happened before in a single day . . . as the ladies left us, Mrs Chamberlain, with a naïve and charming glance, said to me, 'Did you arrange all this on purpose?' "[2] I notice now that friendly evening was 13 October: early the next morning my father would receive the news of the sinking of the *Royal Oak.* So goes it in war.

Treats which came my way from time to time were trips in the company of my parents to various naval establishments and ports, when my father was inspecting new projects—such as the methods to counter magnetic mines, or the development of ASDIC (the system of submarine detection that preceded radar). My mother and I were of course not privy to many of the actual demonstrations: we would be taken on a different programme which often included visiting ships in port at the time. For me it was all riveting: there is an inherent glamour attached to the navy, its ships, and personnel, which captivated me then, and to which indeed I am still in thrall.

One particularly glamorous and memorable occasion came in March 1940, when my father, a cloud of admirals, and I accompanied my mother to Barrow-in-Furness to witness her launch the aircraft carrier HMS *Indomitable:* there are few sights to beat the launching of a great ship, and in those wartime days such a ceremony struck profound chords. A lovely photograph was taken of my mother waving the great ship away: after the war my father painted a charming sketch-portrait of her from it, which now hangs in the Blue Sitting Room at Chartwell.

Not all away days were naval occasions: at the end of January 1940 Winston went to Manchester to address a great meeting of over two thousand people in the great Free Trade Hall. My mother and I, along with Randolph and Pamela, were there to hear him. One effect of the "twilight war" had been to produce a certain amount of apathy nationally, and the theme of his speech was the necessity for greater efforts from workers in industry; he also announced the recruitment of a million women into workshops and factories. At the end he received a tremendous ovation. We had travelled up early that morning: it was a bleak winter's day—we found Manchester shrouded in snow and icy fog—and during the journey my father had been "very fratchetty with his speech on his mind," as I noted in my diary that evening. On our return journey, however, Winston—buoyed up by the success of the speech—was in relaxed form; we dined *en famille* on the train, and although we were all rather tired, we had a happy time together. As the war went on such moments were very precious, and one remembered them.

It was during this winter, on these and other expeditions, that I first perceived my father in relation not only to his colleagues and to service personnel but to the general public, and remarked the effect they had on him—and he on them. I noticed how instantly he was recognized, and how intently people listened to his speeches, or hung on his remarks.

LONDON SOCIAL LIFE was lively: despite the blackout, theatres were full, there were plenty of nightclubs for late dancing after restaurants closed, and many people still gave dinner parties, often organized round a son on leave. Judy Montagu was now rapidly becoming my best friend and confidante; her mother, Cousin Venetia, was most hospitable, and mixed her own glamorous and sophisticated friends in with the younger generation. These included figures such as Lady Diana Cooper, a legend of beauty and eccentricity; Freda Dudley-Ward, a most charming person and for years the Prince of Wales's *maîtresse en titre* (eventually to be displaced by Mrs. Simpson); and Victor Rothschild—Lord Rothschild—secretive, sarcastic, brilliant, and brave (he would be awarded the George Medal in 1944). Quite often we would dine where one could also dance: the Savoy Hotel and the Dorchester, the Café de Paris and Kettners were all favourite places—for Judy and I were not deemed to be "out," and so were (officially) not allowed to go to nightclubs. It is strange to think these social niceties were still observed. Needless to say, the more dashing among us would somehow contrive to sneak off to either the 400 or "Le Suivi" with the favourite young man of the moment: I was always rather prim and would be dropped home first.

Another circle of friends with whom I had countless evenings of enjoyment centred on the Bruce family, to whom I was introduced by Alastair (Ali) Forbes and his sister Iris, who was in London at ballet school. Kate Mary Bruce, handsome and sparky, was one of the daughters of Viscount Maugham (a brother of Somerset Maugham), at this point Lord Chancellor in the Chamberlain government: she was married to Robert Bruce—a very nice if rather bombastic man—and their son David was a great friend of the Forbes family.

The Bruces were immensely hospitable, and I had a lot of fun in their house. A lasting friendship I made at this time was with Robin Maugham, the only son of Lord and Lady Maugham, who was often at the parties in his cousins' house in Cadogan Square, which was just a few numbers away from his own home. Robin was good-looking and full of charm; he would refer engagingly to "my Uncle Willie who writes." He introduced me to his parents, who were civil, but not over-enthusiastic, in their welcome: indeed, Lord Maugham was distinctly chilly—being a great supporter of Mr. Chamberlain, he probably disapproved deeply of my father—so it was more fun to foregather with Robin and his friends and relations in Kate Mary's carefree abode down the way.

A favourite meeting place for our group was the Players' Theatre in King Street, near Covent Garden (then still the great flower and vegetable market). The intimate and cliquey show—"Ridgeway's Late Joys"—was a cabaret-style performance, the audience sitting at small tables and partaking of drinks and snacks while being entertained by a small group of actors who specialized in reviving old music-hall songs. The performers included some already rising to fame, such as Peter Ustinov, Alec Clunes, Bernard Miles, Patricia Hayes, and Joan Sterndale Bennett; they were led by Leonard Sachs on a real honky-tonk piano, and used a minimal wardrobe of Victorian and Edwardian costumes, hats, and caps. It was all very jolly, with maximum audience participation in the choruses and a lot of "in-house" jokes. In this first winter of the war the performances were rarely interrupted (except by false alarms, to which no one paid much notice). Emerging when the theatre closed, usually at two a.m., one would find the market already getting busy, with porters carrying tier upon tier of baskets on their heads. Later, when the Blitz began in earnest, the Players' (like most theatres) carried on gallantly, though it was forced to move its premises to a basement in Albemarle Street, off Piccadilly, where it encouraged its patrons to bring "a pillow and a rug" and to stay the night! The club survived the war and indeed the century, continuing in business until 2002.

More often than not we would go home on foot—taxis could be few and far between—and one of my enduring memories of this period of the war is of how mysterious and beautiful blacked-out London was on moonlit nights. If we had been at the Players', I would be the first to be dropped off; as we were often very late (or early!) there would be no traffic, the only sounds those of voices and distant footfalls. Emerging from streets deep in shadow like dark valleys into the great expanse of Trafalgar Square flooded with moonlight, the classical symmetry of St. Martin-in-the-Fields etched in the background and Nelson's Column soaring away up into the night above his guardian lions so formidable and black—this was a sight I shall never forget.

During these winter months all our lives were touched by the "phoney war"—many, indeed, already transformed. Most of the young men had joined up and many were in training at Pirbright or Sandhurst, or other centres within easy reach of London, or were on embarkation leave pending departure for the Middle East. Of the girls (those who were old enough), some were training in hospitals as nurses, or were already in one or other of the women's services; others were working "for the Foreign Office"—an ambiguous term covering activities not to be defined. For all, pleasures and parties were very much subject to hours of duty.

A major event in mid-December which gripped the whole country was what became known as the Battle of the River Plate—the first dramatic naval engagement of the war. Since October, the German pocket battleship *Graf Spee* had been a formidable marauding presence in the South Atlantic—making a brief appearance here or there, claiming victims (nine in all), and then disappearing into the trackless ocean. Hunting groups of our warships had been seeking her for two months, without avail—until she was "apprehended" on the morning of 13 December by three British cruisers—*Exeter, Ajax,* and *Achilles*—at the centre of the shipping routes off the mouth of the River Plate between Uruguay and Argentina (both neutral countries). A fierce action ensued with much damage and many casualties; the *Graf Spee* made for Montevideo, where she remained for four days, while the British ships—now joined by the *Cumberland,* which took the place of the crippled *Exeter*—waited for her to emerge when the limited time permitted for a warship to remain in neutral waters expired. On the evening of 17 December the *Graf Spee* weighed anchor and steamed slowly out of harbour, watched by huge crowds of spectators; not quite two hours later she blew herself up. Her commanding officer shot himself. I give an account of this famous action because my father, of course, watched it all hour by hour from the Admiralty War Room, and relayed the course of events to my mother and myself. The brilliant victory brought a flash of excitement into all our lives in a dreary time.

We spent this first Christmas of the war quietly in London with all the close family at hand, and also those two Chartwell "regulars" Brendan Bracken and the Prof, Sarah and Vic entertaining us all to Christmas Day luncheon at Westminster Gardens.

CHAPTER 8

A Year to Remember

We began with a storm. We have been in stormy times.
And indeed the winds blow us to the banks of Styx. It can
never be calm again in our lifetimes. Those who die have
the roaring of it in their ears.

—SACHEVERELL SITWELL, quoted in
Splendours and Miseries, Sarah Bradford

AT THE END OF NOVEMBER 1939, RUSSIA HAD INVADED FINLAND.
The British and French governments planned an expeditionary force
to go to the rescue, and public shock and sympathy were widespread:
my mother and I, along with many others, enthusiastically donated our
skis—reminders of carefree snowy holidays—for the Finns defending
their homeland. All efforts official and unofficial were equally un-
availing, and in March 1940 Finland surrendered. But this struggle,
though sobering, was too far away to affect life at home; of much more
immediate impact on our daily existence was the beginning of serious
food controls when bacon, butter, and sugar rationing was introduced
in January.

The year made a very cold start. At the weekends at Chartwell
there was skating, while my weekday life in London was very busy
with Queen's College, piano lessons, learning to drive, and my part-

time war work. In succession Diana, I, and Sarah succumbed to German measles, and I caused a diversion by falling beside a moving train!

I was in a hurry on my way to a music lesson, and at South Kensington Station I ran to try to catch an underground train which had just started to move in my direction: I made a leap to get in—trains did not then have automatically closing doors—slipped, and in falling was carried along by the train; just before the tunnel the platform sloped down quite steeply, and I was deposited lying on the track, uncomfortably near to the live rail. I had the sense to wait for the train to roll over me, and then I scrambled up, dusty, dishevelled, and frightened. The station staff were relieved I was not dead, but were not best pleased with me; after questioning, which involved giving my name and address, I proceeded on my way to my piano lesson—I can't think I made much progress, but my teacher was charming and sympathetic. On my return home about two hours later, I found consternation reigning, as someone from the station had rung the press, who in turn had telephoned Admiralty House.

Towards the end of February a moving and remarkable event took place when the King inspected a parade of the officers and men of the *Ajax* and *Exeter* who had taken part in the Battle of the River Plate. The ships' companies were drawn up on Horse Guards Parade under the Admiralty windows, and quite a number of relations and friends had been invited by Winston and Clementine, as had the wives of the senior officers who had commanded in the action, to watch the parade. While we were gathering well ahead of time, we noticed a small group of women and children being shepherded to a special enclosure on the parade ground—they were the widows and orphans of the men killed in the battle. They looked pretty forlorn, and it was a cold morning: my mother sent me posthaste to the Lyons Corner House in Trafalgar Square, where, after a little persuasion, the management arranged a procession of "nippies,"* guided by me, bearing hot drinks, buns, and

* For those too young to remember: the Lyons's waitresses in their smart black dresses and white caps and aprons were known thus.

biscuits as refreshments for this sad little crowd. The Queen spent a good deal of time talking to them individually; the King inspected the parade, and then decorated some of those who had particularly distinguished themselves. Afterwards the officers and men marched to the Guildhall, through streets lined with cheering crowds, to a luncheon in their honour.

In ordinary times, at this point in our lives I and my seventeen-to eighteen-year-old contemporaries would have been making our "debut," the highlight of which was being presented at Court. Of course, in wartime circumstances presentation parties at Buckingham Palace had been cancelled: however, the young are always ready to have a good time, and their parents ready to help them to do so, so many dinners and some small dances were organized. And despite the rigours, dangers, and shortages of wartime life, one great annual social event— Queen Charlotte's Annual Birthday Dinner Dance for debutantes (popularly known as Queen Charlotte's Ball) at the Grosvenor House Hotel—continued to take place during the war in aid of the famous maternity hospital's wartime services.* In a time-honoured ceremony, after the dinner the "debs" of the year—the Maids of Honour—all in white ballgowns descend the great staircase into the ballroom, and advance towards the huge birthday cake with its appropriate number of candles, which is then cut by the Dance President and Chairman, supported by her Vice Presidents: the serried ranks of debs then make a deep curtsey. After all this the dance gets under way and lasts into the small hours.

In 1940, with the cancellation of the royal presentation parties, Queen Charlotte's Ball was the big social event of the season, and it evoked much excited anticipation and preparation. My mother (who this year was one of the Vice Presidents) allowed herself to be distracted from her very busy life and war work to preside over my dress for the occasion, and to organize a large dinner party at Grosvenor House on the night. I (according to my "dear diary")

---

* The event dates back to 1780, when it was founded by King George III's queen to celebrate her birthday, and continued until 1958 as the first event of the London season.

began dressing at about 5.30 . . . Well, I must say it was lovely to wear such a really beautiful white taffeta hooped dress (slightly off the shoulders!) I wore tiny camellias in my hair—my pearl necklace—my aquamarine & pearl drop ear-rings, long white gloves—& a sweet little diamond naval crown which Vic [Sarah's husband] sent me as a present—the angel! Mummie looked stunningly beautiful in a lovely pale pink gown with sequins embroidered on it.

Our party was about sixteen people, divided fifty-fifty old and young: the "oldies" consisted of family (though not my father, who was working), Brendan Bracken, and some nice and rather grand naval officers, who had been kind to me on various Admiralty occasions, and whom I suppose my mother had conscripted. I was in a state of euphoria—and my cup of happiness overflowed when towards the end of dinner my father unexpectedly arrived to join us for a little while, applauded enthusiastically by the assembled company as he crossed the dance floor to our table. Summing it all up in my diary, I wrote, "I can only say the evening was a dream of glamour & happiness."

In normal times a pleasurable feature of social life would have been country house parties and balls; this year they were few and far between. I do remember a dance in early April given at Petworth House in Sussex by Lord and Lady Leconfield for their adopted daughter, Elizabeth Wyndham; the dance was fun, but the most vivid vignette of that weekend remains my first meeting with my hostess. On my arrival in the late afternoon of Friday, I was shown into a chilly drawing room by the butler, who told me: "Her Ladyship is in the Park on air raid warden duty." So I waited, feeling shy and uncertain of myself, until suddenly the door burst open, and in came my hostess in her warden's getup: trousers encircled with bicycle clips, uniform jacket—and, swinging underneath the steel helmet surmounting her grizzled locks, the grandest and most beautiful pair of diamond pendant earrings I had ever seen in my life!

That visit to Petworth happened to coincide with the German invasion of Denmark and Norway that marked the abrupt end of the phoney, or twilight, war. Denmark was immediately overwhelmed, but the Norwegians fought heroically in their mountain passes. Britain and France sent troops as speedily as possible, and the Royal Navy's role was of paramount importance: consequently Winston was deeply involved in both the strategy and tactics of the operations. The Norwegian campaign, which lasted eight weeks in all, was marked by a series of mistakes, failures, and disappointments largely attributable to lack of air support for land and sea operations. In late April British troops were evacuated from central Norway, and by the first week in May there was a demand for a full parliamentary debate. This took place on 7 and 8 May, and I went with my mother to the House of Commons to listen to my father winding up the debate—which had become a vote of censure. I wrote in my diary: "It was the first time in 11 years that he had wound up for the govt. The House was in a most uncertain, unpleasant & sensitive restless mood. There were frequent interruptions—also quite a lot of cheering. Papa's handling of the actual matter and of the House was nothing short of SUPERB. I listened breathless with pride [and] apprehension."

The vote was 281 for the government and 200 against—the government's majority of just 81 revealing that many Conservatives had voted against their own party or abstained. There was turmoil as the Prime Minister left the Chamber, some Members' singing of "Rule, Britannia!" being drowned by cries of "Go! Go! Go! Go!" It was quite clear that there must be a change of government, and there was a growing demand in the House and press for a National government to be formed. Of course I was gripped and excited by all these events.

On Thursday, the day after the debate, I went in the evening to a dinner party given by Cousin Sylvia (Henley) for her niece, my great friend Judy Montagu. One of my neighbours at dinner—debonair, good-looking, and intelligent—was Mark Howard,* whom I knew

---

* Heir to Castle Howard in Yorkshire. Killed in action in 1944, as was his younger brother Christopher.

slightly already and rather fancied—gratifyingly, I was able to record in my diary that "he made himself v. agreeable to me." On my other side was Jock Colville, one of the Prime Minister's assistant private secretaries: he was later to become a great and lifelong friend, but on this first occasion we were both wary of each other. I suspected him—rightly, on both counts!—of being a "Chamberlainite" and a "Municheer." He wrote in his diary: "I thought the Churchill girl rather supercilious: she has Sarah's emphatic way of talking, and is better looking, but she seemed to me to have a much less sympathetic personality."[1] After dinner we all went on to dance at the Savoy—and later still, "despite a few conscience pricks [my mother's ban on nightclubs being still in force] which I firmly banished, we went on to the 400. Danced, almost exclusively with Mark. V. nice! Home and bed 4 a.m."

On Friday, 10 May, I continued my diary:

> While Mark & I were dancing gaily & so unheedingly this morning—in the cold grey dawn Germany swooped on 2 more innocent countries—Holland & Belgium. The bestiality of the attack is inconceivable. Went to college. A cloud of uncertainty & doubt hung over us all all day. What would happen to the govt.? What is the news from abroad? French towns—open towns—were raided. The rumours of Chamberlain's resignation increased.

The chief factor forcing the Prime Minister's resignation was the categorical refusal of the Labour party to serve in a National government under his leadership. The choice of successor lay between Lord Halifax (the Foreign Secretary) and Winston Churchill. Considerable elements in the Conservative party, and the King, preferred Halifax—who, however, demurred, chiefly on the grounds of the impossibility of leading a government in this situation from the House of Lords. Mr Chamberlain therefore recommended Churchill to the King, who immediately sent for him and asked him to form a government.

That afternoon I had gone down to Chartwell. It was a beautiful summer's evening, and in the gloaming I sat on the steps by the former chauffeur's cottage (where Nana Whyte was installed) and listened through the open window to the radio. As I recorded in my diary, "Just before the 9 o'clock news Mr. Chamberlain spoke to us all, & told us that he had resigned & that Papa was forming a new govt. It was the speech of a patriot."

NATURALLY THE NEXT FEW WEEKS—quite apart from the pace and increasingly dramatic sequence of international events—were full of excitement on my part, and domestic planning for my mother, as we prepared to move into No. 10 Downing Street. All the arrangements were made in a civilized manner—"No-one moves for a month!" my father declared; meanwhile his prime ministerial office was up and running immediately. It included members of his First Lord's team, as well as some of Mr. Chamberlain's private secretaries (including— most wary at first!—Jock Colville). And my father, while continuing to live at Admiralty House, conducted all his business from No. 10. His first and most pressing concern was the formation of a truly National government composed of members of all three main political parties.

Meanwhile events across the Channel were moving fast. On 14 May German forces pierced the French defences at Sedan and thrust forward; on 15 May the Dutch army surrendered and the Luftwaffe laid Rotterdam to waste; in the third week of May Amiens and Arras were captured and the Germans reached Abbeville on the Channel coast; and on 28 May came a major blow with the capitulation of Belgium, leaving the French and British armies fatally exposed. Then followed the epic evacuation of the BEF from the beaches of Dunkirk, when over six days more than 338,000 British and Allied (mostly French) troops were conveyed back to England.

Throughout these weeks Churchill and his colleagues were becoming increasingly aware that bitter divisions within the French government were deepening, and that there was a growing possibility that France might seek to be released from its undertaking not to make a separate peace with Germany. Between the middle of May and 13 June, when he made a last visit to the Reynaud government, by then in Tours, Churchill and his closest political and military team made five flights (several in extremely dangerous conditions) in his desperate attempts to persuade the French to continue to fight—if not in France, then at least in North Africa and their colonial empire—and, above all, to send their fleet out of reach of the Germans. All his efforts were to no avail.

It was against this background of cataclysmic events that our everyday lives proceeded. The pressures on Clementine were considerable, over and above her anxiety for Winston's safety on his flights to France, and the demands of organizing the move to No. 10. Winston told her everything, so she was well aware of not only present but also future threats and dangers. Clementine always reacted swiftly to situations: on Sunday, 19 May, she went to church at St. Martin-in-the-Fields and returned boiling with indignation, and recounted to Winston that she had been so enraged by the pacifist nature of the sermon that she had walked out. Winston told her: "You ought to have cried 'Shame, desecrating the house of God with lies.'"[2]

Normally mistress of herself, my mother was nevertheless given to occasional emotional outbursts: one such caused me (and certainly my father too) acute embarrassment. Shortly after we had moved to No. 10, my father unexpectedly brought David Margesson to luncheon. Margesson had been Chief Whip for the previous nine years, and was now serving Winston (who had a high regard for him, despite their past parliamentary differences) in the same role with integrity and loyalty. However, he had also been one of the principal "appeasers," and on this occasion all Clementine's hostility to the policy of appeasement and to those connected with it—deemed responsible by its opponents for bringing the country to its present dire straits—boiled over, and she flayed him verbally before sweeping out, with myself in deep confusion tagging along behind. As I wrote in my diary, "I was most ashamed and horrified. Mummie & I had to go & have lunch at the Carlton [Grill]. Good food wrecked by gloom." This outburst from the normally immaculately well-mannered Clementine is indicative of the tensions in her life at that time.

Although the press was subject to censorship concerning reports from theatres of war and information relating to service exercises and movements of forces, comment and criticism were unfettered, and the public was kept informed of events at home and abroad: listening to the BBC news programmes was (except for determined ostriches) a mandatory part of everyday life. In his speeches in the House of Commons or over the radio, Churchill gripped the nation, setting before them the gravity of the situation as it developed, and never disguising that harder days lay ahead: people in all walks of life hung on his words, and extracts from these speeches have passed into our literary heritage.

Owing to the pace and pressure of his work, I saw somewhat less of my father in these hectic days when we were still living at Admiralty House, for his duties kept him largely at No. 10; but I listened spellbound to his broadcasts, and was thrilled when my mother took me to hear him in the House of Commons, which she did on 4 June, when he reported to a packed and anxious House the dramatic tale of the Dunkirk evacuation. This speech contained the first (albeit somewhat oblique) warning that Britain might be left alone to face the storm, and he spoke of our determination and ability to "defend our island home . . . if necessary for years, if necessary alone."

It was now that my love and admiration for my father became enhanced by an increasing element of hero worship. I saw how people turned to him in confident hope; and my own daughterly affection became inextricably entwined with all the emotions I felt as a young, patriotic Englishwoman. And of course, it was enormously exciting being so near the hub of *haute politique*. My mother confided in me a good deal, and when I became aware that there was a real and growing fear that France might make a separate peace, having been brought up in an ardently Francophile family I was plunged into anguish, finding this prospect scarcely believable. On 22 May my diary records: "College . . . Papa had left early by aeroplane for Paris. It was terrible flying weather, and I was so anxious. The news is unbelievably bad—one can only hang on by praying it will come all right." On 13 June, he flew to Tours for what would be the last time before Reynaud's government collapsed: "Papa went to France. I do *hate* it when he goes. We all have a ghastly premonition that the French are going to give in. O God! France can't do it! She must go on—she must go on."

By 17 June we had moved into No. 10 Downing Street (accompanied by Nelson, the black cat we had acquired at Admiralty House, who promptly made himself disagreeable to the resident No. 10 cat, dubbed by us Munich Mouser). As is well known, Prime Ministers and their families live "over the shop." On the ground floor are the Cabinet Room, the Prime Minister's private office, and a series of other offices; on the first floor are the beautiful and dignified state rooms, communicating with each other, including a magnificent dining room and a delightful (then white-panelled) passage room, where we always lunched and dined when we were not more than eight. Upstairs from these official rooms was (in our time) the bedroom floor:* with its eggshell-blue passages, tomato-coloured carpeting, and pleasantly sized rooms with sash windows looking out over the garden and Horse Guards Parade, it gave one the impression of a country house. I was ecstatic with joy at the charming bedroom (with a clothes closet I described in my diary as "most Hollywood!") and sitting room allocated to me by my mother quite near my parents' rooms.

Later, when there were air-raid warnings—false alarms or the real thing—one sometimes found oneself in distinguished company in the air-raid shelter. Awakened one night about one a.m. by my mother who told me the sirens had sounded, I descended with her (both of us in our dressing gowns) to find a selection of Cabinet ministers—Sir John Anderson, Mr. Arthur Greenwood, and Mr. Clement Attlee— also in the shelter. That occasion was uneventful, and about 3:15 a.m., after having some tea, we eventually returned aboveground—and my mother and I to our own beds.

---

* After the 1945 election a convenient and labour-saving flat was created on this floor.

During the spring and early summer of 1940, my parents and I spent a number of weekends picnicking in Orchard Cottage at Chartwell, but when the bombing of London started these visits became rare: Chartwell was on the direct target route and, standing on its hill above the lakes, was easily identifiable. Moreover, Winston soon had Chequers, near Aylesbury in Buckinghamshire—the official country residence of the Prime Minister—at his disposal. We spent our first family weekend there from 21 to 24 June: as would be the pattern throughout the war, the party was a mixture of family (Diana and Duncan) and some official guests, plus the private secretary on duty.* We were of course delighted to discover the possibilities of Chequers, and make the acquaintance of the charming, efficient, and diplomatic Scottish curator, Miss Grace Lamont (Monty), who ran the house, and who was to become a great friend of us all.

But this weekend was overshadowed by the dire course events had taken in Europe. On 10 June Italy had declared war on France and Britain; on 14 June the Germans had entered Paris; two days later Reynaud resigned as Premier and was succeeded by the aged Marshal Pétain, whose defeatist counsels had been much in evidence in the last tortured days of the French government; and on 17 June Pétain sought peace terms from the Germans.

My diary records that I spent the Saturday morning touring the house and garden with one of our guests, General Alexander,† whom I thought "so charming & the morning passed very agreeably." Later that afternoon my father was woken out of "his rest by very urgent and distressing news & rushed immediately back to London . . . news bloody awful" (no doubt concerned with the French capitulation).

Sunday, 23 June, started badly: "A wrathful & gloomy breakfast downstairs. Church. Papa returned for lunch. French peace terms an-

---

* While at Chequers, Churchill was immediately contactable, and never other than "hands on" the war. There was a "skeleton" private office, including typists, switchboard operators, a duty chauffeur, and dispatch rider, all accommodated in the house.
† "Alex" (1890–1969): at this point Major General Harold Alexander, about to be promoted to lieutenant general and appointed General Officer Commanding-in-Chief, Southern Command; later Field Marshal and first Earl Alexander of Tunis.

nounced in the evening. They are SHAMEFUL & cruel." All in all it was hardly a "peaceful country weekend"! Happily, our times at Chequers were not always so fraught—but they were always liable to interruption, and business very much came first.

A THRILLING NEW PERSONALITY now entered upon our scene— General Charles de Gaulle. Winston had first met this unusual, taciturn man on 9 June in London, when de Gaulle, hitherto a brigadier and tank warfare specialist unheard of outside military circles, recently appointed as Under Secretary of National Defence, had been sent by Reynaud to report on various developments and to ask for more help. Churchill reported to his colleagues that he had given "a more favourable impression of French morale and determination," and on visiting Briare two days later, he had noticed de Gaulle's air of "confidence and self-possession" in contrast to the other Frenchmen present.[3] On his final visit on 13 June to the rapidly crumbling French government, by then at Tours, he recounted how, as he was leaving, "I saw General de Gaulle standing stolid and expressionless at the doorway. Greeting him, I said in a low tone, in French: '*L'homme du destin.*' "[4] And so, when a week later General de Gaulle arrived suddenly in London, Churchill had already formed a good impression of him, and gave him every support as he raised the standard of Free France—inviting Frenchmen everywhere to join him in continuing the war with their allies.

The British public quickly warmed to de Gaulle and were enthusiastic for the concept of a resurgent France which he embodied. I had to wait till nearly the end of July before meeting "the General," but I had already heard a lot about him from my mother, who from the first took a liking to, and came to admire, this dour man. She was quite unafraid of him, on one occasion reproaching him roundly for uttering sentiments which ill became either an ally or a guest in our country: the General had apologized profusely—and the next morning an enormous basket of flowers arrived for her. He liked and respected

Clementine very much, and after Winston's death wrote to her every year on the anniversary.

I first met General and Madame de Gaulle when they lunched with my parents at No. 10 on 25 July. Beforehand I was much excited by the prospect of at last meeting this intriguing character; afterwards I noted in my diary: "The General is a stern, direct giant. We all thought him very fine." Madame de Gaulle was a dignified figure, but not light in the hand; she must have had a lonely time of it, speaking little English, and living at that time out in Hampstead with their three children and not seeing much of her husband. Elisabeth, the elder daughter, was about sixteen, very shy (and also very clever: she was to do very well when she found her feet and went to Oxford): we asked her to luncheon one day, and afterwards I took her to see a film starring Sacha Guitry, *Ils étaint neuf célibataires,* which I thought extremely funny, but which, I was afterwards informed, would not have been thought in the least suitable for a *jeune fille bien élevée* to have seen. We ended the afternoon with tea at Gunter's, which was always a treat—and noncontroversial! Elisabeth and I were to meet again years later, and cement our warm acquaintance.

I would next meet the General and Madame at Chequers, early the following year, when they came one Sunday to lunch and dine. Lunching with us was also a great friend of mine, Lucia Lawson, who was very beautiful, with black hair, an ivory complexion, and wonderful dark eyes. I was much intrigued to observe that the General could not take his eyes off her—and pleased to learn that this stern man was not at all indifferent to beauty. I myself found him most alarming, and it was not until thirty years later, when my husband was ambassador at Paris, that I had a coherent conversation with Monsieur le Président de la République—as he then had become.

The plight of the French people occupied our anguished interest during these weeks after the collapse of France. There was a real fear that the French fleet might fall under German control, which would crucially—perhaps fatally—alter the balance of power at sea. Then, on 3 July, occurred a dramatic event which echoed round the world:

the destruction by the British navy (after fraught parleyings) of capital ships of the French fleet lying at Oran in North Africa, with the loss of 1,300 French sailors. No single act did more to convince friend and foe alike that Britain was in deadly earnest, and that we would stop at nothing in our fight for survival. That evening we were a small party—the only outside guests the Prof and Brendan Bracken—and during dinner news kept on coming in about the events at Oran: "It is so terrible," I wrote in my diary, "that we should be forced to fire on our own erstwhile allies. Papa is shocked and deeply grieved that such action has been necessary."

The next day my mother took Pamela and myself to the House of Commons:

> It was a very sad day for Papa—he who has always loved & admired the French so much & worked so hard for the entente cordiale.
>
> His statement was sombre—sorrowful but resolved & encouraging. He explained the situation & the government's action to a gloomy, crowded attentive House. When after nearly an hour he sat down—the House began to cheer—the cheering grew & grew, until the House was on its feet—Tories—Liberals—Labour.

Reading some other reports of this historic parliamentary occasion, I find I had given a good account of it. It was indeed extraordinary and moving: my father was heard by Jock Colville to say to a Member as he was leaving the House, visibly affected: "This is heartbreaking for me."[5]

Some weeks later I went with my mother to the White City, where temporary (and no doubt somewhat spartan) accommodation had been provided by French servicemen, most of whom had been taken off the beaches at Dunkirk with our troops after their gallant rearguard action in holding the perimeter against the Germans while the BEF were embarking for home. Now they were in a painful quandary, facing the choice of returning to France or joining the Free French Forces which were being recruited here. General de Gaulle was, at this moment, largely unknown, and for many of these men Marshal Pétain, the hero of Verdun and now head of the French government in unoccupied France, was a figure much venerated, especially in Catholic families. Many of them may have believed that the British forces had abandoned their allies, and the searing events at Oran only just over a month past had been a bitter pill for the French to swallow. The sight of the men my mother and I saw milling about aimlessly in the White City stadium shook me profoundly, and I wrote in my diary: "It was terrible to see how lost they all look. . . . Here we saw men who had lost their country, their faith, their *amour propre*—miserable, disaffected. It made a most profound impression on me. . . . I was quite overcome by the misery of it all."

My life in these months was a veritable roller coaster of contrasts: on the one hand were the occasions such as I have described when I saw some of the war drama close to, and felt emotionally deeply involved; on the other, I had at the same time an intense capacity for enjoyment with my contemporaries—and opportunities were not lacking for us to indulge our (often noisy) high spirits. I was beginning also to savour the zest that flirtations added to life—and to experience the gamut of high hopes and disappointments, dazzling, fleeting moments of success, only too often to be followed by darkest despair, that characterize one's earliest experiences of "that thing called love." We were all, I think, pretty innocent—certainly I was—and I was still not allowed to go out alone with a young man.

Even before the Blitz, rationing and the departure of younger servants into the forces or war factories made dinner parties in private houses fewer and further between; the pleasures and opportunities of country house weekends were much curtailed for the same reasons, in addition to which many people's houses had by now been turned into convalescent homes, or were sheltering evacuated schools, with the family confined to a wing. Moreover, the hazards of wartime travel needed to be reckoned with. In mid-August I set off for Minterne in Dorset, where I had been invited to stay with Pamela's parents, Lord and Lady Digby; my experience of the journey, as recorded in my diary, was not untypical. "Journey from Waterloo to Sherborne scheduled to take 3 hours, in fact took 5 hours, owing to line being blown up between Andover & Basingstoke; the train was diverted & it went to Salisbury & Sherborne via SOUTHAMPTON!! We had a raid warning & had to pull the blinds down—but it was a false alarm. Saw wreckage of 2 planes." However, eventually I arrived safely!

Another dimension to my life was getting used to being "the Prime Minister's daughter": people in all sorts of situations were friendly and kind to me and did me favours because of their admiration for my father (and some, no doubt, out of snobbishness). I also began to be invited to undertake minor public engagements, such as giving the prizes at a local preparatory school, and opening Westerham's War Weapons Week: good training, as it would turn out, for the future— but the cause of much personal alarm and fuss to me at the time.

One particularly thrilling and glamorous occasion for me in early July was when I went up to Liverpool at the invitation of the directors of Cammell Laird to launch a new destroyer, HMS *Gurkha,* built at their shipyard on Merseyside. I had watched my mother at the launch of the *Indomitable* earlier in the year, so I knew the form, and also the emotion and excitement of a launch. It was a beautiful day, and I waved the new vessel away most proudly.* It was at that time customary for the shipbuilders to give the sponsor of a ship a present: my "prize" was a lovely Victorian diamond necklace. After this fairy-tale twenty-four hours I came down to earth with a bump—"Long hot dirty journey home"—but was able to record at the other end: "Mummie & Papa knocked endways by my diamonds!"

On 10 July what is now known as the Battle of Britain began when the Germans launched massive air attacks on our convoys in the Channel and on our airfields. For the rest of that summer, over

---

* The *Gurkha* was named to acknowledge the generosity of the Gurkha regiments who contributed from their pay to replace a vessel of the same name that had been sunk. Sadly, "my" *Gurkha* eventually suffered the same fate.

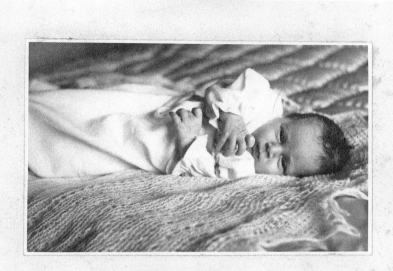

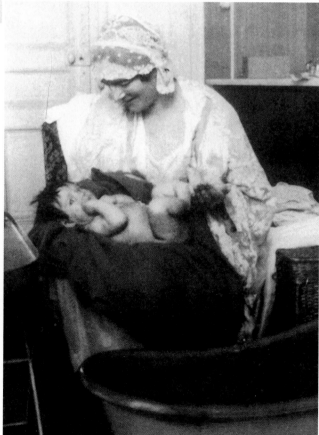

I was born in London in September 1922, the "Baby Bud" of the family. Above is the earliest photograph I have of myself; below, at bath time, not much later.

When I was two, the family moved into Chartwell. The house was somewhat dilapidated when my father bought it two years earlier (BELOW). Here I am with my parents (ABOVE RIGHT) and my eldest sister, Diana (RIGHT). I did not enjoy having my portrait (LEFT) painted: a reluctant sitter, aged four, I was being held by my nanny.

At Chartwell I was introduced to the delights of country life, including feeding chickens with my elder sister Sarah (BELOW) and learning to ride on Judy (ABOVE).

While I helped my father bricklaying (ABOVE LEFT) or played in the snow with Nana (RIGHT), adult life at Chartwell went on. My father painted the visitors assembled for tea on 29 August 1927 from a photograph: (ABOVE, CLOCKWISE) himself, Mrs. Sickert, Diana Mitford, Eddie Marsh, the Prof., Randolph, Diana, my mother, and Walter Sickert. I was there when Diana (BELOW, FAR RIGHT) opened the British Legion building in Westerham—I think I am the little girl on the left in this picture.

My father incorporated in the redbrick walls around
the kitchen garden a tiny one-room cottage that
became known as the "Marycot": here I am (ABOVE),
in a picture painted by my father from a photograph,
giving my first public speech as I laid the foundation
stone. Randolph holds my bouquet. I loved playing
here, but as the years passed I developed more
sophisticated tastes (BELOW).

I spent much of my teenage years riding at Sam Marsh's establishment near Edenbridge (ABOVE) or with my father on borrowed horses (LEFT). When I was sixteen I went to Bertram Mills Circus at Olympia during the Christmas holidays (BELOW), clearly enjoying every minute.

As I grew older, my social life broadened. In the late 1930s my mother and I had three wonderful skiing holidays (ABOVE LEFT AND RIGHT); and I made good friends of my own age, among them Fiona Forbes (LEFT).

My mother's bedroom at Chartwell reflected her lovely colour sense, with arcaded sky-blue painted walls and ceiling, and brilliant scarlet curtains for the bed.

*Summer 1940 in
Breccles, staying with
Venetia Montagu.*
TOP, LEFT TO RIGHT:
*Judy Montagu,
Kathryn Stanley,
Rosemary Scott-Ellis,
and myself.*

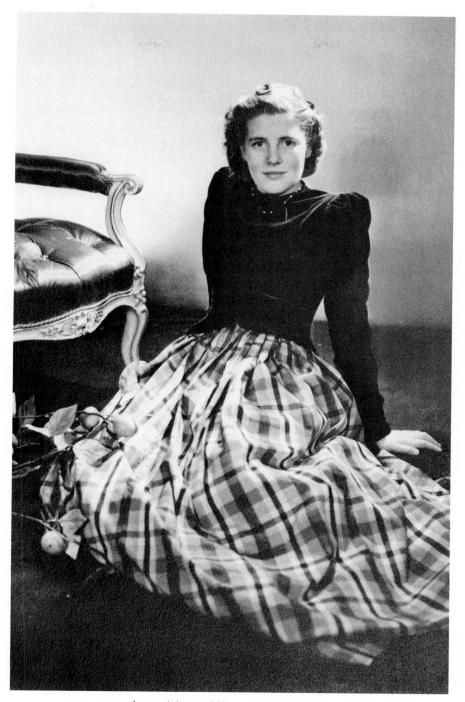

Antony Beauchamp (who would later marry Sarah), just starting as a photographer after his war service, took this one of me in my favourite dress—a sapphire-blue long-sleeved jacket-top over a tartan taffeta skirt.

TOP LEFT: *My mother in the Admiralty House flat my parents occupied in the first months of the war;* TOP RIGHT: *her bedroom in the No. 10 Annexe;* ABOVE: *the dining room in the fortified Garden Rooms at No. 10.*

ABOVE AND RIGHT:
On 4 October 1939 Randolph married Pamela Digby—and I kissed the bridegroom.

LEFT: *Arriving with my parents at the Free Trade Hall. Manchester, January 1940.*

BELOW: *Waving away HMS* Indomitable, *launched by my mother (on my left) at Barrow-in-Furness on 25 March 1940.*

I "came out" at Queen Charlotte's Ball at the Grosvenor House Hotel. Here I am in my ball gown (RIGHT), *and dancing,* (BELOW) *watched by my father: my mother is dancing too, on the right.*

Wartime weekends were usually
spent at Chequers (BELOW), where
I had a top-floor bedroom (LEFT) or
at Ditchley, the Oxfordshire home
of Ronald and Nancy Tree, where
my parents and their guests stayed
when the moon was high. Here I
am (ABOVE) with my
poodle Sukie.

ABOVE LEFT: *Opening Westerham's War Weapons Week early in 1940.* ABOVE RIGHT: *Dancing at Queen Charlotte's Ball, 1941.* RIGHT: *In Cardiff, April 1941, with Gil Winant (far left) and Averell Harriman (right). We were accompanying my father.* BELOW: *As a WVS hospital librarian (LEFT), talking to the visiting minister in charge, and (RIGHT) on leave from the ATS, with my mother and Nana (and Sukie).*

Early days in the army. Our initial ATS training was as much about keeping ourselves and our quarters clean and well presented as about anything strictly military.

*In uniform with Judy Montagu:
note the "fore and aft" caps,
which we could wear off duty.*

*My mother and myself with Admiral
of the Fleet Sir Dudley Pound.*

*Taking leave of my father on the
Duke of York before he set out
for America in December 1941.
Note I am now a lance corporal!*

With some of Pip Section, 481 Battery, at practice camp in Bude, Cornwall, 1943.

two months, the German and British air forces would be joined in daily conflict. My second and last term at Queen's College had just ended, and inasmuch as it was possible to make plans in such uncertain times, it was decided that when the "holiday" months were over I should do a full-time war job, working from home (which was now No. 10). To this end I was interviewed by the very splendid (and, to me, awe-inspiring) Stella, Lady Reading, head of the WVS (Women's Voluntary Service), who said she would take me on at their headquarters in Westminster, working at first in the Registry. With this settled, I spent the rest of this most fateful—but also most beautiful, weather-wise—of summers between London, Chartwell, Chequers, and Breccles in Norfolk (my cousin Judy Montagu's home).

A "peaceful" weekend at Chartwell staying with Nana Whyte in her cottage while my parents were at Chequers was disturbed and enlivened one night by several violent explosions: they turned out to be bombs dropped at Edenbridge several miles off, but they shook the cottage. Nana and I in our dressing gowns watched the brilliant fingers of the searchlights probing the night sky, while planes droned overhead. I reported to my diary that I "felt frightened but excited & robust!" This was a mild initiation.

I spent much of the rest of the high summer at Breccles. Two other girls were also staying, Rosemary Scott-Ellis and Kathryn Stanley; we justified our existence by helping in the mornings with the evacuees, pupils, and teachers from a junior school from London. This involved supervising playtime and working in the kitchen and garden, salting down runner beans, picking fruit, and so on. But that left plenty of time for riding picnics to the Mere, bicycling miles to local cinemas, playing tennis, and entertaining RAF pilots stationed at one or other of the airfields in the neighbourhood—Mildenhall, Honington, Watton (the nearest to Breccles), and Lakenheath—from where they flew in their Blenheim bombers on the now-frequent daylight raids on Germany.

I now appreciate (which I didn't as much as I should have at the time) the generosity of Cousin Venetia's hospitality. She was such a curious personality—formidably gruff and intolerant of our teenage foolishness in some ways; yet (as I discovered later), having herself been a devotee of the "pleasure principle" for most of her life, she was eager to give all the help she could to her younger friends and relations in their zest for fun. She was also strongly patriotic, and more than ready to help the "boys in blue." Despite rationing, her table was well and plentifully supplied: she was knowledgeable about food, and cultivated a prolific vegetable garden as well as producing rabbits, pigs, and game in season. Meals were delicious, and drink flowed freely. The domestic staff was somewhat reduced, but the cook remained, catering both for the household and the evacuees—as did the marvellous Mr. (to us) Clements, Cousin Venetia's long-serving butler, now well over military age. We girls cleared the table and helped with the washing up, but I think Clements, traditionally dressed in striped trousers and tails in the evenings and weekends, scorned our amateur lack of proficiency in these matters, and certainly would not entrust us with the skilled task of "laying up." Both Mr. Clements and Mr. Fit, the somewhat gloomy head gardener, were members of the local Home Guard.

However, Cousin Venetia combined her tolerance in matters of social life with a determination that we should not grow up empty-headed, and time was always found for long and most enjoyable reading-aloud sessions. During those summer weeks she read us Jane Austen (reminding us that these timeless works were written at the height of the Napoleonic wars): she could not resist scathingly comparing us to those "giddy girls," Kitty and Lydia Bennett, who were forever off to Meryton to see what regiments had appeared locally! Nor could Cousin Venetia abide idle hands: she herself was highly skilled with her needle, and worked acres of tapestry carpet while listening to the news and commentary programmes; we too all had to have something—knitting or embroidery—"on the go." We also set ourselves the task of learning a Shakespeare sonnet per day—quite a tall order, and of course we fell behind our schedule; but to this day I have by heart three or four of those matchless poems as companions.

The challenges and demands for bomber crews were quite different from those faced by fighter pilots—the Few—whose tense waiting at the ready for the order to "scramble" and relatively brief bouts of deadly peril and thrill of mortal, often one-to-one, combat needed a different training, and a different sort of courage and endurance, from those required for the long-distance daylight bombing of targets mostly deep in Germany. The crew of a Blenheim bomber was three strong—pilot, copilot/navigator, and gunner: they formed a close team, totally dependent on one another's training, skill, presence of mind, and courage. The crews usually had a certain amount of advance notice of when they would be needed, and were given detailed information about their target, the route to be followed, and any known hazards likely to be met on the way in elaborate briefings, usually the night before the operation planned. Once clear of the English coast, three to four hours' flying over enemy-occupied territory required all the navigator's skill and the utmost vigilance and readiness for attack by enemy planes or anti-aircraft guns. Then came the short, vital time approaching and over the target, usually fiercely opposed; the release of their bombs; and, if possible, an attempt to assess the success of their attack before turning for home. Even then, with "mission accomplished," there would often be the knowledge of one or more planes lost, and damage of varying degrees or seriousness to those remaining; crew members might have been killed or injured and needing whatever care it was possible to give in cramped conditions. The planes involved in the raid, which would have left their home airfield earlier in the day in meticulous order for takeoff, often could not keep together on the homeward flight, and nearly always radio silence had to be kept as they braved the long, hazardous journey home, sometimes limping in after dark or landing at a different airfield. Their welcome home was warm but professionally brisk, and however tired they were, immediate debriefing was required.

Station commanders were all keen on keeping those of their crews who were not on duty for operations or training suitably occupied and distracted, and contacts with the neighbourhood were much encouraged. Most of the squadrons had weekly dances, which were very jolly and noisy and pretty drunken affairs, with sometimes an undercurrent of tension (especially if planes had failed to return), sometimes of relief when, over the noise of the dance music, one heard the throb-throb of a homecomer and was conscious that the flare path had been lit. Local girls were much in demand at these dances, and it was here that we got to know our "special" friends, whom Judy invited back to Breccles to play tennis, swim, lark about, indulge in snogging sessions in the hayloft, or just sit in the garden gossiping. They were charming young men, mostly middle-class, nearly all in their twenties and mostly unmarried.

We spent a lot of our time going to the cinema at Watton, where the films—with the rare exception of a winner like *French Without Tears*—were fairly uninspiring even by our undemanding standards. Other, more unusual entertainments came our way in the form of aerial "beatings up" by our friends: on August Bank Holiday I recorded that

> Watton came and gave us the most superb aerial beating up that anyone could possibly conceive. A flight of Blenheims appeared & one after another swooped down to within 25 or 30ft. of the ground [I think I must have got this wrong—even allowing for skilled piloting and the flatness of Norfolk!]. We all nearly passed out with excitement. It lasted 10 or 15 minutes. Only fly in the ointment was the escape of the horses!

... Which had to be retrieved over the following days from several miles away. On another occasion, a single Blenheim (this time from pals at Honington) swooped down and dropped a letter. I cannot tell if these aerial visitations were deemed to be part of "training"—I suspect they might not have been regarded as such by the commanding officers concerned, but I also suspect blind eyes and deaf ears were turned.

In August I returned home for about a fortnight. During a Chequers weekend, Jock Colville was on duty, and by this time we had both somewhat revised our initial poor opinion of each other. "I like Jock," I wrote in my diary on 10 August, "but I think he is very 'wet.'"* Jock had already formed a kinder opinion of me, writing in his diary in June that he found me "very much nicer on closer acquaintance."[6] Family guests that weekend were Randolph and Pamela (who was expecting her first baby in October); among others who joined us either for luncheon, or to "dine and sleep," were Anthony Eden, Sir Archibald Wavell, Sir John Dill, Sir Hastings (Pug) Ismay, the Prof, Air Marshal Sir Frederick Bowhill, Mr. Ernest Bevin, and Lord Beaverbrook; General de Gaulle looked in for a while on the Saturday afternoon. My diary account of that Sunday told (as did Jock's) of a big air battle in progress: Jock had to ring up Fighter Command at frequent intervals to find out "the latest score," and at the end of the day could report that sixty-two enemy aircraft had been shot down.

On the Sunday afternoon Jock and I set off up Beacon Hill, about an hour's round-trip and the standard after-luncheon weekend walk from Chequers. I recorded that we had discussed marriage—and discovered that he and I had "much the same views as regards this knotty problem—on politics however we differ violently!" Jock wrote: "We sat on the top in the sunshine and prattled gaily, looking at the magnificent view of the plain below. Even though she takes herself a little seriously—as she confesses—she is a charming girl and very pleasant to look upon."[7]

Later that month I returned to Breccles in company with my mother. I was delighted to be reunited with Judy, who bicycled to the station to meet us. The following day—the twenty-fourth—the first bombs were dropped in London. A day or two later in the evening I wrote: "Papa rang Mummie & said that in Ramsgate 700 houses had been blown up by shelling and bombardment. Down here, despite air

---

* Nothing could have been less true. In 1941, at his own insistence, Jock joined the RAF, and after completing his training returned (at WSC's urgent request) to No. 10, until just before D-Day, when he rejoined his squadron to take part in over forty operations before returning once more to the private office, where WSC found him indispensable.

activity & especially during this lovely day one had almost forgotten the war."

After an agreeable long weekend, my mother returned home; Cousin Venetia and Judy warmly and hospitably kept me with them. Warnings and air raids were becoming frequent now in London, and in our safe haven we listened anxiously to the news bulletins. Five days later I wrote my mother a long letter full of our activities, including luncheon in the Mess at the invitation of the Wing Commander—after which, having enjoyed an enjoyable afternoon of tennis and tea, we had been allowed to inspect one of the Blenheims. This was a great thrill, although I confessed that I had found it rather "gruesome & frightening." But the main burden of my letter concerned my increasingly strong feeling that

> I feel I am indulging in escapism down here. For quite a long time on end I have forgotten the war completely. Even when we are with the airmen one forgets—because they are so gay. And then one suddenly remembers that somewhere the sirens are wailing and people are having their houses wrecked—and that millions of people all over Europe are starving and bereaved and unhappy—it is so quiet and I love the country so much—but somehow it's all wrong. May I please come back to you and Papa as soon as possible? I really won't let air raids rattle me—and I care so terribly about the war and everything, and I should like to feel that I was risking something . . .

This letter with its impassioned plea ended, however, on a practical note: "Do you think you would please send me £1-10/-?! Only I haven't got my cheque book here—and so I can't get at my allowance!"

My mother replied at once and at length. With hindsight I see that she (and I expect she may have consulted my father) did not want me back in London just as the air raids were becoming more intense—but she was most understanding of my feelings:

It makes me glad that you are having a happy care-free spell in
the country. You must not feel guilty about it. Being sad and
low does not help anyone. We must decide in a day or two when
you should come back. I will telephone & talk it over with you
my Darling Country Mouse . . .

She described to me the arrangements at No. 10:

We have got quite used to the Air Raid Warnings, & when you
come back you will find a comfortable little bunk in the Shelter.
There are 4, one for Papa, one for me, one for you & one for
Pamela.* The top ones are quite difficult to climb into. Twice
we have spent the whole night there as we were asleep when the
'All Clear' went. Down there you can hear nothing.

My mother also reassured me that she had spoken to Lady Reading
about my proposed work (I imagine they were in collusion)—and that
she had sent me the cheque.

For all of this I thanked her when I wrote again to her on 8 September; but nevertheless I returned to the charge:

I think of you all so often—and I hate to be separated from
you and Papa in these dark days. Please—oh—please, Mummie
darling, let me come back . . . I would so like to be with you and
take my share, and also I do want to begin my work. WOW!
Not make Kitten into 'evacuee Kit'!

My mother had also referred to my father's speech in the House
of Commons on 5 September, when he had announced the exchange
with the United States of fifty old American destroyers for naval bases

---

* Randolph was in the country with his regiment, which would shortly go to the Middle
East, and Pamela was staying with her parents-in-law.

for the U.S. Navy in the Caribbean—a deal of huge importance to us at the time. "I read Papa's speech of course," I wrote back, "and it was so cheering and invigorating. . . . I think it is the best thing I've heard for a long time. What a 'poke-in-the-snoot' for Hitler!"

The succeeding days saw terrible raids on London. The Blitz was starting in earnest, with the capital suffering nightly bombing until 2 November. The "ordering" of my life must have been settled over the telephone: I was to go to live at Chequers for the winter, and work full-time for the WVS in nearby Aylesbury. This would enable me to see my parents and join in their life at weekends—thus considerations of both safety and honour were satisfied. On 11 September, the eve of my departure from Breccles, Cousin Venetia and Judy organized a farewell-cum-birthday party for me, inviting all my new local friends and our gallant boys in blue. It was a lovely party, ending in the early hours with nostalgic and affectionate farewells in the moonlight.

CHAPTER 9

At Chequers

———

I ARRIVED AT CHEQUERS IN TIME TO INSTAL MYSELF FOR MY EIGH-teenth birthday on Sunday, 15 September. There was quite a family gathering—Nana came over for the weekend from Chartwell; Randolph and Pamela were there, and Sarah too; and despite dislocation from air raids, my mother contrived to bring down a delicious cake. There were also gripping distractions: during these days air battles of varying intensity were taking place, and on this Sunday my father (who always liked to see things for himself) drove from Chequers with my mother to the headquarters of No. 11 Fighter Group at Uxbridge, where over a period of a few hours they witnessed the directing of "one of the decisive battles of the war."[1] After their return home later that evening, we learned the tally for the battle: the Germans had lost fifty-six planes; we had lost twenty-five, with fourteen pilots killed.* The Luftwaffe did not repeat these attacks, and—though of course we did not know this at the time—two days later Hitler decided to postpone operation Sea Lion (the invasion of Britain) indefinitely.

I started my work with the WVS at once, driving over to Aylesbury every day (my mother having left her car for me, as she now had the use of an official car). People were pouring out of London as a result of

---

* The German pilot loss was "net," while many of the RAF survivors lived to fight another day. Figures from Gilbert, *Finest Hour*, p. 791, n. 2.

the heavy bombing, and Aylesbury was deemed a safe area: during my first weeks, therefore, I was assigned to the team of billeting officers, whose job it was to accommodate the refugees locally. It was a difficult and ungrateful task, especially trying to keep families together, and relying on persuasion rather than invoking the powers that existed to compel people to take in these unfortunate folk, all of whom had terrible tales to tell of the bombing of their neighbourhoods. At night, even from forty miles away, we could see the flashing from the anti-aircraft guns and hear the distant rumble. All this, I see from my diary, made a deep impression on me:

> Look at the crowds of homeless, destitute, weary people in Aylesbury alone. I have seen more suffering & poverty this week than ever before. I cannot find words to describe my feelings about it. I only know I am moved to a greater & wider realisation of the suffering war brings. I only know that I have learnt more about human suffering & anxiety than ever before.

Any lurking feelings I may have had about being made an "evacuee" from the danger zone of London by my overprotective parents were dramatically banished when a land mine descended upon Aylesbury on the night of 25–26 September hard by the WVS offices, rendering them unfit for occupation! Luckily there was no loss of life; but for a few days there was considerable dislocation in our work, until new premises were found.

Meanwhile my life as a full-time resident at Chequers was settling into its pattern. When my parents, the secretariat, and the guests had all departed and my working week began, kind Miss Lamont took me under her wing, and I breakfasted and had supper with her in her apartment on the ground floor. I often sat with her in the evenings too, listening to the radio or playing cards—she was a charming companion. Just now my sister-in-law, Pamela, was also living at Chequers during the last weeks of her pregnancy, it having been decided that she should have her baby there.

My own bedroom was the "Prison Room," up on the second floor at the northeast corner of the house; it can be reached from a "secret" spiral staircase leading from the Hawtrey Room on the ground floor, though access is more usually from an upper corridor. The "Prison Room" was so named from having been the room in which Lady Mary Grey was confined for two years from 1565 to 1567, in the care of the owner of Chequers, Sir William Hawtrey. Lady Mary, a great-granddaughter of Henry VII, was a younger sister of Lady Jane Grey, who had been executed in 1554 aged only sixteen for high treason.* Some ten years after her sister's demise, Lady Mary rashly married without the consent of the reigning monarch (now Queen Elizabeth), taking as her husband a man both beneath her socially and consider-ably older than she—Thomas Keyes, a sergeant porter of the Royal Watergates at Westminster. The Queen was greatly offended: Keyes was flung into the Fleet prison, and Lady Mary was placed in the cus-tody of Sir William Hawtrey at Chequers, where she was locked up in the chamber thereafter called the "Prison Room." After two years during which she was allowed to go out of doors only for the good of her health, the Queen relented (although Mary was not allowed to see her husband again: he died in 1571), and Mary was confided to the custody of her maternal step-grandmother, the Dowager Duchess of Suffolk.[2]

Such was the pathetic story connected with the bedroom which would be mine for the foreseeable future. I was somewhat isolated up there, as although the servants' rooms were on the same floor, they were on the other side of the house, and the other bedrooms near me were only occupied at weekends; so I was very solitary in my "Prison Room," and it was quite cold (despite an open fire)—but I loved it, and if I gave thought to the earlier Mary who had inhabited it, I felt she

* Lady Jane had been the cat's paw of the Duke of Northumberland and her powerful scheming relations, who had attempted to secure the Protestant succession by declaring Jane Queen on Edward VI's death in 1553. She was Queen of England for just nine days, until Northumberland's army deserted him, at which point the Roman Catholic Mary Tudor (Henry VIII's daughter with Catherine of Aragon) was proclaimed the rightful sovereign, and Northumberland and his associates went to the block.

was a friendly shade—and perhaps liked some company! But the wind "wuthered" round my corner of the house, and I sometimes covered my head with the bedclothes when aircraft (friend or foe?) droned overhead: Chequers lay on the broad flight path to the Midlands, where Coventry and Birmingham were suffering badly.

Though the big house fell silent during the week, it sprang into life every weekend, when a succession of official guests lunched, or "dined and slept," and the business of the war continued unabated. During the summer months there had been many false alarms about the imminence of invasion, and one such occurred the third weekend of September, when President Roosevelt alerted Winston that "a most reliable source" in Berlin had predicted that the invasion would begin at dawn on Sunday, the twenty-second. Jock Colville was on duty early, and in his diary wrote: "The P.M. was rather sceptical . . . [but] kept himself busy telephoning to people about it all morning. . . . I then went and told Mrs C. and Mary who were sitting side by side in the same bed, with trays on their laps, and who treated the whole matter as a most entertaining joke."[3] After luncheon, for those not in conclave, there were walks to the beautiful viewpoints of Beacon Hill or Coombe Hill, and after dinner films were shown in the Long Gallery (they were of widely varying quality and usually too long, and my mother would often escape once the lights were down). Later my father would get back to business with his political colleagues, service chiefs, and planners, working through to the early hours.

At the end of September I was transferred by the WVS from the dramas of billeting to work in the library organized by the Red Cross for patients in the very large hospital at Stoke Mandeville on the outskirts of Aylesbury. The library team was made up of mainly married women with families, working part-time. Our clientele was varied in its tastes and needs: apart from medical and surgical wards with a relatively quick turnaround, there were several big wards of long-term cases, mostly geriatric, evacuated from London hospitals; many of these patients were sunk in torpor or indifference, which we genuinely tried to penetrate. There were relatively few service wards, with cases sent for longer-term treatment from frontline hospitals: these, of course, tended to be the librarians' favourites—some of the nursing sisters occasionally murmuring that more jolly chat was exchanged than books. The work was quite arduous physically, as the hospital was entirely on one level, with long wards giving off the main corridors "herringbone" fashion. We librarians, having loaded our large, heavy trollies with carefully chosen books and magazines, pushed them for what seemed miles along the brown linoleumed corridors, which were in places on a slight slope, so that braking became a problem. We tried very hard to please our "customers," but did not always succeed, and one failure prompted me into verse with this limerick:

> *There was a young man who said 'Hell!'*
> *when I gave him an Ethel M. Dell**—
> *He wanted a tale*
> *by Wren or Taffrail*—
> *And he thought that the Dell was a sell.*

In order to preserve and repair the books we also had to learn bookbinding: Nana Whyte, who came quite often during weekdays to keep me company at Chequers, joined our library team, and was a particularly skilled binder.

A feature of Chequers life at this time was the presence of a platoon of the Coldstream Guards, who were responsible for the general security of the house and grounds. They were supplied on a rotating basis from their London depot in Albany Street, where they were mostly waiting to join their regiment in the Middle East; I gathered that the "Chequers detail" was quite a popular respite from air raids, apart from the unusual interest value. The ranks were encamped nearby in Nissen huts, and the two or three officers lived in one of the lodges, their Mess with its kitchen being in a large tent in the field next to the garden. Their living conditions being fairly spartan, my mother

---

* Ethel M. Dell was a poor man's Barbara Cartland.

offered them hot baths in the house during the week, and quite often at the weekends they would be asked to lunch or dine. The presence of these mostly charming and good-looking young men was very agreeable, enlivening weekday life, and I made some lasting friendships.

Although the tempo of life at Chequers from Monday through Thursday was markedly different from the to-ing and fro-ing of the weekends, even weekdays were not without their alarums and excursions. One evening in October the "young gentlemen of the guard" kindly asked me to dine with them. During the course of dinner our lively conversation was abruptly disturbed by the "swishing crescendo-ing [*sic*] clatter of a bomb uncomfortably near. Everyone ducked ineffectually—& waited—it seemed an age—before a comparatively small bump. . . ." We all went into the slit trench nearby, which was "muddy & spoilt my suede shoes," I complained to my diary. Nothing further transpiring, we resumed our interrupted dinner. The following morning revealed "a LARGE crater about 100 yds from the Mess," caused in fact by one of a stick of bombs that had fallen (fortunately) in the soggy field, causing no damage to life or limb. But at the weekend Jock Colville recorded that the company assembled had inspected the craters, and discussed whether "it was chance that they fell so close"; this was his opinion, "but the P.M. and Ismay incline to the view that it was a trial shot and may well have been done on purpose."[4]

That week was an eventful one for our family also, as on 10 October Pamela, after her long and tedious waiting, gave birth safely to a boy. I recorded jubilantly in my diary: "4.40 a.m. WINSTON CHURCHILL Junior arrived. Hooray. Pam weak but happy. Baby not at all weak & only partially happy!" Some weeks later Churchills, Digbys, and godparents gathered for "Baby" Winston's christening on Sunday, 1 December, which was held at nearby Ellesborough—the Chequers' parish church—after Mattins; many of the congregation stayed on for the christening service. At luncheon afterwards, Winston proposed the health of his grandson and namesake as "Christ's new faithful soldier and servant."

It was round now that the feeling among those responsible grew

that the clockwork regularity of Winston's weekend visits to Chequers, when also so many people vital to the war effort were constantly
present, was a security hazard—most particularly at full moon, when
Chequers could be identified from the air. A solution to this problem was found through the patriotic generosity of Ronnie and Nancy
Tree,* who put their large and beautiful eighteenth-century house,
Ditchley, in Oxfordshire, quite near to Blenheim, at the disposal of
Winston and Clementine, their official guests, and family. I went on
several of these visits, driving over from Chequers to join my parents.
Nancy and Ronnie were the most perfect hosts, and the beauty of the
house—especially coming into its warmth and glow from the chill,
dark outside—remains a vivid memory; the contrast to the drabness
and ugliness of wartime London impressed itself upon us all.

Studying the lists of visitors to Chequers or Ditchley, one can trace
the urgent preoccupations of the moment—and with hindsight see
inklings of what perhaps lay ahead. During August and September
1940, the Air Chiefs predominated—Air Marshal Charles Portal—
"Peter"—Chief of the Air Staff; Sir Hugh Dowding—"Stuffy"—Chief
of Fighter Command; and, a little later on, Sir Richard Pierce, head
of Bomber Command. Leading soldiers were Lord Gort VC; Sir
Alan Brooke, Commander-in-Chief Home Forces; Sir Frederick Pile,
Chief of Anti-Aircraft Defence; General Ismay—"Pug," the inde-
fatigable puller-together of so many threads, a great "troubleshooter,"
and a great favourite with us all. Among the politicians were Anthony
Eden, Secretary of State for War; Ernest Bevin, the stalwart Labour
trades union leader and now Minister of Labour; Oliver Lyttleton;
Max Beaverbrook, brilliant as Minister of Aircraft Production, a
great personal friend of Winston—and always "up to something" (but
what? Clementine's sharp eye was watching!); and Lord Halifax, soon
to be ambassador to Washington. There was also a "regular" from

---

* Ronald Tree was American by birth, but was wholly brought up in Britain and was a
British subject. A Conservative Member of Parliament, he had long supported WSC's
campaign for rearmament. His beautiful and gifted Virginian wife, Nancy, was a
daughter of one of the famous Langhorne sisters, and a niece of Nancy Astor.

Chartwell days—the Prof, soon to be Lord Cherwell and Paymaster General, Winston's chief adviser. Invariably the weekend parties included family members, and quite often a friend of mine—Alastair Forbes or Robin Maugham; Judy Montagu or Fiona Forbes—came to stay; but any friend staying on at Chequers into the working week had to lend a hand at the library, and keep my hours. The continuous weekend entertaining soon proved too much for the original domestic staff, who in any case were proving increasingly hard to get—and there were also considerations of security: so it was decided that it would be appropriate for Chequers to be staffed by members of the women's services, and accordingly volunteers from the Auxiliary Territorial Service (ATS) and the Women's Auxiliary Air Force (WAAF) presently took over the running of the house.*

I knew I could be of use to my mother at weekends, and I did my best in helping to look after the stream of guests; although she did not have the burden of running Chequers, the weekends for her were not restful, for she was always "on duty": her life now, as the wife of the Prime Minister, was increasingly busy, and she was taking on more war work—such as the YWCA (hostels for servicewomen) and later the Aid to Russia Fund—and after a weekend of entertaining, as the war went on she often returned to London as tired as when she had arrived. Needless to say, it was thrilling for me to meet our guests: I got to know the "regulars" quite well—and of course I had my favourites. Although secret business was not discussed at mealtimes, nevertheless the conversation ranged over the war situation—fears for the present and hopes for the future—and it was very exciting to hear of events as they were happening, and sometimes to know a little of what lay ahead. Such was the case on Monday, 9 December, when my father was lunching at Chequers with myself and the Private Secretary: "Papa was worried and preoccupied and told me that at dawn this morning an attack was launched by the British troops in Libya. 'Pray' he said 'for the victory of British arms.' I prayed most

* The arrangement continues to this day.

fervently. Very anxiously waiting." On the Wednesday after I got back from work ". . . Mummie rang up at about 7.45 and told me our army has had a victory [over the Italians]—Sidi Barrani is taken & many prisoners. Thank God—Thank God. It is too wonderful—after this dreary winter with so many blows—I could weep with excitement." My parents returned to Chequers on the Thursday evening: "Papa tells us that approximately *30,000* prisoners have been taken!! Our joy and elation however a little darkened by the sudden sad death of Lord Lothian [British ambassador at Washington]. He will be a great loss." My mother had a sore throat and retired to bed, leaving Jock Colville and myself to dine with my father. "At dinner Papa was pondering who to send to Washington . . . Papa in very bad mood over food and of course I couldn't control him & he was very naughty & rushed & complained to the cook about the soup which he (truthfully) said was tasteless. I fear the domestic applecart may have been upset! Oh dear!"

For the sake of my amour propre, I am glad to be able to recount an occasion when apparently my influence with my father was more successful—though I was oblivious of this until sixty-one years later, when Professor Richard Keynes, whom I had the privilege and pleasure of meeting at Churchill College, Cambridge, sent me the story as told in the Royal Society's biographical memoir of Charles Goodeve.

One Sunday early in 1941 the Prof arranged for Winston to see trials of a new type of anti-tank bomb which were being carried out in a chalk quarry not far from Chequers, and he took me along too. The news of the Prime Minister's visit reached the ears of Charles Goodeve, a Royal Naval Volunteer Reserve officer and a brilliant inventor whose small team had already produced various effective devices in collaboration with Captain G. Davies RN. Both men were working nearby at MDI, the experimental unit at Whitchurch, Buckinghamshire, commanded by Major Jefferis—whence came the anti-tank bomb which was to be displayed this Sunday morning. Goodeve and Davies were trying—so far unsuccessfully—to gain official recognition and backing for a highly advanced anti-submarine weapon which had acquired the name of the Hedgehog: if only the Prime Minister's interest—and hopefully support—could be enlisted, the protagonists of Hedgehog were sure its merits would be recognized. They attended the highly successful demonstration of the anti-tank bomb, and as the Prime Minister, after consulting his watch, remarked that it was "time for lunch" and began to walk back to his car, the Prof introduced Goodeve, who hurriedly described the Hedgehog to Churchill. My father listened with great interest, but said that he was sorry there was not time on this occasion to see this new weapon—at which point, it appears, I had caught up with my father and, grasping his arm, begged him to inspect Captain Davies's bomb thrower, saying there was plenty of time to do so. Somewhat astonishingly, Winston relented, and the whole party proceeded to Whitchurch, where Hedgehog gave a highly convincing display: lunchtime was forgotten, the new weapon received the vital backing it required, and in due course it accounted for a large number of U-boats in the Battle of the Atlantic. I am of course greatly gratified after all these years to know that I had been a small link in this chain of events.[5]

Soon after the beginning of the Blitz, No. 10 became unsafe for habitation, and Winston and Clementine with their immediate personal staff moved into what became known as the No. 10 Annexe. This consisted of a series of offices directly over the Central War Rooms (with which they communicated directly by an internal staircase) and looking out over St. James's Park, which were swiftly converted into living apartments. Winston was very keen on the concept of "business as usual," and for a time continued to hold Cabinet meetings in the Cabinet Room at No. 10, and to entertain with Clementine in the fortified Garden Rooms there; but towards the end of 1940 conditions were such that it was both safer and more practical to transfer the whole of their life to the Annexe. My mother soon made the gaunt, unprepossessing rooms look almost pretty by painting them in pale colours, hanging many of their own pictures, and using much of their own furniture.

These arrangements had implications for my visits to London throughout the war years. Because the Annexe flat had been planned

for Winston, Clementine, and their immediate secretarial and domestic staff, there was no room for a houseguest. Therefore, when I
stayed, I was allotted one of the emergency bedrooms down below in
the Cabinet War Rooms complex, with which the Annexe flat had
direct communication; my clothes, however, were kept (mostly in my
suitcase) in a bathroom used by the women secretaries (which cannot
have been very convenient for them). At night, I would get into my
nightclothes there and make my way "down below." Passing the sentry
on duty at the Annexe front door on my way up and down in my dressing gown and tin hat was a perpetual source of humiliation to me, as
I imagined he must think I was the only "windy" one in the family!

In the last week of December there was a strange lull in war activity on land, at sea, and in the air. Christmas saw a gathering of our
complete close family at Chequers, and the great gloomy hall glowed
with the lighted, decorated tree: "This was one of the happiest Christ-
masses I can remember," I wrote in my diary. "I've never before seen
the family look so happy—so united—so sweet. . . . I wonder if we will
all be together next Christmas?"

CHAPTER 10

Decisions . . . Decisions . . . Decisions

THE NEW YEAR OF 1941 WAS SNOWY: FIONA FORBES CAME TO STAY at Chequers, and we tobogganed merrily on the Beacon, using a sledge made for us by Sawyers, my father's valet.

The victorious surge forward of Allied forces in Libya, which had started before Christmas, was marked by the capture of Bardia on Sunday, 5 January—a day dominated by news coming through at intervals about the progress of the attack:

> After lunch we were in the long gallery. Papa came in & said 'News from the battlefront'. This telegram said Northern section of Bardia defences pierced by Australians. Large numbers of prisoners. Only perimeter defences now holding out . . . At dinner came news—Bardia village taken—further advances. After dinner came the final *triumphant* communiqué 'All resistance in Bardia has ceased'—2500 prisoners—including 2 corps commanders.

A feature of the early part of this year was the arrival from America of personal representatives of President Roosevelt. The first was Harry Hopkins; he was soon followed by Averell Harriman; and in March Gil Winant arrived as United States ambassador, a welcome successor to the anti-British and defeatist Joseph Kennedy (father of a later President). It is impossible to exaggerate the importance of these emissaries in building up the close relationship between Churchill and Roosevelt which would develop as the war progressed; moreover, they also got to know the War Cabinet and Chiefs of Staff. Winston deployed all his personal warmth and charm to win their friendship, and to convince them both of the firmness and effectiveness of Britain's stand—and of our dire need for active and material help. He encouraged these important guests to go out and about in the country, and to visit especially the badly bombed areas, so that they could see for themselves what we were going through, and feel the mood of the people. Nearly every weekend one or other of these remarkable and very different men came to Chequers, so that Clementine and our family also got to know them quite well. Gil Winant was of course here on a long-term basis: looking like Abraham Lincoln, he was the most charming man, with an intense manner (and almost "invisible" voice), and he became a close family friend—especially of Sarah, with whom he fell deeply in love.

Harry Hopkins quickly became a general favourite. The son of a harness maker in Sioux City, he was a social worker and administrator in New Deal days, and through Averell Harriman became close to the President; after his wife died in 1937 he lived in the White House. He was seemingly a most unlikely person to take to the British—our far-flung imperialism and class-oriented society being anathema to him—and indeed he anticipated personally disliking Winston: but mutual liking was instant, and the firm and lasting friendship which soon followed included Clementine and our family.

Winston Churchill and Franklin Roosevelt had first met briefly in London in 1917 when the former was Minister of Munitions and Roosevelt U.S. Assistant Secretary of the Navy. The meeting was not a success: Roosevelt took an active dislike to Churchill, who later actually forgot that they had met at all! But early on in Churchill's time at the Admiralty, the President had initiated a correspondence between them which created a new and important link. Now, by sending Hopkins—his close confidant—the President was seeking to learn more about the man who had rallied his country in its hour of danger, who now held such a dominating position, and who was so obviously keen to establish a closer relationship with him.

Harry Hopkins gave at first a somewhat dour impression, from which soon emerged great personal charm; he was painfully thin, with wispy hair, and he struggled with ill health, which he never allowed to deter him from his work. Poor Harry found Chequers very cold—we would discover him reading official papers wearing a heavy overcoat huddled in the downstairs men's cloakroom, which was beautifully warm as all the hot water pipes ran through it. He had a delightful sense of humour. One day, taking a stroll in the grounds, he approached one of the Coldstream Guardsmen on patrol: "Are there many of you boys around here?" he enquired. "No Sir, only Guardsmen!" came the immediate reply—Harry was delighted.

Whatever his original doubts about Winston, his colleagues, or our country, when Hopkins left us to go back to Washington, at a farewell dinner held for him he said: "I suppose you wish to know what I am going to say to President Roosevelt on my return. Well, I'm going to quote you one verse from that Book of Books . . . whither thou goest I will go; and where thou lodgest, I lodge: thy people shall be my people, and thy God my God." Then he added very quietly, "Even unto the end."[1]

In March the U.S. Congress passed the Lend-Lease Bill, which was of vital importance to us; and shortly afterwards Averell Harriman, the President's personal representative, arrived in London to deal with all matters concerning the operation of Lend-Lease, and to recommend "everything that we can do, short of war, to keep the British Isles afloat."[2] Averell was also a colleague and friend of Harry Hopkins, to whom he was a strong contrast in every way: son of a fabulously rich American railway king, Averell had also made a fortune for himself as a banker and businessman; at forty-nine, he was good-looking, urbane, and full of charm. He came very often to Chequers—a popular guest, and soon a real family friend.

I also got to know our Commonwealth guests. The South African

Field Marshal Smuts, with his calm demeanour and wise judgement (so much valued by Winston), came from time to time; also Mr. Mackenzie King, the Prime Minister of Canada—very nice indeed, but a bit of a "maiden aunt"! A great favourite—and so nice to me—was Mr. Robert (Bob) Menzies, the Prime Minister of Australia. Later, in peacetime, he would bring his charming wife, Dame Pattie, with him, and also his delightful daughter Heather, with whom I would make a long-lasting friendship.

Interspersed with our American and Commonwealth guests, of course, were our own team of political colleagues and service chiefs. Looking back now at the list of Chequers guests, it seems that 1941 was a bumper year—weekends often bringing two waves of guests to lunch or to dine and sleep.

Early in this new year I made another visit to Petworth House, Sussex, for a dance given by Lord and Lady Leconfield. Leaving Chequers early on an icy Saturday morning, I took the train to London. It was the first time I had been in London since the previous August, and I was shocked to see the effects of a winter's bombings: yawning gaps, boards replacing blown-out windows in many surviving buildings, apparently abandoned shops declaring in large letters "BUSINESS AS USUAL," and many entrances shored up by sandbags. This visit also gave me my first view of the No. 10 Annexe flat, where I much admired how my mother seemed to have waved a magic wand over formerly unprepossessing offices. Arrived at Petworth I found an "enormous" house party assembling—some of whom I knew already, including Lucia Lawson and Penelope (Popey) Jowitt;* of the latter I would write in my diary that, as we were supposed to look like each other, I "spent my weekend saying what a charming pretty girl she is!" My hostess's mode of dress again attracted my attention: "Violette [Lady Leconfield] was in excellent form dressed in a pale blue V-necked jumper—loaded with jewellery & wearing scarlet corduroy

---

* Daughter of first and last Earl Jowitt (cr. 1951), then Labour MP and Solicitor General and later Lord Chancellor. Popey and I are still in touch.

slacks!!"* The dance itself was "nothing short of heaven. Positively pre-war. Oh the glamour of not having tickets—& its not being in a hotel. [It is] my 3rd private dance! . . . Retired footsore & weary but very happy to bed at 4.30 a.m."

Two months later I came up from Chequers for another party of a very different character—none other than that hardy perennial, Queen Charlotte's Annual Birthday Dinner Dance for debutantes, at which I and my co-debs had made our debut the previous year. This year my mother, Lady Jowitt, and Mrs. Lawson, with their daughters and attendant young men, made up a large table in the vast (underground) Grosvenor House Ballroom. At the rehearsal for the cake-cutting ceremony in the afternoon, we of the 1940 vintage rather patronizingly agreed, as I noted in my diary, that "this year's debs aren't much to write home about"! Just as we were going down for dinner an air raid began, but we only heard odd bumps and thuds above our chatter and the music. Emerging from the ball in the early hours after the "All Clear" had sounded, our party heading for nightclub life met barriers and closed streets, with ambulances and fire engines clustered round the Café de Paris in Coventry Street, near Leicester Square, which had received a direct hit: it was a place we all knew well, with a famous band, and it was always crowded. Recalling it now, I am a little shocked that we headed off to find somewhere else to twirl whatever was left of the night away.

The changing of the Guard at Chequers brought some delightful friends into my life, and some quasi-romantic interludes—the latter of short duration, as the young gentlemen were in the queue for the Middle East and sterner warfare. One could always hear news from overseas—good and bad—through the regimental tom-tom service: thus I learned that Andy Drummond-Hay had been killed, and that Peter Cooper, to whom I was much attached, had been taken prisoner: I mooned about playing the record he had given me of our "theme"

---

* It was extremely unusual then (other than when "on duty") for grand middle-aged ladies to wear trousers—let alone while also bejewelled! Hence my amazed comment.

song, "All the Things You Are," and writing unsatisfactory letters to which at long intervals I received similarly unsatisfactory answers. Tom Blackwell and Tom Egerton became good and lasting friends; but while they would survive the war, Tony Coates—Jock Colville's first cousin, handsome and debonair—a real *chevalier sans peur et sans reproche*—would be killed in action in Normandy in August 1944. But that was all to come. Meanwhile these young men lunched and dined with us at Chequers when on duty there, and we saw each other on and off in London—leave and air raids permitting: the uncertainties of our lives undoubtedly heightened feelings.

Local dalliances apart, in a period of two months I became engaged to be married—and then disengaged. At the end of March I was invited by Lord and Lady Bessborough* (longtime friends of my parents) to spend a weekend at their home at Stansted Park near Chichester in Sussex for a dance given by the RAF at nearby Tangmere airfield. During that visit I got to know their children, Moyra Ponsonby and Eric Duncannon. Eric, the younger of the two, was nine years older than I; an officer in his county regiment, he was extremely intelligent and cultivated, and much given to dramatic art (he was a near-professional amateur actor). I noted that he was "good looking in rather a lyrical way—very beautiful grey, wide set eyes, melodious voice. Charming & easy. . . ." During the course of dining and dancing and walking and talking we got on well, and "he said as he left 'May I ring you up?' I do hope he will. . . ." Well, he did—and during April he courted me elegantly: a few letters, long telephone calls, an evening or two dining and dancing, and John Donne's *Collected Poetry and Prose,* all of which predisposed me in his favour.

During these weeks the war news was for the most part bad. By the first week in April we had evacuated Benghazi, which Wavell's army had so triumphantly reached in February, and would soon be back in Tobruk, with all the ground we had gained lost to Rommel's advanc-

* Ninth Earl of Bessborough, GCMG, PC (d. 1956), a former Governor-General of Canada, and his French wife, Roberte de Neuflize.

ing German army; British forces sent to help the Greeks in March were evacuating by the end of April. These reverses led to a parliamentary debate culminating in a vote of confidence: the government won overwhelmingly, but still . . . Coventry was savagely bombed on 8 April, and London continued to suffer heavy night raids.

My father, who was Chancellor of Bristol University, decided to award honorary degrees to Mr. Menzies and Mr. Winant. The degree ceremony was planned for 12 April, and in the event we travelled to it via Swansea, which had suffered a heavy raid. The party, which included also Averell Harriman, "Pug" Ismay, Jock Colville, my mother, and myself, travelled overnight by special train, arriving at Swansea early on the morning of 11 April—Good Friday. The devastation was fearful: the centre of the city had not a house standing. The morning was spent inspecting detachments of civil defence workers; Winston drove round seated on the back of an open car, and "wherever he went [people] swarmed around Papa—clasping his hand—patting him on the back—shouting his name." Later that day we travelled on, spending the night in a railway siding not far from Bristol. During the night Bristol docks were heavily bombed: from our safe siding we could hear the distant bombardment, and when the train drew into the station at about eight a.m. fires were still smouldering and wreckage was everywhere. The Lord Mayor and officials who came to meet my father had been up all night; driving to the university we saw devastation even worse than at Swansea. We visited rest centres, and people surveying the still-smoking ruins of their own houses came running to cheer Winston—it was unbelievably moving.

A building next to the university was still in flames, but the degree-giving ceremony went ahead. It was quite extraordinary. People kept on arriving late with grime on their faces half washed off, their ceremonial robes on over their firefighting clothes which were still wet.[3] Afterwards, when we all came out onto the steps of the university, a huge crowd had gathered—"men, women & children—laughing—cheering—waving. And the sun had come out." We went on to Cardiff, where again my father had a "stupendous" reception. By the time we got back to Chequers late that night we were exhausted, and wrung out emotionally by all we had seen in those two days.

During these spring weeks Eric continued his courtship and I certainly became much attracted to him. At the beginning of May, he and Moyra came for the weekend to Chequers, and on the Sunday, in the White Parlour, he asked me to marry him. I must surely have seen which way the wind was blowing, but my diary shows me as being taken by surprise: "This evening Eric proposed to me. I'm in a daze—I think I've said 'Yes'—but O dear God I'm in a muddle." My family and closest friends were all very encouraging and sweet, but my mother was not very enthusiastic (which unsettled me a bit); my father—with other things to think of—was genial, but left it all to her. I vacillated between having real doubts and uncertainties, and—once with Eric—feeling "happy—confident—decided."

The families conferred, and no one could have been kinder or more welcoming than my future parents-in-law; Roberte gave me a beautiful brooch, and it was decided our engagement would be announced the following week. Eric bore me off to Leatherhead to meet General McNaughton, who commanded the Canadian army over here—Eric being one of his staff officers—and once more celebrations and congratulations were showered upon us. One sobering note was struck by my sister-in-law, Pamela, who was staying nearby at Cherkley, Lord Beaverbrook's country house, and came over to see me. I recorded in my diary her wise—if at the time unwelcome—piece of advice: "Don't marry someone because *they* want to marry *you*—but because YOU want to marry them." Her words stuck in my mind.

Meanwhile, on 10 May, Clementine wrote to Max Beaverbrook:

It has all happened with stunning rapidity.

The engagement is to be made public next Wednesday: but I want you to know beforehand because you are fond of Mary—

I have persuaded Winston to be firm & to say they must wait six months—

She is only 18, is young for her age, has not seen many people

& I think she was simply swept off her feet with excitement—
They do not know each other at all. Please keep my doubts and
fears to yourself.

Eric and I left Leatherhead on the Saturday morning to join my
parents at Ditchley. There had been a very bad blitzing the night before in London (in fact it would prove to be the longest and heaviest of
all), resulting in many fires, three thousand people killed or wounded,
and the destruction of, among other buildings, the Chamber of the
House of Commons. In consequence of this mayhem several stations
were closed, and so our train journey to Oxford was by a devious route
necessitating several changes on the way—and it was during this long
and tedious journey that serious misgivings crowded in on me.

At last we arrived, and found a large party already assembled, comprising our contingent and Averell Harriman, plus a mixture of the
Trees' family and friends. Immediately my mother whisked me off to
her room and told me that she had discussed the whole matter with
my father, that they had both been seized with serious doubts about
Eric's and my proposed marriage, and that they wanted our engagement put off for six months. I was of course aghast—but through my
tears and protestations, I was aware of my own doubts and uncertainties crystallizing. My mother asked me directly if I felt certain of my
feelings—and of course I was unable to answer: at this point she perceived (rightly) that I was not in love with Eric, and determined to
do everything in her power to stop the whole affair. Feeling unable to
distract Winston from the war, she commandeered Averell Harriman
(to whom she had confided her anxieties) and asked him to talk to
me: so while she went off to confront Eric with this unpalatable news,
Averell asked me to go for a walk with him in the garden. As we paced
round and round the formal box parterre, he begged me to take more
time to consider this major decision in my life. That night I confided
to my diary: "I can never say just how sweet & sensible & sympathetic
he was. He said all the things I should have told myself."

Eric was of course mortified, but very nice to me—and very angry with my mother! Letters were sent by dispatch rider to the Bessboroughs, and drafted announcements rescinded (despite which there would be a few "leaks" in the press, which added to our general embarrassment). We all got through the evening in civilized fashion, aided by a long film. "Had a lot of cider cup—felt better," I wrote in my diary—but I was perfectly aware I had behaved stupidly and went to bed feeling "crushed, humiliated, but fairly calm."

It so happened that this weekend of my emotional and romantic crisis coincided with a dramatic event in public affairs—and so mountains and molehills acquired their proper proportions. On Saturday, 11 May, Rudolf Hess, the deputy leader of the Nazi party, had flown to Britain, landing by parachute near Glasgow, where he was arrested and demanded to see the Duke of Hamilton. It so happened that the Duke, who was a group captain in the RAF, was commanding a station not far away. Hess, who was in a disordered mental state, had come with the self-imposed task of trying to persuade the British government that Britain could not possibly win the war, and that a negotiated peace was possible—but the prerequisite was that the Churchill government must go. Hess had met the Duke of Hamilton (a distinguished athlete, who had briefly attended the Berlin Olympic Games in 1936), and had found out that he held the appointment of Lord Steward of His Majesty's Household; naïvely assuming that this meant the Duke was in constant attendance upon the King and in a powerful political position, he decided that this was the person who could inform the King of his mission. All this news had been coming through to the private office piecemeal during the weekend; we in turn were regaled with it, and everyone was duly mystified and excited. Churchill sent for the Duke of Hamilton (who, poor man, greatly resented the possible slur this bizarre turn of events might cast upon his loyalty, which was impeccable) to come to Ditchley. He arrived, the object of consuming curiosity, on Monday morning, 12 May, just as the weekend party was breaking up, and my mother and I were departing for London (sans Eric); so our curiosity remained unsatisfied.

I did not linger long in London—though long enough to go with my parents, when Winston arrived back from Ditchley, to view the ruins of the Commons Chamber and St. Stephen's Hall. Just before I headed back to Chequers I went along the passage in the Annexe to the private office and called on Jock Colville, who was not only by now my friend and confidant, but also a longtime friend of the Bessboroughs. He wrote in his diary: "During the afternoon Mary told me her engagement to Eric was off—and that she felt in the bottom of her heart it would never be on again."[4]

AFTER THIS EMOTIONAL and upsetting interlude I found getting back to work quite difficult, particularly as I had told my companions in the library about my engagement, and a number of people on my "rounds" had read the rumours of it in the press: I found all this embarrassing and depressing. At home my family and our visitors were sympathetic and made "hopeful noises"—which did not accord with my mood. However, Gil Winant relayed a welcome message from Harry Hopkins (now back in the United States), whom he had told of my romantic crisis: "Girls as attractive as Mary should get engaged at least 3 times before marrying & and I send her my love."

The President's special advisers had generally taken a very touching interest in my affairs, and I wrote gratefully to Averell shortly after that *mouvementé* weekend. I first of all thanked him for a handsome present of books which he had sent me for my hospital library:

... The patients will be so grateful, and will appreciate them tremendously.

Then I want to thank you very sincerely for your sympathy and helpfulness at Ditchley. I thought it was most sweet of you—when you are so busy [and] have so many important claims on your time—to listen so patiently to a recital of my stupidities and heart-aches! You helped me such a lot—and made

me take myself less seriously—which was an excellent thing!
Thank you again—I shall never forget your kindness.[5]

I remained in a state of vacillation for several weeks, but on 2 June
I wrote to Eric, telling him that my mind was quite made up, and that
I would never marry him. It was a relief to me (and certainly to my
mother) that I had finally decided—but I was very conscious I had not
done well: I had caused unhappiness to Eric, and also discomfiture to
his family, who felt deeply for him, and were mortified that the news
of our private affairs had become public knowledge. Altogether this
was not a happy time for me. I slogged away at my job—with which
I was becoming thoroughly dissatisfied; the war news was unrelentingly dramatic, and not in a good way. We were experiencing painful
reverses in North Africa, Greece, and Crete; on 24 May a capital ship,
HMS *Hood,* was sunk with few survivors by the German battle cruiser
Bismarck—though there was grim satisfaction when, three days later,
the *Bismarck* herself was sunk; and on 22 June Germany invaded Russia.

In the middle of June I went to Norfolk for a weekend with Judy,
to whom of course I had confided the ons and offs of my engagement,
and who listened with infinite patience and good sense as I hashed
over the whole unfortunate affair. It was lovely to be at Breccles again,
and to catch up with many of the local friends of last summer. Judy
(who was a year younger than I) had stayed on at Queen's College,
and was now in her last term there, trying to decide—as was I—what
to do next. During these summer weeks we were much in each other's
company: after my visit to Breccles she came to stay at Chequers, and
it was there that one day we listened to a conversation between my
father and General Sir Frederick Pile, the Commander-in-Chief of
Anti-Aircraft Command. The talk concerned the formidable man-
power requirements of the heavy anti-aircraft batteries which were
the principal defence of our cities and ports—a problem which was
of great concern to my father. General Pile, who had long been fully

aware of this problem, was able to tell him that a project in which he had taken a close personal involvement had just recently, in May, come into operation—namely, the forming of the first heavy mixed (that is, employing both men and women) anti-aircraft batteries, where members of the ATS (Auxiliary Territorial Service) were integrated with Royal Artillery personnel on gun sites, under the command of male officers, to perform all duties and technical operations (including radar) other than actually forming the gun teams, where the physical strength required to operate the 3.7-inch guns and to handle and load the shells was quite beyond the capacity of women. Judy and I were much excited by all this, and intervened to say that we would both like to become "gunner girls"!

We subsequently discussed this idea quite seriously between ourselves, and of course with my parents and Cousin Venetia: all of them approved and understood how we felt. But although I was much taken with the idea of joining up, I did have some serious heart searchings as to where my duty lay. I knew my mother relied a great deal on me, that I was of real help with all the entertaining, and that she also found my presence at home at the weekends as a companion and confidante a real solace: for the demands of security meant she could not talk freely even to old friends. For my own part, I realized of course that I would miss my parents, and the intense interest and excitements that life with them brought me; this consideration weighed far more with me than the thought of any discomforts life in the army might entail. But I genuinely felt passionately about the war—and recently working in a hospital library had come to seem rather inadequate set alongside the challenges and sacrifices confronting so many people. I challenged myself in my diary: "if I really feel as ardently about the war as I think I do—then surely I must give more." After many heart-to-heart talks, Judy and I finally made up our minds and acquired the necessary information and application forms—and in the last week of July I resigned from the WVS.

One Chequers party in that summer stands out vividly—the weekend of 27 July. Of family and old friends there were Uncle Jack, Horatia Seymour (from Chartwell), the Prof (newly elevated to the peerage as Lord Cherwell), and Sir Maurice and Lady Violet Bonham-Carter; at various times we were joined by Pug Ismay, Gil and Connie Winant, Harry Hopkins, and Averell Harriman and his daughter Kathy. To this already dazzling *galère* were added for Sunday night two visiting "stars" from the American media firmament, Quentin Reynolds and Miss Dorothy Thompson, both of whom were doughty advocates of Britain's cause in broadcasts and articles. On Sunday night,

> Mummie came down for dinner looking exquisite as always & in terrific form despite fatigue . . . Dinner (15!) was tremendous success—Papa in best spirits & delightful to everyone. After dinner we all strolled on N[orth] lawn in beautiful gloaming—everyone in good & amusing mood. Papa said 'And why are we in such good spirits tonight?—Because they're not at our throats'. How true—one feels one can breathe for a bit. But even the break is a bit breathless—one knows so well it *is only a pause* . . .

The first weekend in August, I stayed with friends—the Williams family, to whom we had grown close in their days at St. Andrew's, Limpsfield Chart; Melville Williams was now the priest in a Nottinghamshire parish. Before leaving to go north, I wrote to my father: "My Darling Papa, As I am going away I shall not see you before you leave. This note is just to say Goodbye and Godspeed. You will be constantly in the thoughts and prayers of your proud and most loving daughter." My father was on the eve of embarking for a momentous voyage, travelling in the *Prince of Wales* to meet President Roosevelt in Placentia Bay off the coast of Newfoundland. Until the news of their meeting was announced two weeks later, of course I hugged my secret information to myself. I felt deeply anxious, and could not share my worry, as my mother took the opportunity of my father's absence to spend a week at a health farm for a much-needed rest. Of course we telephoned each other, but nothing in our conversations could have given the slightest clue as to what was uppermost in our minds.

Meanwhile, Judy and I reported to the ATS recruiting office in Grosvenor Gardens near Victoria Station to go through the procedures involved in joining up. We had an interview, and a medical examination—which both of us passed, as I noted proudly in my diary: "Grade 1! 'Fit for anything'"—and after which we were told to go home and await further instructions. I went back to Chequers to work out my time at the library, while rumour and speculation about my father's whereabouts were rife in the press—most of it wide of the mark. Suspecting that I must be in the know, several people tried to "pump" me—but I remained resolutely inscrutable. At last, on 14 August, a radio announcement by Mr. Attlee (the Deputy Prime Minister) "told an already speculating world about Papa's meeting with F.D.R. and their 8 point Declaration,"* which, I reflected in my diary, "seems to me like a glimpse of the Brave New World." I sent my father a note:

18TH AUGUST 1941

My Darling Papa,
This is just to greet you on your home-coming.
  Thank God you are safely home; we were so anxious for you.
  For everyone I think your meeting with the President and your joint declaration was a glimpse of the 'Brave New World' which we will all struggle and die to bring nearer. I am so longing to see you.

With tender love from your Mary.

There was much general excitement about this first wartime meeting of Churchill and Roosevelt—to be followed by many more jour-

---

* The Atlantic Charter, which set out Britain's and the United States' postwar aims for world peace: it was to become the basis of the United Nations Charter.

neys, by sea, land, and air, that my father would make in the next few years, in circumstances often of discomfort, and always of danger. After the announcement, silence and secrecy once more descended, until—to the great relief not only of his family but of the entire country—the *Prince of Wales* made safe landfall at Scapa Flow on 18 August.

By that time Judy and I had received our instructions to report to No. 15 ATS Training Centre at Aldermaston in Berkshire on Friday, 5 September, and set about enjoying our last few weeks of civilian life, doing the rounds of our friends and going to many "farewell" parties. I see from my diary that during this time I had considerable misgivings, and that I was full of trepidation at the step I was about to take. I had never even been to boarding school, and the imminent prospect of leaving home for such a totally unknown new world was suddenly very alarming: I wondered how I would cope with its challenges. But I don't remember telling anyone about these ignoble qualms. In any event, both Judy and I were genuinely excited, and buoyed up by our friends' enthusiasm—even admiration—for the step we were about to take. Almost without exception our girlfriends were doing war work—nursing, as air-raid wardens, or driving with the Motor Transport Corps. Some, if questioned, said vaguely "Foreign Office" and discouraged further questioning; we did not learn until over thirty years later that in most cases this meant they were working at Bletchley on the immensely secret Enigma project. Relatively few, however, at this stage of the war were in the women's services, and of these the ATS was the Cinderella, largely on account of the truly unattractive khaki uniform.

However, any doubts or anxieties we may have had disappeared the minute we actually took the plunge—and, looking back, I have always known it was one of the best decisions I ever took in my life.

CHAPTER II

"A Soldier's Life Is Terrible Hard . . ."*

On FRIDAY, 5 SEPTEMBER 1941, I WROTE IN MY DIARY:

> Caught 11.20 from Paddington. Terrific farewell scene. Rose-
> mary S[cott] E[llis], Fiona [Forbes], Ronnie [Buckland, a Cold-
> streamer friend], Nana, Mummie, Cousin Venetia & Cousin
> Sylvia to see us off. Judy & I bore up—& went away saying
> firmly 'No regrets' . . . Army vans to meet us at Aldermaston.

So started our great adventure. That night about twenty of us girls—
mostly between eighteen and twenty-five and from every walk of
life—found ourselves in our wooden barrack room:

> Above each bed are 2 pegs & a shelf & under the bed a large
> hinged playbox . . . the huts are really very nice—& spotlessly
> clean; we have sheets & plenty of blankets. The corporal has a
> little private cubicle at the end. There are 2 stoves I note with
> eager interest thinking of colder weather. The washing arrange-
> ments are really very comfortable. Plenty of 'loos' with plenty of
> Bromo! [Each sheet was marked Government Property—which
> much amused us!] Then a great many basins where one can also

---

* A. A. Milne, from "Buckingham Palace," in *When We Were Very Young* (1924).

wash one's stockings etc . . . & there are drying lines outside. In a separate hut are about 20 baths in little cubicles. *Very* nice. And the water is piping hot!

So first impressions were good.

My first letter home, written that first evening just before "lights out" at ten p.m., was laboriously headed:

PRIVATE M. CHURCHILL

A COMPANY. 3 PLATOON

CLIVE HUT

15 ATS TRAINING CENTRE & RECEPTION DEPOT.

There were about five hundred of us in the camp, in two successive intakes, and we would be there for nearly a month, being transformed from mere civilians into something like soldiers in both appearance and mind-set—the latter being more difficult than the first. I wrote nearly every day to my mother, recounting our daily programme of drills and lectures, the acquiring of our uniform, the endless cleaning and scrubbing—of our quarters, of the NAAFI* canteen, of the pantries and dining halls—and the mountains of washing up. I described to her our daily menu—which was copious and rather good. As our days could start as early as 5:30 a.m., by bedtime we were all exhausted, and there were some homesick tears. We were confined to the camp for the first week, after which we could go to nearby Reading for one afternoon a week: visitors were allowed into the grounds at weekends.

The same day I arrived, I was sent for by the Camp Commandant, whom I described in a letter home as "very charming middle aged & distinguished looking. She saw me alone & said that if I agreed she thought I should remain entirely incognito. I am pleased

* The Navy Army and Air Force Institute, which ran canteens in all service units of any size: they had a pretty middling reputation, but were probably better overseas.

about this—& would you please if you do write me send plain enve-
lopes without the Downing Street address? . . . And would you please
address me Private M. Churchill!! Ahem!" Despite this intention
and precautions, my identity became known within just a few days,
and in my diary for 9 September I wrote: "I'm afraid the cat's out
of the bag—blast it—about me—Still—*C'est la vie.*" Luckily for both
Judy and me, in those first days we had established our credentials
as genuine "floor scrubbers" and nonshirkers. The girls were all very
jolly and friendly—and this new life, after all, was equally strange to
all of us.

Sunday, 14 September, was a red-letter day, as there was church
parade, and we all wore our service dress uniforms for the first time.
That afternoon my mother came down to see us, bearing a picnic tea,
with a delicious cake in honour of my nineteenth birthday, which was
the next day. The following Sunday, both my mother and Cousin Venetia visited us, and I wrote to Nana:

> It is Sunday evening, and I am sitting on my bed in the cor-
> ner of our hut after a lovely supper of Morecambe shrimps &
> cream cheese on biscuits—plum jam & butter on biscuits—and
> a peach! All of which delicacies Mummie & Cousin Venetia
> brought with them. It was simply lovely to see them both and
> we had a very pleasant afternoon strolling around the grounds,
> and then tucking in to a COLOSSAL tea of various delicacies in
> the Chief's office—which she had lent us for the afternoon.

Such pleasant interludes aside, the pace of events was brisk. All of
us soon had very sore arms from a cocktail of inoculations, and those
of us who were volunteering for anti-aircraft duties had to do two lots
of tests—to our great relief, Judy and I were passed as suitable. Each
intake had to put on a concert on the last evening, so there was much
planning and rehearsing for that; and drillings and preparations were
afoot for a visitation from the Princess Royal and the glamorous Director of the ATS, Mrs. Jean Knox. Meanwhile a milestone was our

first pay parade. I confided to my diary: "I feel so grand drawing and 'earning' 11/6d* in cash—O thank you Ma'am!"

The royal visit passed off very well. I was one of those detailed to wait at luncheon in the Officers' Mess, "thank goodness successfully. HRH did not get gravy down her august neck. They had the same menu as us—Pie [unspecified] & Summer pudding." Before she departed, the Princess Royal sent for me: "I thought she was very kind and charming. She asked about Mummie & Papa & whether I was happy & whether the food was good—the beds comfy & the uniform nice to wear." Judy and I were much diverted to see that among the press photographers "dear Cecil Beaton had appeared on the scene—looking very elegant & completely out of place in this galaxy of determined Khaki-clad women."

Later, while we were mulling over the day's events, I was sent for to be told that the War Office had announced that I had joined the ATS, and that the press were coming down the next day to interview me. I was genuinely upset, as I confided to my diary: "Oh how I had hoped it might not happen. That I really could be a person & not a name—that I might be a perfectly ordinary Private. I just said 'Very well Ma'am' and went miserably to my hut where I shed some bitter tears." The next day I did not enjoy at all:

Sat. 27th September. This was quite one of the BLOODIEST days of my life. From dawn till dusk I was pounced at [*sic*] by photographers.
Pte. Churchill—

Parading [with my platoon]
Drinking Tea
Eating Bread
Sitting on bed
Making ?

* This worked out at 1s 8d per day—a little over 5p today, though of course worth much more then, when an agricultural labourer would earn less than £3 for a fifty-hour working week.

Writing letters
Polishing boots & buttons
Scrubbing floors & doorsteps
Emptying dustbins
Saluting

—Oh God taking a bath was about the only portion of my day omitted. I couldn't have felt more mortified embarrassed or miserable . . . the other girls were absolutely charming & understanding about it.

Two days later I would be set upon once again by the press—this time it was the newsreel companies: "Drill competition made doubly hysterical by presence of camera men shooting from all angles. However Platoon 3 won—whoopee!" It was impressed on me by various officers who tried to reconcile me to what I regarded as persecution that the resulting publicity, which was considerable, would be good for recruiting.*

On our last Sunday at Aldermaston my mother, Cousin Venetia, Nana (accompanied by my miniature poodle, Sukie), and Sarah all descended upon us:

Had delicious picnic with grouse & cider—jam tart & figs in grounds. Never have I enjoyed a picnic more—Somehow one appreciates it so terribly . . . Showed Nana & Sarah the camp . . . Tea in Chief's office. She talked to Mummie & Cousin V— Apparently we've done well. Waved all the darlings goodbye— feeling a little blue—Oswestry† is so far away. However—*no* tears. Rehearsal of concert. Tremendous fun. Bed—Tired & happy-ish.

* Many years later, I was really gratified to see in a magazine article about the women's services that a distinct little upward "blip" on a table showing recruitment figures was labelled "Mary Churchill joins the ATS"!
† Small town in Shropshire near the English-Welsh border, whither we were bound for anti-aircraft training.

Two days later our course ended; and on Wednesday, 1 October,

we marched to the station. It was a very calm morning—with a thin mist over a clear blue sky. The country looked so peaceful & beautiful—so 'green & pleasant' and I felt full of hope and courage & pride. The journey was tedious, long & hot, and by the time we had reached Park Hall Camp* & in the dimming evening light saw the vast waste of barrack square & the row upon row of corrugated roofed huts—and the many strange faces—our pride—confidence and courage had ebbed & the self-confident Privates found themselves rather frightened—very tired new gunners. I felt very very miserable.

Thursday and Friday were

Days of loneliness & gloom. Strange faces—strange customs strange places—& I summoned all the courage I could to face it—& suddenly by Saturday it began to get better—we began to know the people in our room—so nice & gay—tough & fun. We began to catch on to the new rules & regulations. Our plans straightened themselves out . . . Judy & I feel happy & begin to settle in contentedly.

We were to be at Park Hall Camp for over two months—and long, physically hard, and action-packed they would prove to be. We all lived in "spiders"—complexes of barrack rooms (mostly double-bunked, sleeping from twenty to over thirty girls) which gave off the central ablutions block; the ATS had their own restrooms and dining halls, but shared with the men the huge NAAFI and the other amenities of this bewildering hutted garrison township, with its church hut, cinema, theatre, and hospital. All our operational AA training was conducted by male instructors, and apart from lectures many cold hours

---

* A very large army establishment, about two(?) miles out of Oswestry. Several heavy anti-aircraft regiments and ATS "specialist" personnel (which included us) underwent training courses there.

would be spent by us novice "gunners" on the vast windswept barrack square either drilling or learning our roles on the various instruments: Judy and I were predictor operators. In view of the wintry cold, the issuing to us of battle dress (like the men's) was most opportune, as very necessary layers of warmth could be put on under our "battle blouses."

Days started at 6:30 a.m. and, with suitable breaks, lasted until 6:00 p.m.; in between these hours one expended a great deal of energy simply getting from place to place. After we were "stood down" in the evening, we might cram in a visit to the somewhat limited delights of Oswestry, getting back in time to go to regimental dances which took place several times a week. After the first of these, which Judy and I went to with some trepidation, I wrote: "Greatest fun. I danced with several charming people—and a particularly fascinating Sergeant Berry escorted me most considerately 'to my lines' . . . I retired to bed in the pitch dark at 12.15."

Families in the neighbourhood who were friends of our parents were quick to get in touch with us—the Scott-Ellises at Chirk Castle, the Ormsby-Gores at Brogyntun, and Lord Dudley at Himley Hall— offering very welcome breaks from camp life. On several occasions my mother and Cousin Venetia came up to stay at Chirk or Himley, and we were able to get local passes and spend some time with them. Sometimes friends turned up doing occupational courses—Michael and Jakie Astor and Hugh Fraser managed to track us down, and took us out to dinner. But it must have been very tough going for the great majority of the girls who had no local contacts; the almost "family" loyalty which developed once one was posted to a specific battery was totally absent here, and so it was unsurprising that at the end of November I told my mother that eleven ATS (not from our group) had run away in one week, and that I had spent a long time trying to persuade one of ours not to do the same "by cajoling, comforting, scolding & general 'boosting' up—and I hope to God she hasn't hopped it this evening." (I have forgotten what the outcome of my efforts was!)

I was not without low moments myself—and this went for Judy too. Nevertheless, I wrote in my diary in the train on our way home for our first leave: "Mummie & Nana are wonderful & send a constant flow of letters & parcels. Time flies—[but] there never seems to be a moment to write or read. . . . But it is a wonderful life & I only pray for courage to stick out the black moments." I firmly averred that "as long as I live I shall never—never regret joining the ATS"—and I never did.

In the middle of October Judy and I, with others deemed suitable, were elevated to the inspiring rank of local/unpaid/lance bombardier; we proudly sewed one stripe on our uniforms and started on an NCOs (Non-Commissioned Officers) course. This was a step up, making life more interesting—and even harder work, for in addition to the customary lectures and drills, we were all detailed for various duties such as "defaulters" and sick parade; most demanding of all was to be on "fire picquet" for a whole week, which Judy and I duly were: "I really could have wept," I wrote to Nana on 28 October, "—because it means CB [confined to barracks] for a week (which excludes even garrison cinema, post office & theatre) and perpetual turning out at night if there are sirens . . . when we have to galvanise ourselves (& still more difficult 10 peculiarly nitwitted disorderly ATS) into efficiency & tear about with crowbars & hoses & axes (very dangerous)" for training purposes.

Also in October we had our first spell of forty-eight hours' leave—not a moment of which was wasted. Arriving in London on the Friday evening, we went straight to a party my mother had organized for some of our London friends; she had also gathered up Cousin Venetia and Nana, and the next day we all went down to Chequers to make the most of the precious hours remaining before we rumbled back north through Sunday night. "The journey back wasn't too uncomfortable, & we arrived just in time," I wrote to my mother. "We went to bed mighty early on Monday night, and slept like two large logs all through a raid warning & the distant Merseyside blitz."

But I had been much upset to see how "very tired out and exhausted you were, Darling Mummie." And I continued my letter:

Do spare yourself all you can. I love you so dearly, and I cannot bear to think of you being so tired and pressed by work. How I wish I could be with you to take the entertaining off your hands. I sometimes think I should not have joined up when there is so much I can do at home—and yet I feel that really I am doing the right thing.

Despite her increasingly busy and burdensome life, my mother made time to write to me, usually every few days. About this time she had taken on the chairmanship of the Red Cross Aid to Russia Fund (which came to bear her name), and on 26 October she wrote to me from Chartwell:

> *My own Darling Mouse,*
> *I was so very happy when I got your letter & so much ashamed that I have*
> *let a whole week go by with[out] writing at all. 'The aid to Russia Fund' has*
> *almost overwhelmed me, but I am still treading water frenziedly. Cousin*
> *Venetia & I are certainly coming to see you next weekend & we will write*
> *or telegraph plans. I hope you had an amusing evening with the Astor boys.*
> *I wonder which was most fun, the Astor boys or Sergeant Davis? I am*
> *having a cosy restful weekend with Nana, Yellow Cat, (Paddy [my Lakeland*
> *terrier] with remains of lumbago) & Sukie [my miniature poodle] very*
> *French & frisky! Papa is having a masculine party at Chequers. I'm afraid*
> *you are having air-raids. How far off was the crash you heard? Next Tuesday*
> *the King & Queen are lunching with us at Downing Street.* I will write*
> *& tell you what 'Their Majesties' said & if they enjoyed Mrs Landemare's†*
> *cooking! I'm doing 2 'Aid for Russia' broadcasts this coming week . . .*

True to her word, my mother wrote to me from Chequers an account of the King and Queen lunching alone with her and my father:

---

* Whenever possible my parents continued to entertain in the fortified Garden Rooms at No. 10.

† Mrs. Georgina Landemare, a wonderful cook and charming personality. As a girl she had started as an under-kitchenmaid in a grand kitchen, and had risen "through the ranks"—and married the French chef M. Landemare. In the thirties she used to come for special weekends to Chartwell, but from the outbreak of war she came to cook for my parents full-time.

Mrs Landemare was in a flutter & produced a really delicious luncheon, & it was really all most enjoyable becos' the Queen is so gay & witty & very pretty close up, tho' Alas the silhouette is not quite as it should be . . . It was the first of a series of really bitterly cold days & she was dressed in a pale grey voile gown & I think a straw hat! Papa tried to interfere with the Menu, but I was firm & had it my own way, & luckily it was good.

The Queen asked about you & admired a photograph of you scrubbing . . . The King did not say much. He looked rather thin & tired . . . Princess Elizabeth & her sister are being educated 'at Eton'! That is, the Vice-Provost of Eton & one or two of the most agreeable & brilliant Masters go to Windsor Castle two or three times a week & instruct them & they enjoy it very much. I think they have the most amusing lives with lots of dogs (altho' they are only those horrid 'Corgies' [*sic*]) & poneys [*sic*] & a delightful Mother . . .

Towards the end of October Sarah joined the WAAF (Women's Auxiliary Air Force) as Aircraftswoman 2nd Class Oliver, and went to do her initial training at Morecambe (on the seafront, where it was bitterly cold and she suffered agonies from chilblains!). Her very sudden decision to join up was prompted by her decision to end her marriage to Vic, which had been unravelling for some little while. American citizens had been ordered to return to the United States, and Sarah knew she could not consider leaving England: this prompted her to ask her father the only favour she ever asked of him—namely, that he would facilitate her speedy entry into the WAAF (which she said she chose because of the uniform!). Vic, hoping that she would change her mind, stayed on in England.

In the summer of 1940, Sarah had already confided to me her anxiety as to what she should do if Vic decided to return to America, so I had known for some time that things were not well with her—but when the actual break came I was deeply upset. In fact, all the family were dismayed and sorry, as they too had become attached to Vic. My mother must have told me the real reason for Sarah's precipitate action after discussing it with her, for Sarah wrote to her from Morecambe:

> I have had a sweet letter from Mary—she told me you had decided to tell her after all—I think perhaps it was best—she is very grown up—it is sad though because she was genuinely fond of Vic—she seemed somehow to know him much as I knew him . . . it hurts less if people think kindly about him not harshly about him. Whatever has happened he has meant much to me in my life.

I must have nurtured fond if unrealistic hopes for their relationship, for in the New Year of 1942 I wrote to Vic (who was playing at the London Hippodrome) and received a warm and affectionate reply:

17/1/42

> *My darling Mary,*
> *Words fail me to express my deepfelt thanks for your very sweet letter. You are the only one of your family who has written to me, and, I hope has not changed, in spite of the grave, please God, only temporary change in my marital status. Alas, I cannot describe to you the agony through which I have gone since your dear sister decided to leave my house . . . Sarah was and is everything to me. The sun rises and sets with her—I only live because there is a faint ray of hope that she might forget and give me another chance . . . But whatever happens, Mary—your letter has given me courage to wait an eternity.*
>
> *Bless you and thank you so much. Vic.*

For all her decisive action, Sarah too was tormented with doubts and unhappiness about the breakup of the relationship, as is clear from a letter I wrote her later that year, after we had managed to combine some leave time together, and she had unburdened herself to me:

"then—and most important I want to tell you how terribly I feel for you. I know just how unhappy you are—& what agony you are going through. Perhaps I understand because I am so deeply fond of Vic, & I know what a sweet & vulnerable person he is."

But all was to no avail: although throughout the war their separation remained unknown except to closest family and friends, Vic and Sarah were eventually divorced with the minimum of attention in 1945. They remained on friendly terms always.

My mother was the chief retailer of news between her daughters, while our father wrote political and home news to Randolph, then serving as a staff officer in Cairo. Every now and then I would write him a short letter, such as the one I penned just before his sixty-seventh birthday when I had had a spell of leave:

> *My Darling Papa,*
> *I am just writing this little note to tell you how happy I have been during the last seven days—and also how unhappy I am to be away for your birthday.*
> *I shall be thinking of you on Sunday so much—many, many happy returns—darling.*
> *This buttonhole is a very small present—but it brings you more loving thoughts than I can ever write.*
> *God bless you—darling Papa.*
>
> > *With Love from your*
> > *Mary*

On his birthday—30 November—he sent me a telegram: "Am wearing your lovely flower. Fondest love. Papa."

That our father was well aware of his children's doings is illustrated in the letter he wrote to Randolph on 30 October:

Your sisters have chosen the roughest roads they could find. Mary is acting Temporary Unpaid Lance Bombardier and will

in five or six weeks probably be promoted Sergeant. I hope she
will presently be posted to a mixed battery in one of the parks
near London so that we shall be able to see something of her on
her leave. These two months of Amazonian Sparta have made
a man of Judy and also contrariwise improved her looks. Sarah,
casting aside about £4,000 of contracts, is undergoing austeri-
ties with the WAAF. We think they are very heroic. They are
certainly braver than the lady in *The black Mousquetaire* who 'did
not mind death, but couldn't stand pinching'.

Towards the end of our time at Park Hall Camp an emergency
arose which I recounted to my mother on 1 December:

My own Darling Mummie,
It really is TOO dreary—Here are Judy & I & 30 odd girls isolated for ten
days owing to there having been two cases in the camp of Cerebral Spinal
Meningitis; & one case was in our barrack room. Yesterday was unbelievable.
The girl was carted off to hospital in the morning, & in the evening, her
diagnosis having been ratified, we had to move lock, stock & barrel into this
new spider. We are in separate beds—& OH HEAVEN Judy & I have a
tiny room to ourselves! It is too maddening that we are missing the end of our
course—but naturally it can't be helped. The girls are going on (in a select
group) with their work, and as there is no sergeant attached to us Judy & I
are in charge of the whole lot & have more responsibility than before . . . We
have to take them for drill, respirator practice and we're going to give them
full length lectures.

   We are having what is known as 'rather a time' with them—as they are
cross and fed up—and as we have to have all the windows & doors open—it
is VERY cold, and naturally it is dreary for them to be able to go neither to
the NAAFI nor the cinema; & so they grumble a great deal, fight continually
& occasionally burst into tears—all three of which functions seem to have to
be chaperoned by the bombardiers! Life is hectic.

   Darling—I do beseech you not to worry—they have never known a case

to occur again in the same room—& our isolation is purely precautional
[sic]. We are well looked after. We gargle 3 times a day & the M.O. visits us
every morning. We live in a veritable GALE of fresh air—& we are on the
whole cheerful & not at all alarmed . . . No more news at present—I must go
to sleep.

> *Masses of love & kisses from your happy kitten.*
> *Mary.*

P.S. We are called the 'untouchables' & our Sergeant Smith (male
instructor) walks round with a bottle of diluted potash with which he
wipes the predictors after we've been on them!!!

As I did not want to worry my mother unduly, I did not tell her
in detail about what had been a fairly horrendous night. The girl who
was taken so ill was in fact in the bunk above mine, and I had climbed
up to see if I could help her; as one could not put on the lights as blackout screens were all taken down for ventilation I tried to comfort her
by holding her in my arms. Judy and several other girls tried to help
too, but it took us all some time to realize (by torchlight) that the case
was really serious: then we could not find a senior NCO, nor did we
know where the ATS officers slept, so that it was nearly daylight by the
time we got help and the MO was summoned.

I think the War Office must have contacted my mother, who reacted predictably: Judy and I were embarrassed and enchanted in
equal measure to observe her, escorted by the commanding officer, the
ATS senior officer, and the sergeant major, walking across the barrack
square to our barrack room within twenty-four hours of receiving the
news! She did not stay long—and I have to say that although the authorities were annoyed by her turning up in such an irregular fashion,
they never took it out on us—and nor did our companions.

During our "imprisonment" we were all cheered by visits from our
friends in the camp: these were conducted at "long distance" after parade hours when our chums would stand outside the barrack-room

windows (not nearer than fifteen feet or so) and engage us in cheery shouted conversation. I told Nana that "Sergeant Taylor [my pal of the moment] was too sweet & brought masses of chocolates & books!"

Finally our incarceration, and our time at Park Hall Camp, came to an end. We all received news of our postings: Judy and I were to join 469 Heavy (Mixed) Anti-Aircraft Battery at Enfield, on the northern outskirts of London. Before reporting to our units, we were granted a spell of leave; but when I arrived home at the Annexe it was to find luggage stacked in the corridor and much to-ing and fro-ing. My father was off that very evening, 12 December, to the north by train to board the ship that would take him to visit President Roosevelt. I was much cast down to realize I would hardly glimpse him—and my disappointment must have shown in my face, for he said: "Come with me on the train—at least we can dine together!" So I did just that.

As we rumbled north that evening I would have caught up with the series of events on all fronts which had taken place since my father and the President had met in Placentia Bay in August—by far the most important being the attack by the Japanese on the American fleet in Pearl Harbor on 7 December which had brought the United States into the war. We had suffered some grievous losses at sea: in the Mediterranean the aircraft carrier *Ark Royal* had been sunk; later the battleship *Barham* was lost; and on 10 December our most powerful battleship, the *Prince of Wales,* and the battle cruiser *Repulse* had been sunk off Malaya with heavy loss of life.

Early next morning we arrived at Gourock, on the Clyde, and my father and his party were taken by tender to board the *Duke of York* (sister ship of the *Prince of Wales*—a melancholy touch). I took leave of my father on deck before returning home with anxious thoughts for the travellers setting forth on their dangerous—and, as it would turn out, extremely rough—voyage.

CHAPTER 12

Battery Life

———

AT THE END OF OUR LEAVE JUDY AND I, EXCITED AND DISTINCTLY nervous, reported for duty to 469H(M)AA Battery at Chaseside, Enfield. Before I left home I wrote to my father, who was still on the high seas:

> *My own darling Papa,*
> *Just a little letter to tell you I love you, and that I hope you are well*
> *and have enjoyed the journey.*
>
> *I so much enjoyed my trip with you to Scotland—although it made*
> *me sad and anxious to leave you.*
>
> *Today Judy and I join our battery, which is situated near Enfield;*
> *I am so much thrilled by the thought of being in action.*
>
> *And the fact that I shall be so near home makes me very happy indeed.*
> *Please take care of yourself, and come back soon.*
>
> > *With love and kisses from your own kitten—*
> > *Mary*
> > *WOW!*

My mother, in a letter to my father the following day, wrote:

Yesterday Mary's leave came to an end; I took her & Judy in
your car & deposited them as night was falling at their new
camp near Enfield—In the gathering darkness it looked like a
German concentration camp. It is a big piece of waste ground
surrounded by suburban villas in the distance.—It has a high
iron fence all round with barbed wire & locked gates . . .

Although first appearances were so dismal on a drear December
evening, the gun site was in a pleasant open situation, and the living
conditions were a marked improvement on our Park Hall accommodation, as I told my mother, to whom I wrote the day after our arrival:

There are about 120 ATS*—& we inhibit 1 spider *comme a la Oswestry*—BUT

1) We sleep in single beds & 25 per room.
2) The rooms & passages are much more cheerful—being
   painted white & green.
3) Each AT has a box & shelf & hooks.
4) The floors are ordinary boards which just need sweeping
   & occasionally scrubbing. Hooray!
5) Attached to the spider is a lovely rest room—with comfy
   chairs & a stove.

Thank God—the curse of NAAFI is not upon us. There is a
small—but nice YMCA (delicious cream buns!) . . .

---

* A heavy mixed anti-aircraft battery was composed of eight 3.7-inch guns, with about
600 personnel, of which about one-third were women, commanded by a Royal Artillery major and several RA officers. The senior ATS officer was a junior commander
(equivalent in rank to a captain), with about six ATS subalterns. The battery occupied
two gun sites in the same area, with four guns on each site.

We shall only be able to get out 2ce a week from 4 to 11 & we don't know which days.

The girls here seem very charming & I really think it will be thrilling, interesting & fun here.

The next day I managed to get home briefly, and wrote to my father about battery life:

10 DOWNING STREET,
WHITEHALL.

My darling Papa,
I am at the Annexe for a few hours 'off duty'—and I find there is an
opportunity of writing to you.

I was on duty at the gun site from 1 o'clock today. The 'manning team' sleep
in a little concrete warren—ready (fully dressed in battle regalia!) to rush
to the instruments. Twice during the night Judy and I took our turn to do an
hour's stretch at 'spotting'—and watching for anyone suspicious on the gun site.

The battery I am with seems very agreeable. There is a great deal of work
to do, for besides manning the guns we have fatigues and guarding duties to
do. I am sure I shall be very happy there, and I am thrilled and proud to be
part of the aggressive defences of London.

I hear that your journey was delayed by bad weather—I do hope when
this reaches you that you will have arrived safely. It is very sad that we shall
all be separated for Christmas—but I hope and pray we shall be re-united
soon.

With loving thoughts and kisses from
your proud and devoted soldier—
Mary

I told my mother I would be "manning" on Christmas Day itself; my father being away, she decided to remain in London, inviting Nana to come up from Chartwell to be with her. On Christmas Day she wrote to me:

10 DOWNING STREET,

WHITEHALL.

My own darling Mary,

Yesterday at four o'clock Papa rang up from The White House. He might have been speaking from the next room. But it was not very satisfactory as it was a public line & we were both warned by the censors breaking in that we were being listened to.

Nana & I are all alone this Christmas, but we are not lonely because we feel Papa is serving the World & you and Sarah are also, & are happy in your work. We shall be here till Saturday when we go to Chequers till Tuesday morning.

On Boxing Day [Saturday] Diana, Duncan, Pamela, Archie Sinclair, Ivor Churchill & Mr. Winant are lunching with us at Downing Street. It would be lovely if you and Judy blew in then or any time . . .

Tender Love my own Darling & thoughts & Kisses—your present is here. I don't send it as it would probably get lost in the turmoil of the Barrack Room.

The present referred to was a lovely turquoise-and-gold Victorian necklace from Mummie, Papa, and Nana.

To assist in our celebrations at the battery, my mother sent an out-size cracker and some delicious goodies. On 28 December I wrote to tell her how well they had gone down:

Thank you too for the food and the enormous cracker you sent to the barrack room. The girls were simply delighted & we had a lovely party on Christmas evening & the officers came & we pulled the cracker and ate the cake. I am very well—but tired as there were very gay exhausting parties both on Christmas and

Boxing night and last night [27th] (after bundling down with the rest of the cast to perform our pantomime at the Battery hospital) I was manning on the predictor & so had an interrupted & short night. I am just going to have a lovely hot bath and retire to bed.

Meanwhile, across the world, my father had Christmased at the White House, and on 26 December he had addressed both Houses of Congress:

. . . How wonderful Papa's speech was—& how thrilled and proud it makes me to know that he has 'conquered America'. But how I long for him to be back.

Isn't it lovely—I and Judy have got 24 hours leave from 1 p.m. on 31st!! Whoopee. Goodnight—darling Mummie— Love & Kisses.

On New Year's Eve I wrote to my father:

My own darling Papa,
. . . Many, many congratulations on your two wonderful broadcasts [he had addressed the Canadian parliament on 30 December]. Whenever you speak free peoples everywhere lift up their hearts, and we in the fighting forces turn to our tasks with fresh courage and determination.

I have just had twenty four hours leave and I went home to see Mummie who was very well. I am back once more in camp just starting on a twenty four hour stretch of duty.

Happy and Victorious New Year—darling Papa.

With love and kisses from your
Mary.

When my father returned home on 17 January we were all so much relieved—it had been a long absence.

———

JUDY AND I would be with 469 Battery at Chaseside for nearly ten months. It was, on the whole, a happy time—and certainly a busy one. From the local underground station (about a quarter of an hour's walk away) we could be in central London in just over an hour, and usually had evening leave two or three times a week. Unless we had a special late pass, however, we had to be back in camp at eleven o'clock, which somewhat restricted our night life, entailing much anxious checking of the time and frantic rushing for the station.

Battery social life was very jolly, with fairly frequent all-ranks dances in the NAAFI. Outsiders could be invited to these, including American soldiers from a nearby unit; these visitors jazzed things up considerably, as many of our own gunners were married or not dance-inclined. Even so, girls predominated, and rather than be "wallflowers" danced with each other. Our officers also attended these dances, and naturally there was considerable competition to dance with our very handsome major; my section officer Mr. Green was also very good-looking and intelligent, which made long nights on duty less tedious. Predictably I fell for him—he was married (of course)—and I confided to my diary that I rather envied Mme. Vert.

But the focus of my off-duty life was home. As always, the atmosphere there was like a barometer which reflected the war news, which in the early months of 1942 was unrelentingly bad. Late in January Rommel launched a new offensive in the Middle East and drove our forces back to Tobruk; in the Far East the Japanese were advancing through Malaya while we were falling back towards Singapore, which surrendered on 15 February—an event pronounced by my father little over a month afterwards as "the greatest disaster to British arms which our history records."[1] Towards the end of February I had twenty-four hours' leave: I lunched alone with my parents. "Papa is at a very low ebb," I wrote in my diary. "He is not too well physically—and he is worn down by the continuous crushing pressure of events. . . . He has not weakened—never for a moment—but he is desperately taxed. O God, we need him so much—spare him to us."

Meanwhile, on the family front there were tensions and difficulties. Randolph had been granted two months' home leave, and at the end of January had made a powerful and pugnacious speech in a House of Commons debate on a vote of confidence.* However, as well as laying into his father's and the government's critics in Parliament, he had publicly attacked Lord Chatfield (recently a member of the War Cabinet) in a speech at the end of February, which naturally embarrassed Winston; and he also enraged his father by violently attacking his colleagues and criticizing the conduct of the war.

A further cause for friction and unhappiness between Randolph and both his parents arose from the fact (which he discovered on his return home) that Pamela had for many months been having an affair with Averell Harriman—a situation which was widely known in social circles, thereby adding to his hurt and humiliation. Randolph was convinced that his parents not only knew about the affair, but actually condoned it. Winston and Clementine were in an impossible situation. I do not believe they knew about the relationship for quite a long time after it began—and when they did, they did not want to believe it: Averell's and Pamela's behaviour was perfectly discreet, and he had been from the first persona grata at Chequers and No. 10—and indeed, needed to be so. They were devoted to Pamela (who was a model daughter-in-law in her relationship with them), adored "Baby" Winston, and hoped against hope that Randolph and Pamela's differences could be healed and the marriage saved. Diana and Sarah knew about the situation long before I did (I think Sarah told me); all three of us were indignant on Randolph's behalf, and loyally took his part.

Pamela's relationship with Averell not only destroyed her and Randolph's already rocky marriage, but was also the cause of a series of

---

* Randolph had been elected in 1940 at an uncontested by-election as Conservative Member of Parliament for Preston.

scenes at No. 10 when Randolph would turn up at the Annexe and provoke violent arguments with his father; after one particularly volcanic episode, Clementine, fearful that Winston might have a seizure, banned Randolph from their home for the rest of the war. On my own various visits to the Annexe, I either witnessed or heard distressed accounts of these appalling rows, and became furious with Randolph for causing such mayhem and misery.

Towards the end of March I had seven days' leave, on the first evening of which my mother took me to see Vivien Leigh in Bernard Shaw's *The Doctor's Dilemma:* returning home rather late, we found that

> Papa, Diana & Duncan had already started dinner. Evening from here on was not a success. Papa tired, low & cross, had a row with Mummie. Then battle royal ensued between Papa, Mummie & Diana over Randolph. Randolph must go & rejoin his regiment if he is to save Papa from public resentment & disapproval which just at the moment he can ill afford. [I imagine I was referring to Randolph's attacks on members of the government.]

Stirred up by this fracas, I wrote (I suspect a heated) letter (which does not survive) to Randolph, "begging him to rejoin his regt."

Two days later, when I was alone with my father after dinner, he told me Randolph had shown him my letter: he strongly reproached me for such an unsisterly action, and "proceeded to show me two secret telegrams [from Cairo] which explained how justified R was in being over here." I complained to my diary that I thought "R would have had greater dignity than to go running to Papa. I must say I didn't know he [Randolph] set all that store by what I said or thought." I poured into my diary the details of the severe scolding I received from my father, which of course upset me deeply:

> It all hurts so much. I so much wish this bust up hadn't happened. But I DON'T regret writing that letter ... But darling

Papa—if only you knew how reluctantly I did it [and] how grieved I am you're angry with me. Well—then—in the middle of Papa lecturing me in walked R & Pamela. It was a little strained—but all right on the whole. I went to bed after about a quarter of an hour—R leaves for Cairo tomorrow—I said goodbye—Il y avait un peu de gêne—Papa in a hoarse whisper tried to make me say something about it [the letter]—but I wouldn't . . . [Later] I weakly capitulated & vaguely promised I'd write to R about it. I went to bed feeling calm but a little saddened. *I will not relent.*

The next day I accompanied my parents to Caxton Hall, where my father was to address the Central Conservative Committee. Just before we left home, "Papa came in looking frightening & said 'Have you written that letter?' I said 'No' firmly. But I felt sick at heart." As for Randolph himself, in April, shortly after his return to Cairo, he joined a parachute detachment of the Special Air Service (SAS), formed by Major David Stirling with the express object of operating behind enemy lines in the desert.*

Happily for me, my leave was not entirely composed of family commotions! I shopped and bought a glamorous dress (according to me); became godmother to a school friend's baby daughter; went to a luncheon and reception with my mother at the Soviet Embassy; and was taken by her to see another play—*Old Acquaintance* by John van Druten, starring Edith Evans. I also went to a party, staying up all night with Ali Forbes and other jolly friends, going to two nightclubs and finally eating an enormous breakfast at Lyons Corner House in Leicester Square:

Coffee, Sardines-on-toast, Waffles & butter & treacle. Oh heaven. And this perfect meal gave me the poetic brainwave

* At the end of May Randolph incurred fairly serious injuries in an accident while returning from a long-range raid on Benghazi; after some weeks in a military hospital in Cairo, he was invalided back to England until October 1942.

[shades of Wordsworth] of seeing the dawn from Westminster Bridge!!! So we walked down Lower Regent St. & down the Duke of York's steps & through St. James's Park and across Parliament Square to Westminster Bridge. What a lot one misses by taking taxis at night in London. How lovely the night is—& what fun walking the deserted streets. I had brought a pair of low heeled shoes & made John put the others in his pocket. Just before dawn on Westminster Bridge wasn't a let down—it was still & chilly & mysterious . . . And then—as the sky was growing paler we went home. Judy & I both agreed it was a perfect night & had hot baths. Mummie's comment was: 'Well I don't mind you coming in at five, but at six—I draw the line—& what must the marines [on sentry duty at the Annexe] have thought!' Went to bed from 8.30 till 12 & felt awful when I woke up.

My parents, Nana, and myself were all at Chequers for the weekend, and to my joy, Sarah had some leave as well and came over on Saturday. She was now commissioned and doing highly secret work in photographic interpretation at Medmenham near Henley, only about an hour from Chequers. I was delighted to find I was sleeping in my old bedroom—the "Prison Room"—and went to sleep watching the firelight play on the old beams.

On Saturday I went with my father when he inspected the Second Division, which was stationed in Oxfordshire, preparing for overseas service. On the way my father talked again about Randolph and was "very cross," but "I didn't answer back or argue at all—out of wisdom I hope—perhaps cowardice—yet somehow I felt hopeless about making Papa see it at all as we see it." I reflected that in fact I had come to care for Randolph more than I had in earlier times (the age gap of eleven years having put him beyond my reach as a child),

and now I seem to have alienated Randolph—& which grieves me to the heart—hurt & angered Papa & destroyed that understanding & sympathy that really had grown strongly between us—& which alas had naturally diminished a little as we see so little of each other—& now this has dealt it a blow. However later he was sweet to me—but I felt a little chilled inside & fearful.

That evening Lord and Lady Louis Mountbatten arrived for dinner. He was then Chief of Combined Operations—good-looking and most affable: "Sarah & I both fell for him in a big way! [I remember we somewhat disrespectfully dubbed him "Glamour pants"!] All through dinner news of the St. Nazaire raid* kept coming through. Thrilling."

I stayed up talking to Sarah very late, and on Sunday morning "I woke about 9. Had breakfast in Sarah's room—after we went into Mummie's room & gossiped & greased our faces." The rest of the weekend was pleasantly uneventful, with two of my friends, Ali Forbes and John Bruce, coming down from London for luncheon. After dinner Saturday and Sunday we had films—*Les Misérables* ("which I thought bloody awful—Papa the sweet, said 'Fine film'") and *Wuthering Heights*. It had been lovely for me seeing Sarah, and having a good "catch up": we confided to each other that we were "both *dreading* going back."

IN FACT ONE'S SPIRITS revived quickly after a spell of leave, once one was back in the hustle and bustle of camp life. During the spring and early summer the battery received several visits from VIPs—which always involved a great deal of dashing round smartening up ourselves and the camp: all this caused a bit of grumbling, but these visitations kept us on our toes, as we always gave our guests a demonstration "Stand to" and "Action stations," and a dummy run on an imaginary target. The first of our VIPs were my parents, who came in early April: I, of course, was beset by anxiety—but in fact my comrades really seemed quite pleased to show off our skills. In the event it wasn't only

---

* The raid by a destroyer and commando force was mounted by Combined Operations. Its purpose—successfully achieved—was to destroy the only dry dock on the Atlantic coast big enough to accommodate the German battleship *Tirpitz*.

our skills that were shown off: there were some building works in progress on the site, and—to my embarrassment, but everyone else's delight—my father stopped, seized a trowel, and laid a line of bricks!
Some time later he made a return visit, bringing with him my "favourite American," Harry Hopkins. I think the officers and senior NCOs
quite enjoyed these visits, and they certainly caused less general anxiety
than descents upon us by "top brass"—such as when General Pile
(Commander-in-Chief of AA Command) inspected us, accompanied
by sharp-eyed colleagues. "Tim" Pile, although diminutive in stature,
was a great character; on this occasion he called Judy and myself forward and asked us how we were getting on, remembering that it was his
visit to Chequers which had inspired us to volunteer as AA gunners.

When we arrived at 469 Battery, Judy and I both kept the rank
of lance corporal we had acquired at Oswestry. However, quite soon
I was made up to a corporal: this caused me embarrassment vis-à-vis
Judy, for up to now we had kept pace with each other. In this smaller
unit, however, promotion was governed not only by merit, but by the
appearance of vacancies (each unit having its set "establishment" of
NCOs). Judy did mind my being promoted ahead of her—as did I—
but she accepted it with generosity; it did not ruffle our friendship, and
quite soon she too put up her second stripe. Then, two months later,
to my great astonishment, I was promoted to sergeant—which meant
not only a third stripe, but my having to live in the sergeants' separate
quarters and Mess, and taking on a quite distinct role with different
responsibilities. I remember a tearful (on both our parts) conversation: again, Judy's loyalty and generosity saved our relationship, which
was of great importance to us both. Luckily, she was regarded as a great
character, and was immensely popular with the other girls and gunners—much more so than I was (I fear I was thought overbossy and
too big for my gaiters).

My mother wrote me a remarkable letter about this time in re-
sponse to news of the first death in action of an ATS on a gun site.
I quote it because I think it casts an interesting light on her almost
"Roman matron" reaction:

My darling Mary,

Perhaps I may see you before you get this letter. But I want you to know my feelings when I read of the death in action of Private Nora Caveney*—My first agonizing thought was—it might have been Mary—my second thought was satisfaction & pride that the other girls on duty continued their work smoothly without a hitch 'like seasoned soldiers'—& then private pride that you my beloved one have chosen this difficult, monotonous, dangerous & most necessary work—I think of you so much my Darling Mouse. I know you never regret your choice. Give Judy my love—

I hear Mrs. Casey† visited your Battery and saw 'Mary's rosebud face looking sternly past me'!

Although I managed to see my friends quite a lot, any time at home was precious to me; even if I was going out with someone for an evening, I nearly always went home first. Best of all for me, and always highlighted in my diary, were the times I could spend alone with either or both of my parents. On one such evening when I went home, I found my mother was still at Chequers, as she had been ill, so I rang her up; there was a dinner party at the Annexe that night, and "Papa sent for me to talk to him while he was dressing for dinner. O heaven—something of that companionship has come back; I was able to say I had written to Randolph, who has joined a sort of armoured skirmishing-cum-parachute corps. O darling Randy—how terribly proud I am—we all are." The dinner guests were Richard Casey,‡ Oliver Lyttleton,§ and Anthony Eden,¶ and it was obviously a jolly party:

---

* Nora Caveney was serving in a heavy mixed anti-aircraft battery at Southampton when, on duty during a German air attack in April 1942, she became the first female soldier killed in action in the war. She was just eighteen.
† Wife of Mr. Richard Casey: see next footnote.
‡ Australian, recently appointed Britain's Minister Resident in the Middle East.
§ Minister of Production in the War Cabinet.
¶ Foreign Secretary.

"Mr Casey is young & charming, Oliver is as invigoratingly witty as ever. How we all laughed—a good dinner party."

In the early summer of that year we had a spell of lovely fine weather, and one evening I was home early enough to go for a long walk in St. James's Park with my mother before dinner, "which was deliciously peaceful because Mummie & I & Papa were alone together & we dined on this glorious June evening in the garden [at No. 10] & Papa was pleased about my guns [an emblem awarded me that day and placed above a gunner sergeant's stripes] & so was Mummie & we were all so together." But not all our evenings were so tranquil! To Judy, who was away on a course, I wrote describing another evening in the same week:

On Wednesday I went home again and Mummie, the Dove [Judy's and my odd soubriquet for my father] & myself were all alone which was rather heavenly. We dined in the garden of No. 10. Papa and Mummie were in terrific form . . . one or two enjoyable flare-ups—during one of which Mummie said: 'Oh you old son-of-a-bitch!' Dinner ended in mellow & happy silence. Papa sank into the *New Yorker*—Mummie & I after 5 minutes rose to go: 'Don't leave me' said the Dove pathetically. Mummie contemplated him with a judicial eye: 'The trouble is Winston—you [would] like 20 people to come and watch you read the *New Yorker!' Quelle famille!* & how I adore them.

But another occasion, little more than a week later, was overcast by events, as I noted in my diary:

Went home to dinner. Mummie & Papa alone. The news is bad* & he was in very low spirits. He was unhappy & tortured & Mummie and I tried so hard to comfort him. He may go to

* At the end of May Rommel had renewed his offensive in the Western Desert; on 15 June *The Times* reported that the Battle of Libya was being fought with new intensity. Tobruk would fall on 20 June.

America on Thursday [he did, by flying boat]. Brendan* arrived
& was cheerful & encouraging. I left with a very heavy heart—
but Papa's last words to me were: 'Now not a word—& no one
must see in your face how bad things are.' They won't!

Looking back, these summer months with 469 Battery at Enfield
flew by: we certainly expended a lot of time and energy dashing to
London and back. My diary, however, is full of introspective and self-
critical outpourings: I had to hug to myself my anxiety when my father was on his travels, and my small steps up the ladder of promotion
brought their own difficulties for me. Once, some months later, after
I was commissioned, I would confide in Major Tony Hogg, the senior instructing officer at the AA training camp at Arborfield, who
became a friend and confidant of both Judy and myself; he wrote to
his wife:

> I've had a most interesting talk with Mary C. this evening,
> who's been behaving rather loudly and badly lately and who I'm
> afraid is going to get a wigging from the S.C. [Senior Com-
> mander ATS] tomorrow. She's really a very nice and charming
> child who can state her case as well as any barrister. She says
> she's tried all ways of behaviour, but every one of them seems
> to be wrong as people will put interpretations on them. If she is
> quiet and unassuming they say she is smug and stuck up, on the
> other hand if she's noisy and matey with all and sundry they say
> she does it to draw attention to herself . . .

However, by and large these months at Enfield were happy—
certainly busy. My fellow gunners (male and female) were a friendly
lot, and long hours of duty were made less tedious by my mild *amitié
amoureuse* with my section commander.

It would indeed have intrigued me and been the cause of much

* Brendan Bracken, Minister of Information.

merriment among my family and friends if I had known that about this time I had been momentarily part of Adolf Hitler's thinking. Over sixty years later I would learn this from an extract from *Hitler's Secret Conversations:*

> By far the most interesting problem of the moment is, what is Britain going to do now? . . . At the moment, the British are try-ing to wriggle out of their difficulties by spreading the most varied and contradictory of rumours. To find out what she re-ally intends to do is the task of the Wilhelmstrasse [foreign ministry]. The best way of accomplishing it would be by means of a little flirtation with Churchill's daughter. But our Foreign Office, and particularly its gentlemanly diplomats, consider such methods beneath their dignity, and they are not prepared to make this agreeable sacrifice, even though success might well save the lives of numberless German Officers and men.[2]

Towards the end of June I had seven days' leave which quite for-tuitously coincided with my father's return from Washington, where he had spent ten days conferring with President Roosevelt. The news from the desert war was bad, and it was during this visit, on 20 June, that the grave tidings of the fall of Tobruk had been received. My fa-ther travelled home by flying boat, landing in Stranraer harbour at five o'clock in the morning of 27 June; there he boarded a train for Euston, where he arrived in the late afternoon. My mother took me and Uncle Jack with her to the station, where Pamela joined us, and where members of the War Cabinet, the Russian and Chinese ambas-sadors, and various other persons soon gathered: "I was feeling so ex-cited & relieved that Papa is home. When the train drew in, Mummie & I got in to welcome him. Poor darling—not a very gay homecom-ing. His enemies have lost no time in his absence. . . ." Indeed, a major parliamentary row awaited him! On 25 June a motion had been ta-bled in the Order Paper of the House of Commons that "this House, while paying tribute to the heroism and endurance of the Armed Forces of the Crown . . . has no confidence in the central direction of the war."

My daughterly indignation spilled over into my diary:

It is strange to reflect that in the middle of world war Sir J. Wardlaw Milne*—Roger Keyes† etc. etc. could find nothing more glorious to do than table a vote of censure in Papa's absence & in the middle of a battle which sways to and fro & which so far has proved disastrous to us. It is stalling [sic] that when all Papa's abilities & energies should be now bent to retrieving the military situation he has got to fight a battle at home. How our enemies must be rejoicing—wherever they are—at this vexation. How our friends must be bewildered & Puzzled.

My father went straight to a Cabinet meeting, but later that evening we all repaired to Chequers. I noted that "Papa is well—but terribly worried & perplexed & harassed. He thinks tactical errors lost us the first part of the Libyan battle."

Chequers proved a true haven (as on so many occasions) from outer storms, although my father immediately started working on his speech for the vote of censure debate, and visiting colleagues mixed with the family as people came and went. During the weekend Diana and Duncan came down; Nana Whyte was there, and Sarah, just starting some leave, appeared from Medmenham—on a motorcycle! We stayed up till about two, gossiping: over a late breakfast in my mother's room on Sunday, I noted with delight that "Papa has brought Mummie 4 lovely dressing gowns from America—they are beautiful." We played cro-

* Sir John Wardlaw-Milne, chairman of the Conservative Foreign Affairs Committee (1939–45). Increasingly critical of WSC's conduct of the war, it was he who tabled the motion of "no confidence in the central direction of the war."
† Sir Roger Keyes, formerly a friend and supporter of WSC (see note on p. 111), seconded the motion.

quet before lunch, joined by the Prof; later, we had "the chief bomber*
and the chief fighter† to dinner & Oliver Lyttleton.... After dinner
[we] saw moderately good film—Kipps—Bed V. late. Battle rages in
Mersa Matruh." On the Monday,

> Mummie, Sarah, Nana & I & Papa—in fact everyone—decided
> to stay at Chequers. Lovely day. I spent most of it idling happily
> in deck chair on lawn. Went for a twirl on Sarah's motorbicycle.
> V dangerous & uncomfortable. Great fun tho'. Went for a walk
> with nana to Beacon Hill. James Stuart (Government Chief
> Whip) came for dinner to confer about the debate ... Mum-
> mie & Sarah departed for London. Papa, Mr Stuart, Nana and
> me [sic] saw Lloyds of London [sic]. Rather good. Papa enjoyed it.
> After the film, Papa had bad news of the battle. He & I and Mr.
> Stuart walked up & down the lawn. It was a soft night with high
> clouds & a moon gleaming through the rent in the ceiling [sic].
> Papa was unhappy and anxious. It is so frightful that he has to
> deal with this political crisis when he should be concentrating
> every faculty on this battle. I left him still pacing unhappily up
> & down. Oh darling—would to God I could help you.

The debate was on the Wednesday and Thursday of that coming
week. Nana and I went to the House with my mother on both days: for
me the most memorable speeches were those of Sir Roger Keyes, who,
while professing lifelong friendship and admiration for Churchill, delivered a rambling attack on ways and means; Hore-Belisha—a former
government minister who joined in (I judged his "a *despicable* speech—
slimy—clever—opportunist—ugh!")—and (most exciting) Aneurin
Bevan, whom I heard for the first time and

---

* Air Marshal Harris ("Bomber" Harris), appointed Commander-in-Chief, Bomber
Command, in February 1942: transformed Bomber Command into an effective weapon
against the enemy.
† Air Vice-Marshal Sholto Douglas, Deputy Chief of the Air Staff and Commander-
in-Chief, Fighter Command: responsible for rebuilding fighter strength after the Battle
of Britain.

who made a poisonous speech. Point by point one could destroy his speaks [speech?] pointing his phrases with little gestures— with a tone of w[h]eedling spite ... As I sat in the Gallery & listened to all these carping voices, I watched the unhappy set of Papa's shoulders—& my heart went out to him in his anxiety & grief. I know his mind is more with the battle in Egypt than here in the House. Sometimes I could scarcely control myself for rage at these little men who have only jibes and criticisms to offer.

This was the second day of the debate, and Sarah had joined the family support group; after luncheon we returned to the fray. I noted that I

put on a sterner hat for the afternoon instead of the hyacinth creation[!].* Felt terribly tensed up. Mummie obviously feeling the strain. The House was terribly crowded—Members standing at all the doorways. In the galleries Mr. Winant & Mrs W, M & Mme Maisky, Averell [Harriman], Kathleen [his daughter], Quentin Reynolds,† Nancy Tree [our hostess at Ditchley]. Papa rose to speak at 3.30. His speech was a remarkable performance. Measured—exact—reasoned—dignified—& throughout an undertone of unalterable determination & sober hopefulness ... The House listened in rapt attention. Except for some of the critics—Eddie Winterton‡ shrugging his shoulders & cracking his long fingers & smirking at the House. But Aneurin Bevan listening carefully & liking Papa's points and jokes—but maintaining his opposition standpoint. And then the division 475

* I find it interesting to be reminded of how formally and tidily we dressed, despite clothes rationing (hats, incidentally, were not rationed).
† American journalist and broadcaster.
‡ Edward Turnour, sixth Earl Winterton (1883–1962): as an Irish peer, he sat in the House of Commons, where by 1951 he had sat continuously for longer than any other sitting Member. He had famously clashed with WSC in the House in 1911, accusing the latter of disorderly interruptions.

to 25. And not as many abstentions as had been expected.—
Felt dazed & elated . . . Went to Papa's room—He was pleased.
Mummie & Sarah went on home. I stayed & had 10 mins all
alone with Papa. A crowd had gathered outside the House &
Papa was greeted by happy smiles & encouraging waves. One
man shouted 'You stick to it Sir!' Papa very much moved.

With all this political excitement, and several late parties thrown
in, this had been a very eventful—and quite exhausting—leave! But it
was not long after my return to the battery that we faced the culmination of all the technical training and practice, all the humdrum routine of alternate manning and camp duties, when—at last—we went
into action "for real" in the last week of July: it was a "first" for us all,
and PIP section (mine) was on duty. Two nights later we fired again.

The next day, 31 July, Judy and I had to hare off to Reading to be
interviewed by an OCTU (Officer Cadet Training Unit) board as
possible candidates for commissions. On our way back to camp (combining this with a wild Polish party!) I had a short time with my father:
"He & Mummie arrived back from lightening [*sic*] visit to Chartwell—& he took me into his room & told me 'I am going to Egypt to
try & win this battle* & then I'm going on to meet Stalin.' . . . I kissed
him goodbye with a heavy heart." This was to be a long absence—over
three weeks. But about a week after I had taken leave of him, I wrote
in my diary: "It's out in the papers now about Papa—it's a wonderful
relief to talk about it—it's been like a suffocating secret." And then on
24 August came a joyful, thankful entry: "On 9 o'clock news—Papa is
home. THANK GOD. Felt hysterically relieved."

---

* The Battle of Alamein. The First Battle of Alamein, in July 1942, had halted Rommel's advance in the Western Desert: the Second, fought in October and November,
would turn the tide of the North African campaign in favour of the Allies. It was on
this visit to the Middle East that the command structure of the armies was reorganized,
with General Montgomery taking command of the Eighth Army.

CHAPTER 13

An Officer and a Gentlewoman

D URING JULY, AFTER A FURTHER INTERVIEW, JUDY AND I WERE accepted as suitable "officer material." Our training course was scheduled for early October; meanwhile our battery life continued much the same. One excitement was an impromptu visit to the site by my father and Harry Hopkins: Papa rang me up and announced their imminent arrival. Fortunately Major Paul Hodder-Williams was "unchippy," and did not take amiss this somewhat incorrect procedure.

The site was wrapt in sunny Sunday afternoonishness [*sic*] & Papa and Harry & Tommy [Thompson, naval ADC] all rolled up about 5.30. Papa was in his sunniest mood & wearing a pale grey suit. Harry charming & debonair as always. It was a lovely visit & much more fun than when all the brass hats came trapesing [*sic*] round behind. The alarms were rung & we did a short show, which went very well. Then a quick tour of the camp which ended up in drinks in the Sgts' [Sergeants'] Mess. I felt so proud & happy that Papa should have thought to visit me.

I was to see Harry again that week:

Went on 24 hours [leave]. Oh heaven. Transatlantic lunch! Very hush hush! Papa/Harry Hop:/Admiral King,* General Marshall† & Mummie. All most charming & kind. Mummie & I then went off together & saw "Uncensored".‡ Very exciting & moving. Walked home . . . Judy arrived for Dinner at No. 10. Averell [Harriman] & Harry at Dinner & also Max [Beaverbrook]. Gay & interesting dinner.

Next morning "I slept till nearly 9. Delicious breakfast in Mummie's bed. Fried bacon & egg, brown bread/butter white currant jelly, coffee—*Peach!*" It is a measure of how drab wartime food could be that even breakfast menus featured in one's diary.

This last lap of our time at 469 flew by. On the face of it, they were happy weeks, excitingly enhanced on several occasions by our battery being in action—but my diary reminds me also of my anxieties for my father; of my being ill for a week in the camp hospital with some "bug"; and of inner storms—including a crisis in my religious faith—all of which I poured into my diary. I must also have moaned to my mother about the frustrations of camp life, because I find a letter from her dated 27 August which shows her wise and calming attitude:

My Darling Mary,
I am sure you will find everything much easier when you are an Officer—
and you have earned it. I hope you will go soon, but don't fret my dear One
if you do have to wait—becos' remember if you live to be a hundred you can

---

* Fleet Admiral Ernest King (1878–1956): Commander-in-Chief of the U.S. Fleet and Chief of Naval Operations, 1942–45.
† General George Marshall (1880–1959): Chief of Staff of the U.S. Army, 1939–45, and later Secretary of State, 1947–49: his plan for the economic recovery of Europe after the war became known as the "Marshall Plan."
‡ Film released in 1942, set in occupied Belgium, directed by Anthony Asquith.

never again have the experience of the past year. And I want you to leave
with 'Flying Colours' & be remembered by all with love & respect.

My enforced rest in the camp hospital was a most salutary experience: as well as suffering from a microbe, I think I was dead tired from
dashing to and fro from London, and too many late nights (whether
in nightclubs or on duty at the command post). Anyway, after about
a week I emerged considerably calmer in spirit and with my faith restored, as I asserted in my diary: "Now I shall cling to my religion
humbly and earnestly acknowledging that I cannot stand without it."
Nearly seventy years later, I know this is true for me still.

On 15 September I was Orderly Sergeant, and I celebrated my
twentieth birthday. I had telegrams from all my family, and a letter
bearing a proposal of marriage from a charming young officer I had
known slightly in Chartwell days. (This was romantic but not trau-
matic—I said "No" politely by return of post—and was good for morale!) My mother sent a delicious cake for us all to enjoy.

In the last week of September I had seven days' leave—the prospect of which had shone like a beacon through the somewhat fraught
weeks I have described. Arrived home at the Annexe,

I tore off my uniform & hid away every vestige of Khaki.
Changed into my civilian self. Mummie, Papa, Anthony Eden
for lunch. Afterwards Mummie & I went shopping. Took sky
blue jersey material to 'Rita' who is going to make it up in
most glamorous & slimming (!) style.* Then to MOLYNEUX†
& Mummie has given me a day dress. wow! My first dress from
MOLYNEUX.

---

* Clothes were rationed on a points/coupons system from June 1941 to 1 February 1949.
† Captain Edward Molyneux was one of the great couturiers of the thirties, with salons
in London and Paris. My mother had many of her clothes from him. In due course Molyneux would make my wedding dress.

It was understanding, as well as generous, of my mother to give me some lovely clothes: genuinely proud though I was of my military uniform, khaki was not an enhancing colour.

Both Judy and I had mixed feelings about taking a commission—but it was time to move on. Our last day with 469 Battery was on 5 October, which started normally but was then interrupted when we received a

sudden summons—'Will Sgt Churchill & Cpl Montagu pack their kit & go to BHQ [Battery Headquarters] at once.' Fled to Command Post & said goodbye to best part of section. Had so much I wanted to say & couldn't. Wrung their hands chokily—everyone very sweet. Greeny charming & me tearful—clutched his hand said goodbye Sir—& just ran as tears ran down my cheeks. Because despite the fact that I want to go now—I hate leaving 469 and the girls & the instruments & a life that has taught me so much & given me so many opportunities . . . Finally departed on lorry & Pip Section waved us goodbye—and I felt determined but sad as I lost sight of their gay smiling faces. No—I'm glad to go & sad to go . . . But as the lorry drove us over to BHQ I knew this is an end chapter of my life.

JUDY AND I REPORTED the following afternoon to No. 2 ATS OCTU at the Imperial Service College at Windsor. We were in the same company but in different platoons and rooms:

Dreary girl (vicar's daughter) & *charming* fany [FANY]* in my room . . . Before I went to bed—but last thing—I took down my

* FANY: acronym of the First Aid Nursing Yeomanry, a British women's ambulance unit formed in 1907. Its title was later changed to the Women's Transport Service, but the name FANY stuck. Its members served as drivers and welfare workers; many worked for SOE (Special Operations Executive) as wireless operators and cipher clerks, and some as agents (many of whom operated in France).

sergeant's stripes & golden guns. I minded that terribly. I am so proud of them & they mean such a lot to me—They were mine of my own getting—& winning & keeping. So I went to sleep not Sergeant Churchill—but Cadet Churchill.

The officers' training course lasted two months and involved an intensive programme of lectures and presentations, interspersed with parades and guest nights; there was a lot of gym and PT (which I always hated). We spent a lot of time making and keeping ourselves immaculately smart (we found a laundry in the back streets of Windsor where we took our collars to be starched), and the white bands on our caps needed frequent changing. One was always conscious of being watched and assessed: I found it quite trying, and did not shine particularly.

Wartime Windsor had several amenities from our point of view. Fuller's Tea Shop with its famous walnut cake was much patronized by the cadets; the Theatre Royal (then as now) produced excellent plays; and over the bridge in Eton High Street the Cockpit—where one was in crowded competition with Eton boys and their parents—served copious teas. With those friends who had cars (and petrol) one went further afield to the Hind's Head at Bray for luncheon, and we trained up to London from Windsor or Slough. Chequers too was only about an hour away—I would meet the duty car at Slough and soon be home sweet home.

Mrs. Roosevelt paid a visit to England that October, and spent a weekend at Chequers. I dashed home after church parade on the Sunday, and found a large party gathered—the Edens, the Portals, Gil Winant, Robert Hopkins (Harry's son), and Elliott Roosevelt (second of the President's surviving sons). I recorded the event enthusiastically in my diary: "M[ummie] & P[apa] & I were at the door to welcome Mrs R—She is so natural & Kindly & exudes energy & life. Lunch went off very well. Scrumptious food—had double helpings."

During this last week of October, in North Africa the Battle of Alamein was raging, and on 4 November the Eighth Army inflicted a severe defeat on the German and Italian forces under Field Marshal von Rommel: it was to prove the turning point of the war. Two days after these tremendous tidings my parents gave one of their few "social" luncheon parties at No. 10. The guests were Harold Nicolson;* two old friends, Eddie Marsh and Horatia Seymour; and two "fringe friends," Lady Kitty Lambton and Lady Furness, both of whom had just escaped from the South of France. It so happened that I arrived from Windsor towards the end of the luncheon, which I described as "exceedingly sticky." I further labelled Lady Kitty as "crazy as a coot" and Lady Furness as "very beautiful & sane." Brendan Bracken (then Minister of Information) had appeared, and my father had told him to arrange for the church bells throughout the country to be rung the following Sunday (this was Friday) to celebrate our great victory. Some hesitation about this idea had been expressed by the company in general—but my father was determined.† After the party broke up, however, I noted in my diary that "Mummie [was] being violent (quite rightly I thought) with Papa" about this: my mother was more cautious, and fearful lest something might occur which would make nonsense of a premature display of triumph. On this occasion, her forceful arguments prevailed. But it was not long before the bells did ring out—on Sunday, 15 November—by which point the British army had once again entered Tobruk, and the enemy forces in North Africa had lain down their arms.

I was just now much in love with a very good-looking, very nice, and excruciatingly dull American officer I had met when I was with 469, and most of my London evenings were spent with him, Judy, and a fellow-officer friend of his. Much encouraged by me, he duly proposed, saying however that he did not want to "rush me." I spent hours pouring my feelings out to long-suffering Judy, and practicing writing "Mary Conklin." My mother invited Ed to Chequers for the weekend of 7 November, when I had some leave, and my diary entries for those

---

* Harold Nicolson (1886–1968): author, critic, and National Liberal MP. Married to Vita Sackville-West, poet, author, and gardener.
† Up to now church bells had been silent—they were intended to be rung to warn that the invasion had started—but those dark days had passed.

days show how my dilemma came to its eventual inevitable conclusion. Ed brought me what was in those days a collection of very welcome presents: "a tin of peanuts, pr. of silk stockings, packets of hairpins, lipstick—too lovely,"* I commented: but even driving down from London I became aware of my rising irritation at his "sweet, minute & leisurely way of recounting the most trifling details of his life . . . 'when I was a youngster . . .'" Both my parents were exceedingly nice to him: my father listened to his long-winded stories with what I regarded as angelic patience—but he had scolded my mother for inviting Ed, "because then I'd marry him & go to America & he'd be miserable & I'd be miserable too. . . . When I went to see Papa he was so sweet & did his duty as a father! 'Now don't you go marrying that young man—He's very nice but you wouldn't like American life . . . etc.'"

Sarah also came for part of the weekend, looking really exhausted and ill. Before dinner on the Saturday, my father told us that American and British forces would attack the North African coast at dawn the next day. "We all felt a little breathless all evening I think. Sarah it now appears has been doing the intelligence work [interpretation of aerial photographs] for it under lock & key for the last 2 months! Sensation!!" Later that evening I had a long heart-to-heart talk to Sarah and spilled out to her my mortification at realizing that my rapidly cooling feelings for Ed were "just a CRUSH dying & I had so believed it was the *real thing*! Sarah was sweet. Long fascinating gossip—I made up my mind irrevocably then—the answer is NO."

The next day Sarah had to leave early.

Ed & I breakfasted in sunlit dining room in an empty silence that fidgeted me . . . Papa left to entertain General de Gaulle at No. 10. G de G wasn't told of attack because of security! This was to be a soothing down luncheon. The news broke too wonderfully—Mummie & I listened to the radio messages &

---

* Rationing even extended to makeup: there is a mention in my diary about "my quota" being in at Cyclax.

instructions to the people of North Africa. Dear God—what wonderful news—When I think of the sad & disappointing news we have all waited on at Chequers—& now . . . Victory— we are all so happy & excited. Mummie & Ed & I all went for a long, lovely Sunday morningish [*sic*] walk. At lunch I nearly went mad at Ed's narrative[s]—& hustled him off to catch a train. I was rather glad when he was gone.

Oh dear: poor Ed! A few days later I "wrote & said 'no' as simply & unwoundingly as possible."

The lectures and training at the Windsor OCTU usually ended at midday on Saturday, so I often got home for part of the weekends. Sunday, 15 November, was rather special because there was a church parade: "As we paraded the chimes from Windsor began—Victory Bells*—our own College bell clanged discordantly but still the *thought* was there!!" After the service I dashed back to Chequers, where, because my mother was away, I had to officiate as hostess at a large party assembled for a conference with my father. As I confided to my diary, I

felt inefficient & overwhelmed by lunch party of 17 with which I had to grapple. But WHAT a party. I sat between 'Glamour-Pants' [aka Lord Louis Mountbatten] and Sir Charles Portal— great fun and very hilarious—the rest of the party was:

General Smuts (so gay & v kind to me & full of life & vigour);
CIGs [General Sir Alan Brooke];
Pug [General Ismay];
Tommy [Thompson];
Mr Peck [John, Private Secretary on duty];
Brig. Hollis [Sir Leslie, chief assistant to General Ismay];

* For Alamein: the subject of the heated discussion between WSC and CSC at the luncheon at No. 10 on 6 November 1942, of which an account appears earlier in this chapter.

Gen. Smith (Gen Eisenhower's 'shadow' here) [General
    Bedell Smith, Chief of Staff to General Eisenhower];
General Gale [General Sir Humphrey Gale, (British) Chief
    Administrative Officer to General Eisenhower];
Sir Dudley Pound [1st Sea Lord];
Papa;
Lady Portal.

It was an enjoyable exciting lunch. Afterwards talked to Lady
Portal till second session of conference ended around 4.30. '16th
Front Now' having been planned. Everyone left. Felt depleted.

A great excitement for me this winter was my inclusion in the invitation to my parents from the King and Queen to a Thanksgiving Day
party for American officers at Buckingham Palace. In the event, my
mother was ill in bed, and so I went alone with my father. It was the
first time I had ever been presented to the King and Queen, and, as I
confided to my diary, "I couldn't have been more thrilled if I'd been in
white satin & feathers (tho' of course that would have been rather gay).
And I felt so proud at going with Papa." The princesses were there too
(up from Windsor Castle, where they lived during the war:* it must
have been one of their first official appearances). I enjoyed myself immensely, not only with the American guests, who were charming and
easy to chat up, but with the British ones, quite a number of whom
I knew. I was thrilled, of course, to meet the latest hero—Squadron
Leader Nettleton VC† ("so good looking AND married—tant pis," I
remarked in my diary!). My father had to leave after a short while, but
he left me "under the friendly wing of Mr. Winant, who was looking
more like Abe Lincoln than ever." I had been unaffectedly thrilled
by the whole plush and gold setting, and by my first close-at-hand
glimpse of the Royal Family.

---

* Princess Elizabeth joined the ATS as a commissioned officer in 1945.
† Squadron Leader John Dering Nettleton had been awarded the VC in April 1942 for
"unflinching determination as well as leadership and valour of the highest order."

This 30 November was my father's sixty-eighth birthday, and, as she had done every year since 1940, my mother organized a lovely dinner at the Annexe for close family and one or two old friends. Since 1940, also, my father's birthday had almost become a national institution, and greetings poured in from far and wide—not only from relations, friends, and colleagues, but also from countless members of the general public, often accompanied by presents. Despite rationing and austerity, people sent him delicacies of every kind—not only grand and sophisticated presents of oysters or rare vintages, but more homely and just as much appreciated gifts of butter, cream, and eggs. Mrs. Landemare had a field day, and we all had a scrumptious dinner. Apart from the "principals," the party was Diana, Sarah, Pamela, Uncle Jack, Venetia Montagu, Brendan Bracken, and myself. The charmless rooms of the Annexe flat looked really pretty and glowing by candlelight, bedecked with masses of flowers. When we all drank my father's health we thought of "absent friends," and of all those who were with us in spirit—and this year a gleam of victory caught our glasses.

A few days later Judy and I graduated at our passing-out parade as officers and emerged as that lowest form of army life—newly fledged second subalterns (one pip). I was certainly not sad to leave OCTU: I had not enjoyed the course, and knew I had not done particularly well. Both Judy and I were impatient for the next step—which was to get back into Ack-Ack, which involved a further period of technical training. So after a week's leave we were posted to an anti-aircraft training regiment—205H(M)AA—at Arborfield, near Reading.

WE WOULD BE TEN WEEKS at Arborfield, and for me it was not on the whole a successful or happy interlude. There were about forty in the Officers' Mess, of which about a third were permanent staff (instructors and so on); the rest were an ever-changing population of male and female officers attending the various courses and awaiting postings to their respective batteries. I missed the conviviality of the Sergeants' Mess at Enfield, and I was bored by and not good at the technical course subjects; Judy, on the other hand, shone to such an extent that Captain (later Major) Tony Hogg, who befriended both of us, contrived to have her posted at the end of the course on to the permanent staff, with the prospect of her becoming an instructor. Moreover, Judy's affections were fixated on a charming RAF pilot, whom she had originally met in Norfolk (Bruce Grimston from Gorhambury near St. Albans, which was reasonably accessible), while I was footloose and fancy-free, and very much on the lookout for "romance."

Apart from Tony Hogg (very much married, and in any case our "guru" figure) and one or two others, there were not many kindred spirits in the Mess, although there were plenty of unattached (genuinely or merely perceptibly) officers from various regiments stationed round. I was, I'm sorry to say, in a "bolshy" mood, and elected to have a highly visible "walk-out" with a very good-looking (and similarly "bolshy-minded") battery sergeant major on the permanent staff, whom I had taken up with at one of the sergeants' dances at the camp. It didn't amount to much: we used to meet in the evenings and, he having acquired a bicycle for me, ride out together to some quiet country pub; and at camp dances we would dance a great deal together, which gratuitously drew attention to the situation. There was nothing in military regulations specifically to forbid officers and other ranks associating—but it was certainly discouraged, particularly within the same unit. Judy from the first disapproved of this "carry-on"—and so did the ATS Senior Commander, who sent for me and left me in no doubt that in her view it was an unsuitable friendship: in a martyred mood I therefore gave up seeing him off duty. (I fancied I was "in love" with him and that my affection was genuinely returned; I learned later, to my humiliation, that he had done it "for a bet.")

Soon after our arrival at Arborfield it was Christmastime; we had a few days' leave and Judy came back with me to Chequers, where there was quite a gathering of the clan over several generations: Uncle Jack and Aunt Nellie Romilly; Diana and Duncan with Julian (aged three); Sarah; Pamela with "Baby" Winston (two and a half); Brendan Bracken and the Prof; and—since business was as usual—delightful

Leslie Rowan from the private office. Dear Monty Lamont made the gaunt house glow with a huge Christmas tree, garlands, and lights, and with so many separations one really appreciated "being together." In writing to thank my parents for their generous present, I said: "It was sweet of you to think of a cheque, because although I can be quite economical here as there are no shops, and the Garrison cinema only charges 1s 6d a time—still on the whole being 'an officer and a gentle-woman' is more expensive than being a rude rough sergeant!!"

Early in the New Year I was again at home, and learned some disquieting news about my father's health. On the Sunday I

went for a long & lovely walk with Mummie after lunch. We talked entirely of the family—& especially of Papa. It appears that he MIGHT get [a] coronary thrombosis—& it might be brought on by anything like a long/or high flight. The question is whether he should be warned or not. Mummie thinks he should not—I agree with her.

Looking back, I see this is a very good example of my mother's calm and resolute stoicism. I reflected in my diary:

It is frightening & yet I feel perfectly calm. Funny how I fuss & fret about comparatively small things & yet this shadow & menace to someone I love so much much more than life itself doesn't throw me out of gear—I just feel numb & calm—And yet how desperately, longingly hopeful that it will be all right.

This knowledge, of course, made the few of us "in the know" even more anxious whenever my father had to fly. From this time on, persuaded by his doctor, Lord Moran,* and close colleagues, he travelled as much as possible by sea.

* Charles Wilson (1882–1977), created first Baron Moran in 1943. President of the Royal College of Physicians 1941–50, he was WSC's doctor from 1940 to the end of his life, and accompanied him on nearly all his travels from 1941 onwards.

But it was by air that he went on 12 January to North Africa to meet President Roosevelt for the Casablanca Conference; ten days later he went on to Turkey to meet President İnönü; and from there he went on to visit the Eighth Army in Tripoli, before flying home. The news of his journeyings was not made public until 27 January, so until then I gleaned information about his movements only spasmodically when I visited home, keeping my anxiety to myself in the intervals; and it was over the radio at lunchtime on 7 February that, to my intense relief, I heard of his safe arrival back in London. I was given permission to go to London for the night; Diana and Sarah were also at dinner, and I reported in my diary: "Papa in excellent form—sang Poultry and Half a woman & half a tree [two of his favourite Edwardian music-hall songs]."

However, the strain and fatigue of his travels contributed to my father becoming ill. On 18 February my mother had told me he had a feverish cold; this developed into pneumonia, and the next day saw the first of a series of doctors' bulletins. I went home two days later, a Sunday, and on the way up,

in the train reading the official bulletin about Papa I got into a sudden panic. Might this be the beginning of the end? Arrived home M was ready for church. In her lovely dark cloth coat trimmed with beaver & the flame coloured scarf bursting out—beaver muff & hat. To me Mummie has all the lovely graces of life—tempered with a steel-like integrity. We two went to service in the Royal Military Chapel [at Wellington Barracks]. It was rather lovely & comforting. M is not *seriously* worried about Papa—but he is pretty ill. I was shocked when I saw him. He looked so ill & tired—lying back in bed. What beautiful hands he has. I found the house frightening—nurses' caps, kidney bowls & bedpans. In the office slips of paper with bulletins, messages, fond enquiries.

It was not until March that the last bulletin was issued, the doctors feeling confident that my father was at last restored to health.

Judy's and my time of serving together was now coming to an end. At Arborfield I'm afraid we had been regarded with some disapproval by our seniors and betters—the general consensus being that we were all right apart, but tended to be noisy and boisterous when together. Judy, however, was to earn golden opinions for her actions in Reading one afternoon: a sneak raider dropped some bombs—one just opposite where she happened to be; she was involved in the aftermath, and was later commended by the authorities for her assistance. I wrote in my diary that she "had behaved with wonderful & typical presence of mind & returned white and unconsciously shocked" from this unpleasant experience.

As planned, Judy was to remain on the permanent staff at Arborfield, where her technical abilities would be fully employed; so we had a tearful parting of the ways at Wokingham Station on the evening of 22 February, when I departed with my new battery, 643 Heavy (M) AA Battery RA, on our overnight journey to the practice camp at Whitby on the Yorkshire coast. It had been wonderful for us to have started our army life together; Judy's presence had been a salvation to me in my slightly conspicuous situation, and our friendship would remain important for both of us always.

BEFORE I LEFT ARBORFIELD I had spoken to my mother, whose reassurance about my father's health enabled me to leave for Whitby with an easier mind. Of course, I missed Judy enormously, not least because I could talk to her about family matters which I confided to nobody else; however, luckily life at Whitby with my new battery, where we were all new to each other, was completely engrossing and very hectic, so I did not have much time to mope, and very soon we had all "shaken down" together nicely—although I shared a room with a maddening colleague, about whom I complained bitterly in my letters home and to my diary. (I have no doubt my feeling was shared—these things are usually mutual.)

The ATS billets were in requisitioned boardinghouses and cheap hotels on the seafront, totally exposed to the wild and bitter winds. We kept warm largely by moving about constantly (sometimes "at the double") between billets, dining halls, Messes, and—above all—the guns and command post, which were up on the cliff which towers above the town, and which one reaches by means of 199 steep steps.* These had to be climbed twice a day, and more if one was on special duties, so that by the time we left Whitby we were truly "fighting fit." I think we all enjoyed our month there: Whitby is a charming town, full of character and cosy pubs, and the sea air was wonderfully invigorating. Also, I made a very nice friend, John Archer, a captain in one of the other batteries.

The bulletins about my father continued to improve, and in her first letter to me in Whitby, on 24 February, my mother wrote to me:

First of all I write to tell you that Papa is I think really better. The doctors still give out the 'no change' bulletin because the temperature has not completely gone down, but I can see for myself that he is better. His face looks quite different. He has lost that weary look. I know, my darling, this will relieve you. I have really been very worried about him.

I am longing to hear how you are, and all you are doing, and how you are settling down. I love detail about everything if you have time.

As soon as my father was strong enough, my mother moved him down to Chequers, from where she wrote to me on 9 March:

Here are Papa and I living for a whole week at Chequers. Most unusual—by the time it is over I shall have settled down & be quite enjoying it! Papa is progressing very slowly but (I hope & believe) safely through his convalescence to his normal strong state of health. Yesterday morning as Papa could not go to his

* To date there is still no lift!

weekly luncheon with the King—the King came here & paid a morning visit in the White Parlour a la Jane Austen.

Meanwhile our battery's time at Whitby was coming to an end, and I summed it up in my diary:

What shall I remember about it?—feeling v well—steps & more steps—sun drenched fresh spring days—convoys moving slowly & fatefully out at sea—enjoying my work & it troubling me— enjoying increasingly John's company . . . And the guns firing & crashing [practicing on targets] & me never really getting used to it—& endless professional jokes—battery gossip—battery problems—battery life. Moments of homesickness—long let- ters from Mummie & Judy—bracing myself to go to S. Wales [where 643 was to be deployed].

I was much absorbed too during these weeks by *War and Peace,* which I was reading—predictably falling in love with Prince Andrew, and seeing myself as "Princess A . . . & everyone saying 'Moshka' & 'Little cousin' & 'Princess' to me!"

A spell of leave followed Whitby, and I remember standing in the corridor of a crowded train, clutching a large parcel of lobsters and crabs I had acquired as a present for my parents (the lobsters' whis- kers escaped from their package, and caused a stir among my fellow travellers). To my great joy, Judy also had leave just now (before going to a gunnery instructors' course), and that evening our dinner party was just my parents, Judy, and myself: I reported that the lobsters and crabs were "very pink & popular!" I spent the weekend at Chequers, where Uncle Jack, who had been ill, was recuperating; Ali Forbes also came to stay, as did Averell Harriman and his daughter Kathleen (Kathy), and the Prof. My poor mother had retired to bed—the strain of my father's illness, and her own load of war work and engagements, had temporarily quite worn her out.

I and my colleagues of 643 Battery converged a few days later on our new site—West Nash, near Newport in South Wales, where we would form part of the defences of Cardiff. Our camp seemed very remote: it was also five feet below sea level, the seawall being a prominent feature of the landscape. Our first task was to clean up the camp, living quarters, and cookhouse—upon which we found that the camp drainage system left much to be desired. Living conditions for the troops were not good; buses were distant and erratic, rendering our nearest "metropolis," Newport, although in fact only seven miles away, almost unreachable; even the nearest public telephone was nearly two miles away at the local post office.

Still, the girls set to and made the best of things. They soon persuaded the drivers of the local trains to stop and give them a lift to Newport! We made our own fun in camp too, including a dance—although I can't remember where we got "outside talent" from: very likely a neighbouring battery or other service units—at which a local band played all the current favourites. I noted the event in my diary: "Dance in the evening—quite a success in the end. Girls enjoyed it. Felt how much more I'd enjoyed camp dances when I was a glorious O/R [other rank]. However it was madly energetic & gay."

I had been told while I was still at Whitby that I would shortly be posted to a London battery—481, in Hyde Park. I had quite mixed feelings about this. I felt genuinely sad at the prospect of leaving all my 643 pals so soon—more especially as living conditions for them were so unsatisfactory. Also, I was only just "finding my feet" and learning my job as an officer (apart from my technical role as a plotting officer), and now I got a bad attack of "Fright & jitters" at the thought of going "to a long established bty & once again to start to try & break down a hostile, expectant & you-wait-&-see atmosphere—& once again to feel terribly new & an outsider."

I also felt embarrassed by my "special treatment"—though on this score my colleagues were charming and most understanding. They knew I had no part in these special postings which kept me in the London area: the powers-that-were had, I think, decided that my presence near to home would be a solace and pleasure to my father, and his needs featured large in people's minds. I found this story, which illustrates how people felt about him, in my diary. While my father had been on his travels in February, my mother took Nana to see a play: "In the audience was a whole submarine crew & their girl friends. Their Petty Officer introduced the men to Mummie. She said they were charming & at the end the Petty Officer said 'Will you tell your husband that we dive for him.'"

My posting came through on Saturday, 10 April, and that evening the girls gave me a party. After warm farewells all round I left 643 the next morning and, having paid a flying visit to my parents at Chequers, I reported on the Monday to 481 Battery in Hyde Park, with whom I would serve for nearly two years at home and abroad.

Our half battery of four guns,* with the supporting encampment of Nissen huts, was north of the Serpentine, behind Speakers' Corner and opposite the Dorchester Hotel in Park Lane, where today there is a great empty space used for mass demonstrations and pop concerts. Between us and the Serpentine was a rocket battery, manned by the Home Guard: on the occasions when both batteries fired, the racket was considerable. I had a friendly welcome from my fellow officers, and settled down quite quickly. Although not comparable to the Blitz of 1940–41, the spring and summer of 1943 brought quite a lot of air raids and 481 was in action on a number of occasions.

Our commanding officer was Major Stan King—a formidable six-footer whose bark was every bit as good as his bite, and who rejoiced in the nickname "Phyllis." The senior ATS officer was Junior Commander (equivalent to Captain) Molly Oakey, who was charming and efficient, and with whom I quickly made friends. Besides myself there was one other ATS subaltern and three or four RA officers. I settled in quite quickly: of course it was lovely for me being so near home. Not long after my arrival my parents visited us one evening: it was a "great success," although I also noted in my diary that I "was shocked to see Papa looking tired & old." But four days later he was off again (in the

---

* The other half was at Burnt Oak, in the northwest suburbs of London.

Queen Mary) to visit the President: "Went with party to station. Felt panicked inside—& rather desolate standing on the platform in pitch darkness with the train drawing out—Bon voyage my darling. Brendan [Bracken] deposited me at [the] battery."

While my father was away, 481 went to practice camp at Bude on the north Cornish coast, and it was while I was there that his whereabouts—conferring with the President in Washington—were announced. He would also visit Algiers and Gibraltar before arriving home in the first week of June. In his absence, on 9 May came the tremendous news of the surrender of the German army in Tunisia: for the second time the church bells were rung in celebration. And on the home front there was more cause for celebration, for on 18 May, Diana's third child—a daughter, Celia—was born; I went and visited them, and found Diana sitting up in bed "looking beautiful, happy & peach-like. The baby is adorable."

Quite fortuitously I had twenty-four hours' leave at the time of my father's arrival home from these latest travels. I had stayed overnight at the Annexe, and at a quarter to seven in the morning there he was— "Well & in wonderful spirits. I lay in a sleepy haze in Mummie's bed & he padded up & down in his blue rompers* & told us the news." The rest of this joyful day was given over to vanity: "Shopped bought new hat, belt, shoes etc. Went with Mummie to Molyneux & saw about *lovely* new dress. Most excited. . . . Lunched at home—Mummie & Papa, Oliver† & Moyra Lyttleton, Duncan. After lunch—packed & re-transformed myself into AT officer. Returned 481. . . . Everyone sweet about Papa being home."

At the end of June there was a lovely and triumphant family occasion for us when my father was made a Freeman of the City of London. Sarah and I in our uniforms accompanied our parents in an open lan-

---

* These "rompers" were officially called WSC's "siren suit" and were modelled on the "boiler suit" he used to wear while bricklaying: he wore them at Chartwell and Chequers. The daytime ones were made of suitable weight, and usually approximating to an air force blue. For dinner at home he had luscious velvet ones (CSC used to take great pleasure in organizing these)—usually dark green or deep red (with slippers to match).
† Oliver Lyttleton, Minister of Production.

dau from Temple Bar to the blitz-scarred Guildhall, where other family members were among a great gathering of government and civic guests. It was an intensely moving occasion. The casket in which the scroll recording the Freedom was presented had been made from oak salvaged from the roof of the Guildhall after the destruction wrought by the air raid in 1940. After the speeches and ceremonial we all transferred to the Mansion House for luncheon with the Lord Mayor: wherever my father went or appeared he was greeted with vociferous cheers by the other guests and onlookers. One felt so moved and proud looking back on all the events of the last three years, and the part he had played in them, and it was so gratifying to see the people recognizing this. Although there would be more trials and tribulations to come, there was a sense now that victory surely lay ahead.

During these summer weeks my parents and I (duty permitting) saw several plays: *This Happy Breed* and *Present Laughter,* both by Noël Coward, and *The Watch on the Rhine* by Lillian Hellman. These evenings at the theatre were a real relaxation for my father, and of course great treats for me when I was included.

Early in July, I had some of my own friends at Chequers for a weekend. They included Robin Sinclair, a flying officer in the RAF (son of Sir Archibald Sinclair, the Liberal leader and a close friend of my father's ever since their days together on the Western Front in the First World War), and Robin Maugham, whom I had not seen since the first year of the war: now a captain and back from the Middle East, where he had been wounded, he was far from well and relapsed into bed for part of the weekend. On the Sunday Noël Coward came down ("Very charming, queer & gay," I noted in my diary). That evening after dinner he obligingly sang and played for us (there was a grand piano in the Great Hall): he had a brand-new song—"Don't Let's Be Beastly to the Germans"—which was received enthusiastically by us all.

But after this pleasant interlude we heard on Monday the tragic news of the death the previous day in a plane crash in Gibraltar of General Sikorski, head of the Polish government-in-exile and

Commander-in-Chief of the Free Polish Forces. My father was shocked and saddened—he knew Sikorski personally and admired him greatly, and they had established a rapport which was of importance given the complications of Polish affairs, particularly vis-à-vis the Soviet Union. Also killed in the crash were the general's daughter, his political liaison officer, and Lieutenant Colonel Victor Cazalet, MC, MP, a friend and country neighbour and, incidentally, my godfather.

While life for all ranks in the Hyde Park battery had great advantages from the point of view of access in off-duty hours to entertainment, shops, and general contact with civilian life, our location also placed particular pressures on us: we really had to be on our toes as a "showpiece" for the relatively new phenomenon of mixed anti-aircraft batteries, which were of interest both to our own military pundits and to overseas official visitors. This made site life quite demanding: "Phyllis" was a great stickler not only for our personal smartness and deportment at all times, but also for the general appearance of the gun site. Stones forming the edging to flower beds at the camp entrance had to be whitewashed, and roads and pathways kept swept; on the eve of any special visitation potted plants (according to season) were hastily planted in among the regular shrubs and plants by "volunteers," and there was a good deal of grumbling about "eyewash." Our most important (and most popular) visitor this summer was Queen Elizabeth: with her were the Princess Royal and the Director of the ATS, Mrs. Jean Knox, plus a positive gaggle of male "top brass." Despite an unhelpful downpour, I was relieved to be able to report to my diary that "everything went off all right."

CHAPTER 14

"Subaltern George"

I SEE FROM MY MILITARY RECORD THAT FROM 29 JULY TO 20 SEP-tember 1943 I was officially "Attached to the Personal Staff of the Minister of Defence." This meant that on 29 July I left my battery without explanation: in fact I knew that I was to go with my parents on a voyage to North America, and that I would act officially as an ADC to my father. Although I was of course much excited by the prospect of this journey, I was genuinely concerned about the "right-ness" of this arrangement; however, over the next weeks I would feel that I was able to make myself useful, as well as having a most thrilling and interesting time.

I spent a few hectic days at home reorganizing my uniform (less emphasis on battle dress and gaiters; addition of tropical kit), in the course of which I spent a lot of time at that excellent establishment in Piccadilly, Austin Reed (where my orders were labelled "Subaltern George" for security's sake).

On 4 August my father was on the eve of his departure by sea, with many colleagues and a large staff, for the Quebec Conference with President Roosevelt and the Canadian Prime Minister, Mr. Macken-zie King. My mother retired to bed to garner her energy; to our *petit comité* for dinner of my father, myself, Sarah, and Uncle Jack (who were not coming on the voyage) was added an unexpected guest—Brigadier Orde Wingate, the brilliant and fearless commander of the Chindits, the guerrilla forces in Burma. I was deeply struck by him, as my diary entry late that night records:

The 'Clive of Burma' came almost straight from the plane [in his crumpled tropical uniform—summoned by WSC]. He is a triple DSO. Looks like Lawrence & is a *Tiger* of a man. We were all greatly impressed. I can see Papa has great things in mind for him. He is to come on the trip. Mrs Wingate [after frantic telephonings from No. 10] was snatched off the train from Scotland southbound & instructed to wait at Edinburgh. Very dramatic & exciting. He looks terribly strained & ill & I do hope the sea voyage will do him good; 11.30 [pm] we left. Dark starless night. Sarah came to the station. On train 1st Sea Lord/ Brigadier Wingate/Averell [Harriman]. I am so excited I can hardly believe it's all true.

I continued my account on the morning of 5 August: "It is cold & wet and we are speeding along the coast Northwards. The sea looks pretty rough. We picked up Mrs Wingate at Edinburgh . . . of her more later." By the end of that day we were well ensconced aboard ship:

Arrived Faslane 14.30. Went aboard *The Maid of Orleans* [a tender]. At Faslane came the news CATANIA IS OURS! Went up the Gairloch & there was the Q.M. [*Queen Mary*]* in the Tail of the Bank opposite Greenock. Nearly two years ago it was here I went aboard *The Prince of Wales*—a lance corporal & said goodbye & Godspeed to Papa setting out for the first of his many heroic & fateful journeys. How wonderfully our prayers have been answered so far. Dutch notices are plastered all over the ship to kid everyone it was Queen Wilhelmina coming aboard. (Their figures at any rate are not dissimilar).

---

* The *Queen Mary* was used as a troopship during the war, ferrying large numbers of Allied troops between North America, the UK, Australia, and North Africa.

. . . Our suites are luxurious and most comfortable. I am in a little green room next to Mummie . . . The 'special' party is over 200 strong—among Cs [Chiefs] of Staff & their Staffs are Kathy H[arriman] & the Dam Buster*—who I met this evening & seems delightful. *To dinner.* Averell & Kathy/CIGS [Alan Brooke]/Lord Leathers [Minister of War Transport]/Tommy [Thompson].

The food is UNBELIEVABLE. White rolls & masses of butter.

Shipboard life was indeed very agreeable. Well wrapped up, despite "dirty weather & a fairly heavy sea which grew worse" we tramped the deck: our escort at times could very clearly be seen wallowing in heavy seas, "coming over green." Various permutations of the party lunched or dined with my parents, and I happily noted "Papa in a benign sunny mood." For myself, I had a lovely time being entertained in the wardroom, touring the ship, and enjoying the company of Kathy and Dam Buster, and of charmers like "Pug" Ismay and Peter Portal.

Mrs. Wingate, who was about twenty-six, lovely to look at, and with a melodious voice, started out with a romantic aura and received a universally friendly welcome from all and sundry; however, as the voyage progressed it became painfully clear that she was immensely impressed with herself, and was a bore and a prig to boot. Brigadier Wingate, next to whom I sat at dinner one night, I found "extremely interesting but very intense. God! what a ménage with Mrs W. . . . But he is not so tiresome. I wonder if he will be a great new figure." Major General Wingate, as he would soon become, was supported by my father and became a popular hero with his exploits in Burma, but was killed in an air crash in the jungle in March 1944. My father called him "a man of genius who might have been a man of Destiny."†

---

* Wing Commander Guy Gibson VC, who commanded the audacious and costly bombing on 17 May 1943 of the Ruhr dams: WSC wanted him to have a break from operations, and he was en route for the United States and Canada on a "goodwill" trip. Tragically, he was killed in September 1944 when his aircraft ran out of fuel and crashed in the Netherlands.
† Jock Colville told me this, and I recorded it in my diary on 1 April 1944.

We made landfall on the afternoon of Monday, 9 August, when I went up onto the bridge with Guy Gibson "and watched Canada appear. Saw 2 whales. It was lovely & most impressive steaming into Halifax harbour with our US Navy escort 'line astern.' Mounties in scarlet & blue patrolled the quayside." Although elaborate security arrangements had been made, the true identity of "Colonel Warden" (my father's pseudonym for this trip) had become known, and there was a large and enthusiastic crowd at the railway station as well as the official welcoming party to greet him and "Mrs. Warden" and their colleagues. After civilities, we all boarded a long and most wonderfully comfortable train, and started on our seven-hundred-mile (and twenty-two-hour) journey to Quebec.

At journey's end our party was met at Charmy (a little station nestled below the Heights of Abraham, famously stormed by General Wolfe in 1759) by the Prime Minister of Canada, Mr. Mackenzie King,* the provincial Governor and his lady, and divers "personalities," and whisked up to the Citadelle, which stands so imposingly on the cliffs above the St. Lawrence River and dramatically dominates the old city of Quebec. At that time the Citadelle was a royal residence,† and the King had offered it to my father, his family, and his immediate entourage for their stay: the rest of the large party was accommodated in the Château Frontenac, a large and luxurious hotel quite close by. Despite its stern exterior, the Citadelle inside is a charmingly arranged house, from which one can emerge on to the long, wooden-planked terraces which command wonderful views over the city and river. It was after dark when we arrived, and I remember my mother and I stood for quite a long time looking out over the twinkling city lights below us—after four years of blackout at home it seemed a wonderful sight.

The Conference itself, between President Roosevelt, my father, and Mr. Mackenzie King, was not due to start until the beginning of

---

* William Lyon Mackenzie King (1874–1950), Liberal Prime Minister of Canada, 1921–26, 1926–30, and 1935–48.
† Now it is one of the residences of the Governor-General of Canada.

the following week, and while the staffs were completing their plans and agenda the President invited my parents and myself to stay with him and Mrs. Roosevelt at Hyde Park, his family home on the banks of the Hudson River. We would travel there by train, and my father conceived the delightful idea that on the way a detour could be made so that he could show us the Niagara Falls. However, my mother was in no fit state to travel—indeed, she was completely exhausted: already tired when she went on board the *Queen Mary,* she had hoped to recoup her energy during the voyage, but unfortunately had suffered a series of sleepless nights—so she decided to stay in Quebec and rest up in order to be ready for the considerable demands the conference period would make on her in terms of entertaining and being entertained. My father was dreadfully disappointed, and though I offered to stay with her for company, she insisted I go with him. So we reluctantly left her in the good care of Grace Hamblin, Lord Moran, Mr. Mackenzie King (who was quite a cosy old thing), and several very nice Canadian ladies.

We left in the early evening, and as the train slid through lovely countryside it was really touching to see that "little groups of people gathered at the side of the track to wave at Papa." In my diary I am ecstatic and excited by it all, and "this journey especially—just me and Papa *à deux* is a real treat for me. He is being so sweet & kind—calling on me at 8 on Thursday morning [12 August] to see that I was getting ready & had eaten breakfast." At Victoria Park we left the train and were

met by the Mayor of Niagara & a battery of press hounds—I was bunched—Papa too with gladioli—& then we saw the Falls. *O they are wonderful.* We then drove on & saw the Rapids from various viewpoints & then went to Brock's Monument & looked down on the river Niagara—broad & peaceful after all its convulsions & swirlings flowing into Lake Ontario . . . Back in the train & travelled through the state of N.Y. & then followed the Hudson to Hyde Park.

As a newly commissioned officer at the end of 1942, I accompanied my father to military exercises in the north of England. Here I am keenly observing the proceedings.

ABOVE: *Leaving No. 10 with my father to hear him speak in the House of Commons, July 1942.*

TOP: *My parents, Sarah, and I on the way to Guildhall to see my father receive the Freedom of the City of London. My father was light enough of heart to have some fun with his top hat.*

The Queen visited 481 Battery in July 1943. OPPOSITE: *Here I am in the lineup with Molly Oakey on my right; Major Stan King stands behind the Queen.*

ABOVE: *An artist's impression of the command post at my battery during an air raid when my father paid us a visit. General Pile, C-in-C Anti-Aircraft Defence, is standing behind him. I am the plotting officer marking the position of our target on an illuminated glass tabletop.*

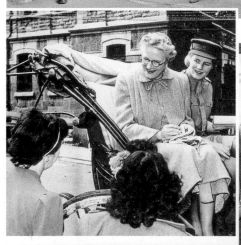

TOP AND ABOVE LEFT: *We arrive in Quebec for the First Quebec Conference in August 1943.*

ABOVE: *Brendan Bracken, "Pug" Ismay, and myself during one of our long train journeys.*

LEFT: *With my father on the observation platform outside the rear coach. Inspector Thompson stands behind.*

ABOVE: *My father and I downstream from Niagara Falls, August 1943.*

We went home on HMS Renown (RIGHT); *during our voyage I celebrated my twenty-first birthday, and cut a hastily assembled cake with a midshipman's dirk* (BELOW).

During redeployment in 1944, 481 Battery found ourselves in a field a few miles from Chartwell! My parents visited us, and saw the battery in action against a flying bomb (V-1).

Meeting my parents at Euston Station on their return from Quebec, September 1944.

Visiting Paris after the Liberation. ABOVE: *Watching General de Gaulle and my father walking down the Champs Elysées on Armistice Day, 11 November 1944.*
(Left to right:) my mother, Mme. de Gaulle, Beatrice Eden, myself, Lady Diana Cooper.

With my parents and the Edens leaving the Quai d'Orsay, where we were all accommodated during the visit.

On my way to serve in Europe: embarking with other members of
481 Battery, 25 January 1945.

With my father and Anthony Eden, viewing the ruins of Hitler's Chancellery in Berlin during the Potsdam Conference, July 1945.

July 1945: *from the beach at Hendaye with my mother* (LEFT) *to the house near Potsdam where I stayed with my father* (BELOW).

Outside our house near Potsdam I am presented to President Truman.

Berlin, 1945: taking part in a victory parade (LEFT); with Anthony Eden (BELOW), surrounded by servicemen all keen to be in the photograph of this momentous occasion.

In 1945 I visited my old French holiday governess, Mme. L'Honoré (LEFT). She was now in a nursing home—but sparkling as ever.

An outing with my mother in a speedboat resulted in a fall that sadly put her out of action for the rest of our holiday.

BELOW: *The page from my album recording my first meeting with Christopher Soames.*

flew to Paris morning. Sunday not before

Christopher Soames for a few minutes— the meeting was uneventful, I was rather flushed after a large lunch. My hair needed doing — I was wearing this dress — which all goes to drew Mama was right when she told me the old Scottish Proverb

and so we that Saturday. We left on morning, but I had met

"IF YOU'RE TO HAVE A MAN — HE'LL COME DOWN THE LUM (Chimney)" !

ABOVE: *Driving with my father through Berne on his official visit, September 1946.*
BELOW: *Sarah and I go to Buckingham Palace with our mother in July 1946 to witness her investiture by the King with the GBE.*

THE TATLER
LONDON and BYSTANDER One Shilling and Sixpence
NOVEMBER 20, 1946 Vol. CLXXXII. No. 2369

Miss Mary Churchill Announces Her Engagement

Miss Mary Churchill, Mr. Winston Churchill's youngest daughter, announced her engagement on the day this photograph was taken of her attending the wedding of Lord Burnham's daughter, the Hon. Leslie Lawson, and Lord Woolton's son, the...

LEFT: *An engagement picture.*

BELOW: *At our reception at the Dorchester Hotel.*

Leaving 28 Hyde Park Gate with my father on my wedding day, 11 February 1947.

Outside the church.

Leaving St. Margaret's Westminster, where my parents had also married.
Behind me is Judy Montagu, my only bridesmaid, and behind her my father.

*Christopher and I began
our honeymoon in
Lenzerheide in
Switzerland—where I had
enjoyed that last wonderful
skiing holiday with my
mother ten years earlier.*

Below the President's property, which stands on quite a high cliff, is a halt, and there the President himself, driving his jeep, met us, with Mrs. Roosevelt and Harry Hopkins, and whirled us up the steep, winding, narrow track to the mansion. Cocktails were served at eight, and the other guests were the U.S. ambassador to Eire, "Mrs Delano Roosevelt [the President's mother] and Admiral Brown, the Pres's PA. I sat next to the Pres. He was most kind charming & entertaining."

The next morning Mrs. Roosevelt was kindness itself and took personal trouble to see that I had a good time, notwithstanding her many preoccupations, as she was very shortly to depart on a long tour of overseas U.S. establishments. "Rigged out in her clothes I rode her horse called 'Here's How' accompanied by a very nice corporal; then Mrs R. drove us (my father and myself) down to her own house Val-Kill across the valley from the mansion, where we saw again her personal private secretary/PA, Miss Malvina Thompson" (who had accompanied Mrs. Roosevelt on her visit to England in October 1942).

The weather was hot and lovely, and after a long swimming session when "I got happily & heavily waterlogged" we had a "delicious picnic luncheon—Chowder & Hot dwgs [*sic*]. Wow!" I then artlessly described Mrs. Roosevelt's companions, "Miss Marion Dickerman— charming & cultivated woman showed me the house which she shares with Miss Cook (a sinister looking old thing, with glittering eyes, white hair & brown skin—she terrified me & I had my doubts about her)." After more swimming, and playing deck tennis with "Mrs R & the children (a niece + 2 friends & very nice)," we had tea and then "returned to change for dinner. Again [I] sat next to [the] Pres. who I find more & more delightful & enthralling. Papa v. sleepy—went to bed early—So did we."

On the Saturday it was again very hot: there was more riding and swimming, and a

picnic lunch at the Pres' pavilion . . . Corn & water melon. The Pres. & Mrs R, Papa & self all drove through beautiful country with lovely 'Colonial style' churches to the Morgenthaus* for tea—or rather mint juleps. Back just in time to change & pack. Dinner. Departed [by train] at 10.30—wishing Mrs R Godspeed & good fortune on the brink of her voyage.

Back in Quebec, we were much relieved to find my mother looking much better, although while officially "resting" she seemed to have had quite a busy time. I was touched and so proud when she told me that my father had said that he had liked having me with him alone during our Hyde Park visit.

The Conference now got going in earnest: the President arrived on the seventeenth, when the galaxy of politicos and "top brass" was at full strength. At this point a new and most charming person made his appearance on our scene—General George Marshall, the American Chairman of the Joint Chief of Staffs Committee.† One night at dinner "I was delighted to find myself next to Lord Louis Mountbatten . . . who is such fun & makes me laugh. After dinner the Pres. talked to me for quite a time—I find him so stimulating & gay. O *what* a wonderful time I'm having—I can hardly believe it's true." The Conference agenda concerned the planning of Operation Overlord (the code name for the Allied invasion of northwest Europe) and the setting up of the command for Far Eastern operations, and a few days later "Papa told us of Dickie's [Lord Louis's] appointment as Supreme Commander of the Far Eastern Pacific—We all drank his health."

During all these days while the Conference was in progress, my mother and I were swept up in a bustle of being lunched or dined by our kind Canadian hosts; my parents also gave some lunches and dinners where I was *de service,* and I spent two days on my own visiting Canadian Women's Army Corps (CWAC) units and establishments. My mother and I did a bit of sightseeing, I made my first broadcast, and (I see from my diary) we did a good deal of shopping: after four years

* Henry Morgenthau (1891–1967) was Secretary of the Treasury from 1934 until the end of the war.
† See footnote on page 222.

of ever more stringent wartime rationing at home—not only of food and petrol, but since the summer of 1941 clothing as well and from early 1942 even soap—one eagerly seized the opportunity to stock up on nylon stockings (no tights then), lingerie, and other items once so much taken for granted—for oneself and as presents for family and friends at home.

When the Conference came to an end with the departure of the President on the night of 24 August, my father and his staff and close colleagues were only too ready for a letup, and he was happy to accept the invitation of Colonel Frank Clark (head of a vast firm producing wood pulp for newsprint) to stay at his fishing lodge on the Snow River up in the Laurentian mountains. Accordingly that evening I drove with my parents, accompanied by Lord Moran, John Martin (Private Secretary), and Tommy Thompson, the sixty miles or so to La Cabanne. The keen fishermen among the Chiefs of Staff, Sir Alan Brooke and Sir Charles (Peter) Portal, were already up at Lac des Neiges, a large lake further up in the mountains, where their skill and tenacity over the next few days resulted in their catching a great number of fish. Those of our party who wanted to fish went up daily to Lac des Neiges: my mother mostly stayed at La Cabanne, but I tried my inexpert hand at the sport—with less than outstanding success: I reported to my diary that after a whole day's fishing I had caught "1 fish, 1 sardine, the same guide 4 times, & 2 logs." The President had requested that he be kept informed of the fishermen's fortunes: "Be sure to have the big ones weighed and verified by Mackenzie King," he cabled Winston on 27 August;[1] the same day the latter reported: "Subaltern and I have caught a few, and the change and air are doing us all good."

It was indeed lovely after the long sunshine days in the bracing mountain air (much cooler in the evenings) to return to La Cabanne with its blazing log fires and creature comforts. I noted with satisfaction in my diary on 29 August that

Papa has broken the back of his broadcast—it really is a joy to see him having a good time. He is loving it up here & is really

relaxing—he was in terrific form today—He looked a delightful figure in a blue siren suit with an exceedingly tight fitting
tweed overcoat (buttoned with difficulty) & his old hat sitting
bolt upright in a boat & tearing down the lake to fish far into
the evening.*

My poor mother, however, was so overtired that she was not able to
really relax and profit from this short holiday. She was in a highly nervous state: I was unhappy to see her so, and at a loss as to how best to
help her. Needless to say, when we were back "on duty" again she was
able to do and be all that was expected of her (and all that she expected
of herself—which was even more).

I left La Cabanne ahead of the main party, as General Marshall
had arranged for me to visit some establishments of the Women's
Army Corps (WAC) at Fort Oglethorpe in Georgia; so on Monday,
30 August, I returned to the Citadelle to "turn myself around." During the short time I was there Malcolm MacDonald (the British high
commissioner) turned up quite unexpectedly to say "Goodbye" to
me—which I thought extremely civil: "He was more kind to me than
I deserve & said I'd done very well & in fact this suddenness & his ap-
parent sincerity quite overcame me." I know I appreciated this kindness very much, because during these weeks I had been faced with a
succession of challenges—speaking to the press; making unscheduled
speeches; meeting literally hundreds of people and trying to respond
adequately to their warmth and kindness. It was a constant revelation
to me just how greatly my father was admired, and also how Britain's
lonely stand in 1939–40, and the courage of civilians under bombardment, had really gripped people's imagination.

Returned from my "flying commission," I rejoined my parents and
went with them on 1 September to Washington, D.C., where we were
guests of the President at the White House for ten more days. Mrs.
Roosevelt was by now away on her travels, but we were most kindly

---

* WSC's fishing attire had obviously been improvised locally.

and efficiently looked after by a fellow guest, a delightful distant cousin, close friend, and neighbour (on the Hudson) of FDR's—Miss Margaret Suckley, who had been invited especially for that purpose (we had met her already on our visit to Hyde Park); Elliott and his wife, Ruth, also came on many of the expeditions. There followed an action-packed week of engagements within and outside the household, lunching or dining with our host;* while my father conducted "business as usual," my mother and I were diverted and entertained round the clock, visiting the sights of Washington (all new to me), and one day lunching with General Marshall at the Pentagon, from where the President himself collected us in order to take us to George Washington's home, Mount Vernon.

We made two memorable day trips. The first, on 6 September, was to Boston, Massachusetts, where my father was received at Harvard University and presented with an honorary doctorate, and made an important speech. The second expedition, two days later, took my mother and me on a flying visit to Williamsburg, the colonial capital of Virginia—one of the most astonishing and convincing reconstructions of a period and a whole way of life. While we were in the Raleigh Tavern, I noted in my diary, "a strange man looked into the room [and said]: 'It's just been announced on the radio that Italy has surrendered unconditionally.'"

During these days and on our visits to Hyde Park I was to see much of FDR, and I recorded my own jejune judgements of him. "I still find the Pres [sic] magnetic & full of charm," I wrote in my diary on 3 September; "his sweetness to me is something I shall always remember—But," I went on,

he is a 'raconteur'—& it can be tedious—But at other times it is interesting & fun—I wonder if recounting anecdotes etc is an American trait? . . . But what a cultivated animal FDR is . . . and

* While not wishing even after half a century to seem ungracious, we sampled the really nasty food produced by the famous-for-it Mrs. Nesbitt (the President constantly complained about her capacity, but Mrs. Roosevelt resolutely refused to get rid of her).

a cute, cunning old bird—if ever there was one. But I still know who gets *my* vote . . . Every evening FDR makes extremely violent cocktails before dinner in his study. Fala [the President's black Aberdeen terrier: a national celebrity] attends—& it is all very agreeable & warm. At dinner Mummie is on his right, & several nights no other outside guests being there I've been on his left. I am devoted to him & admire him tremendously— He seems to have fearless courage & an art of selecting the warmest moment of the iron—Papa & he are an interesting contrast.

At Sunday luncheon on 5 September the several other guests included Mrs. Ogden Reid (a vice president of the *New York Herald Tribune*). "She calls the Pres 'Franklin' & then allows her paper to write filthy articles about him. Papa had a good 'go' at her," I wrote indignantly. However, Mrs. Reid and the President shared critical views of British policy in India, whose peoples she considered were brutally oppressed by the British. The subject was raised after luncheon as we sat on the verandah: my father asked her whether she was referring to "the brown Indians in India, who have multiplied alarmingly under the benevolent British rule? Or are we speaking of the red Indians in America, who I understand, are almost extinct?" Mrs. Ogden Reid was totally disconcerted by this, and the topic was dropped: but FDR was delighted and laughed uproariously.[2]

Later I tried to analyze

all I feel & think about FDR—not that it matters—but I am so intrigued. To me he seems at once idealistic—cynical— warm hearted & generous—worldly-wise—naïve—courageous— tough—thoughtful—charming—tedious—vain—sophisticated—civilised—All these and more for 'by their works ye shall know them'—And what a stout hearted champion he has been for the unfortunate & the battling—and what a monument he will always have in the minds of men. And yet while I admire him intensely, and could not but be devoted to him after his great personal kindness to me—yet I must confess [he] makes me laugh & he rather bores me.

Presently Mr. Roosevelt left us installed in the White House and went to Hyde Park, where we were to join him later to take our leave before heading for home. During our remaining days in Washington a considerable whirl of gaiety and entertainment had been arranged for me; I was also taken to see some factories and war plants, such as the torpedo yards at Alexandria which I thought "rather a grim factory but very interesting." Another day, at Bendix Radio Towson plant, I was greeted by the assembled workers "and to my horror had to say 'a few words' to 2000 men & women—I don't know how I did it. I only pray it was all right. I felt quite sick with nerves." After I had been round the workshops I faced a press conference, where I had to field "sticky questions about women's conscription."* In the afternoon I visited the other half of the same works in Baltimore: "Here there were fewer [workers] & the work is heavier. Nor was there quite the same atmosphere of friendliness. I felt nervous & unhappy . . . I spoke & fear it was not as good as the last—tho' I said more & meant it just as sincerely." I was truly gratified and grateful when some months later I saw a letter that Miss Frances Perkins, the U.S. Secretary of Labor, had written to our Mr. Ernest Bevin (her opposite number) on 11 November, in which she said:

How useful young Mary Churchill was to us during her visit here. She went to several plants at my invitation . . . Her effect on all the workers, and particularly women workers, was excellent. She was intelligent, modest, dignified and showed herself familiar with machinery and its problems. She treated the girls like any other girl and made a great hit. We all felt her work was useful.

* Women had been liable for conscription in Britain from 1941.

As my father would say in such circumstances: "A little bit of sugar for the bird!"

On 11–12 September my parents and I travelled overnight to join the President, arriving at Hyde Park early in the morning: it was a sunny but chilly day, and we spent the morning driving round the estate with FDR at the wheel, his dog Fala beside him; then "we lunched (in arctic chill) at his own cottage (higher up the hillside than Mrs R's Val-Kill)." After luncheon,

> Papa presented a charming sight . . . flat on his back in a patch of sun (shade is v cold—sun deliciously warm here)—Warming his tummy after the chilling atmosphere of the verandah. I lay near him and we gazed up at the very blue sky & the green leaves dancing against it—flecked with sun. He described to me the colours he would use were he painting—& commented on the wisdom of God in having made the sky *blue* & the trees *green*. 'It wouldn't have been nearly so good the other way round' . . . To me these moments with Papa are the golden peaks of my life.

At dinner, the President (duly primed)

> proposed M & P's health for it is the 35th anniversary of their wedding. Mummie told me Papa had told her he loved her more & more every year—How well I believe it—What those two mean to each other is something even I can only guess at. [After dinner] FDR drove us down to the train & off we went with the lights twinkling on the Poughkeepsie bridge & the moon shining down on the broad Hudson.

Our train journey north to Halifax took the whole of the succeeding day and night, broken occasionally by chances to stretch our legs. (Pug Ismay and I and a few others nearly got caught out at one station, and had to make a dash to jump back on the moving train.) We were not out of touch from world events, and on 13 September I noted in my diary: "News from Italy continues to be most serious—Salerno must be grim." Having arrived in Halifax we went aboard HMS *Renown* about midmorning on 14 September; but in fact,

> until the very last moment Papa was uncertain whether he would not have to fly owing to the battle news from Italy being so disquieting. However, in the end, I am relieved to say, the original plans were carried out ... At 3 o'clock we sailed. The band played 'You fair Spanish ladies', 'O Canada'—& as we took up position in midstream heading for the open sea the band struck up 'Should auld acquaintance be forgot'. It was a lovely afternoon. Clear skies—bright sunshine—a soft breeze—Ship-yard workers (men & women) cheering. Papa went out onto the Bridge & I went too. What a wonderful land we were leaving. The shores looked so lovely as they receded very gradually. And then the ship began working up speed. I was changing for din-ner & Papa sent for me to walk with him on the Quarter deck. I dashed up & we walked up & down & watched the sunset to-gether. For me that was one of the moments of my life I cherish.

During the voyage, which would take nearly six days, our party—which consisted of my parents and myself, John Martin and Les-lie Rowan, Pug Ismay, Lord Moran, Brendan Bracken, and Tommy Thompson—always met for dinner in the "cabin" dining room. On the night of the 14th

> and every night Papa proposed 'The King'—sitting down—according to true Naval tradition. And then we started [in-structed by my father] on the Duke of Wellington's Peninsular [War] toasts—'Our Men; Our Swords; Our Religion; Our-selves; Our Women; Absent Friends'—and drank a different one every night. After dinner Pug, Papa, John & I (in a duffle coat) paced the Quarter Deck doing Cavalry drill! Papa was in the highest spirits & when we returned to the Admiral's Cabin

he showed us the basic principles of cavalry drill in matches—&
afterwards the layout of the Battle of Omdurman. Tomorrow
I am 21. Papa told me he was under fire for the first time on his
21st birthday. Hooray I beat him by just over a year!

The next day I celebrated my twenty-first birthday:

Quite a remarkable 21st birthday all things considered . . . Sweet
letters from M & P—£100 from Papa towards a hunter—and M
tells me that exquisite aquamarine set is mine. [I had seen it on
approval at home before we left.] A golden key from the Wardroom Officers, and a small, damp & v. sweet kitten (christened
Quadrant [code for the conference]) from the Ship's company
& lovely cards from all the messes. I certainly never expected
such kindness & everyone was absolutely *charming* to me.

In the afternoon there was a tea party, attended by the WRNS officers on board (who were on cipher duties); a birthday cake had been
rustled up, and I cut it with a midshipman's dirk. In the evening I
went for drinks in the Wardroom and "they'd all sung 'Happy Birthday to you!' & '21 Today'!"

One morning we all assembled to watch (and hear!) target practice
with the great fifteen-inch guns. I also had a thrilling and interesting time being shown all over the ship: one such exploration, however,
nearly had a bad ending. About five o'clock one afternoon I was standing with one of the officers ("Schoolie," the instructor lieutenant commander) on the quarterdeck—where neither of us should have been, it
having been placed out of bounds while the ship executed a zigzag, the
usual tactic against submarine attack.

The sea was grey & heaving and a brilliant light gleamed on
the waves—& the wake of the ship was white & aquamarine.
It was fresh and lovely. We talked of this & that & threw cents
overboard for luck. And then with no premonition, but with

mild interest I said: 'Oh look' & we watched for a split second the huge green white lipped wave ... We'll get wet I thought & suddenly both of us gripped the top wire [of the guard rail]—& then all thought was interrupted & the world was just an ir- resistible weight of warm wetness—my hands were torn from the rail—it might have been a bit of cotton I was holding—& I was swept along—completely conscious & certain I was going over[board] & suddenly I felt a wire and held on—the force subsided—and suddenly I could get up—soaked & feeling hi- larious & light-headed. We walked in. And the risk & gravity only impressed itself on me as I saw the faces of the Cmdr. & a Wren officer—white & terrified the latter—grim & rather frightening the former.

I was rapidly taken below and made to have a hot bath, after which in the wardroom I was plied with first a strong Scotch and then a brandy. It was decided not to tell my parents at this point about my narrow escape, but appearing at dinner with my hair still wet and in a dress, I was scolded by my father for wearing civilian clothes without his permission. That night I reflected that I had "bought my luck pretty cheap. . . . The Cmdr had said 'Now you know a little what "preserve us from the perils of the sea" means.' My prayers this night were not long or complicated—but I meant them."

An amusing diversion for us on the voyage was an exchange of sig- nals between *Renown* and one of her escorting destroyers, HMS *Orwell*, which was carrying as passengers Petty Officer A. P. Herbert (Mem- ber of Parliament and a well-known author) and a fellow MP, Major Sir Derrick Gunston, returning home after a parliamentary mission in Newfoundland. A signal in their names (carefully concealing by means of Greek mythology the identity of its addressee) was received:

> *Respectful salutes and greetings.*
> *Return, Ulysses, soon to show*
> *The secrets of your splendid bow.*

> *Return and make all riddles plain*
> *To anxious Ithaca again.*
> *And you, Penelope the true,*
> *Who has begun to wander too,*
> *We're glad to meet you on the foam*
> *And hope to see you safely home.*

My parents were delighted of course by this signal, and my father set us all to devising a suitable reply. My contribution was chosen to be sent. It was as follows:

> *Ulysses, and Pempy too,*
> *Return their compliments to you.*
> *They, too, are glad to wend their way*
> *Homewards to Ithaca after a stay*
> *With friends from where the land is bright*
> *And spangled stars gleam all the night.*
> *And when he's mastered basic Greek*
> *Ulysses to the world can speak*
> *About the plots and plans and bases*
> *Conferred upon in foreign places.*
> *We thank you from our hearts to-day*
> *For guarding us upon our way.*
> *To chide these simple rhymes may be chary*
> *They are the first attempts of Mary.*

(The last two lines were supplied by my father.)

I was the next person to receive a signal, A. P. Herbert recalling that Ulysses and Penelope had a son, Telemachos:

> *Telemacha, the sailors send*
> *Their greetings to a fighting friend.*
> *The Major adds a smart salute*
> *To any Lady who can shoot!*

> *And I, poor scribbler, must give place*
> *To one who writes with such a grace.*
> *Why not (when Mr Masefield's passed)*
> *A Lady Laureate at last?*

Reading my diaries again nearly seventy years on, I sometimes feel a jarring note in all this jollity and jokiness set against the gravity of events and the daily toll of loss in terms of human lives—but then I recall what my father said to Sarah when she accompanied him to Cairo in November 1943:

> War is a game played with a smiling face, but do you think there is laughter in my heart? We travel in style and round us is great luxury and seeming security, but I never forget the man at the front, the bitter struggles, and the fact that men are dying in the air, on the land, and at sea.[3]

On the morning of Sunday, 19 September, we sailed safely up the Clyde and anchored off Greenock. All our party attended morning service onboard: we sang "Eternal Father, Strong to Save" and gave thanks for our safe homecoming. Afterwards my father addressed the ship's company—then "Hats off!" and three cheers for him—before we disembarked and went ashore and joined the special train for the last lap home. There was a big party at 9:30 that evening at Euston of family—Diana and Sarah—and government colleagues to welcome us all.

On the Tuesday my father went to the House of Commons to give an account of his travels. I sat with him "while he dressed & then said 'Goodbye' & signed off as ADC. He was so sweet & said I'd done all right. If I've pleased him—then that's OK by me. Returned to 481. Everyone v. sweet. Have got a cold."

CHAPTER 15

Testing Times

———

URING OCTOBER AND NOVEMBER THAT YEAR, AND AGAIN IN the spring of 1944, there were quite a lot of air raids; we had one or two near misses to our site, and 481 fired on several occasions. My father would quite often visit us unannounced, and if the raid was at dinnertime, he would bring along a guest or two as well: he was particularly pleased when he had American or other overseas guests, who were not familiar with that still-unusual military entity, the "mixed" battery. Not content with viewing the activity only in the command post, he would visit the gun teams when they were firing. One evening in early October I was off duty and dining at home when there was a raid; we could hear the "local" batteries in action, and I was much put out at being "off site." Among our guests was Sir Alan Brooke, CIGS, and my father decided to deliver me back to the battery himself and to take "Brookie" along too to see what was going on. We arrived to find that 481 had indeed been in action, had fired about 140 rounds, and was still "standing to": they stayed quite a long time, but (to my father's disappointment) there was no further action for us that evening. However, he "got lucky" on several other occasions, writing to Randolph (who was with Marshal Tito in Yugoslavia) on 4 April 1944: "Sometimes I go to Maria's battery and hear the child ordering the guns to fire"—which, touchingly, greatly delighted him. My battery colleagues took all these visits in their stride, although I was, at times, considerably embarrassed.

Among daytime visitors there were marked contrasts. Visiting military groups were sent by the War Office, as were a few gaggles of women officers. The latter were quite often a little "prickly," as mixed batteries were deemed in some quarters to get too much attention—a view well illustrated by the account of an officer from an anti-aircraft battery at Dover telling an American what he thought of London's defences in Irwin Shaw's novel *The Young Lions*. "They're so busy planting rhododendrons around the emplacements and shining the barrels so they'll look pretty when Miss Churchill happens to pass by that there's b— all gunnery."[1]

The variety of individual VIPs was striking, from Field Marshal Smuts to Mr. Irving Berlin (of "Alexander's Ragtime Band" and "White Christmas" fame), who brought a group and performed extracts for the whole battery from his latest show, *This Is the Army, Mr. Jones*, to the Regent of Iraq—on whose visit I reported to my father: "The Regent of Iraq paid us a visit. He looked stunned & mystified. I think he thought the battery was a new way of organizing a harem, and he gave the Major some interested looks!"

As well as these fleeting visits, the battery brought me another lasting friendship that began with the arrival in September 1943 of another ATS subaltern, Susan Rhys Williams: the daughter of most distinguished parents, and a granddaughter of the exotic Elinor Glyn. She was dark and most striking-looking, immaculately neat, and already well versed in the technicalities of anti-aircraft gunnery. She came to us at a sad moment in her life, not long after her beloved elder brother had been killed in action with the Welsh Guards. Susan was greatly liked and esteemed by everyone—except the major, who persecuted her most unkindly: she was calm and resolute, at one point putting in an "official" complaint about him! She and I shared a Nissen hut in Hyde Park, and later a tent in the fields of Kent.

Also on the personal front, this winter I had a rapprochement with Randolph which made me happy—indeed, he used me as a go-between with Pamela over some matter in their now-fraught relationship. "R was terribly pleased & sweet to me. I'm so glad I made it up with him," I wrote in my diary on 11 November. And there were some nice off-duty evenings. I described one such on the eve of my father's departure on his travels once more: he himself was in bed with a slight temperature as a result of an inoculation, but the rest of us evidently had quite a hilarious evening: "Dinner was gay & fun: Max [Beaverbrook], Anthony & Beatrice [Eden], Sarah, Mama & self and later Uncle Jack. Max was in riotous form; Anthony spilt us lots of beans about the Moscow conference.* Max had brought a Magnum of champagne, [and] Anthony some caviar—so we were very 'kept.' Pug [Ismay] came in after dinner." The next day my father left, with Sarah as his ADC, for journeys that would last over a month: they would take him to Cairo, thence to Tehran (for a "Big Three" conference) and back to Cairo again before returning home. I said goodbye to him that evening, noting in my diary: "It always is a wrench."

During the weeks of my father's and Sarah's travels, my mother filled me in on news which I could not gain from the official press reports. Winston was already staving off a sore throat when he went on board *Renown* again for the first lap of his circuitous journey, and this had developed into a heavy cold in Cairo, which he had not thrown off before his flight and visit to Tehran, where he met President Roosevelt and Marshal Stalin between 28 November and 2 December (and incidentally celebrated his sixty-ninth birthday on the 30th). After the strains and stresses of the Conference, he returned to Cairo for further days of discussion with the President. From there he planned to visit the battlefront in Italy, and despite the advice of Lord Moran and other colleagues he set out on the tenth—but arriving en route at "The White House" (General Eisenhower's villa overlooking the sea near ancient Carthage), he felt so ill that he went straight to bed. The next morning he had a high temperature and pneumonia was

* Moscow Conference of Allied foreign ministers, 18–30 October 1943.

diagnosed; his condition continued to deteriorate, and the first official bulletin announcing his illness was released on 15 December. The next day, it was decided (by the Cabinet) that my mother should fly out to be with him, accompanied by Jock Colville from his private office.

I had permission to be absent from my battery to see them off; meanwhile, a thick fog having descended on a very cold southern England, we waited for hours to hear of an airfield which was operating. My mother was busy with her packing and preparations; the morning's bulletin was not very good, and my morale was low, when suddenly Max Beaverbrook appeared—sized up the situation, saw I was *de trop,* whirled me off to his flat in Stornoway House, "and in an incredibly short time filled me with chicken & cheese & whisky—comforted me *à la* Max ["Aw! It takes more than some lousy microbes to get the better of your father!"] & returned me. Departure again postponed."

At last we were informed that Lyneham in Wiltshire was "open," and set forth by car at 4:15 p.m: the journey took four hours through "swirling fog." After dinner in the officers' mess, the travellers were zipped into padded flying suits and I drove with them out to the Liberator aircraft (it was unheated and there were no seats, only some rugs and air force blankets on the floor). After I had seen them tucked in, I was taken up to the control tower "to watch take-off—and at last as it heaved off the ground, I could not but feel happy long & hazardous though the journey was—I don't know how—I just *knew* it would be all right, as I stood a little desolate & heard the plane drone away, I felt happier than I had done all that day." Later the next day I was back at 481: "Everyone sweet. News came at last that Mummie had arrived—thank God—it was so comforting to know they were together." The following day Leslie Rowan of the private office read me a message from my father: "Your mother is here. All is joyful. No need to worry. Tender love. Papa."

Needless to say, all the stay-at-homes involved were greatly relieved—and meanwhile it was Christmastime! Preparations to celebrate at the battery were hectic, with dances, concerts, elaborate

decorations, masses of special "off-ration" festive food and drink ga-
lore. On Christmas Eve, despite feeling rather sleepy,

> Molly [Oakey] & I made a dash for St. Martin's-in-the-Fields &
> arrived (having suffocated by pressure in the U/ground)—late.
> Church full to the doors. We stood right at the back. It was a
> lovely and moving service—I found myself swaying with sleep &
> weariness—& was thankful for a pew at last. I'm afraid I wasn't
> a very active participant—I just stood & let the simplicity of
> the service—its comfort & beauty wash over me . . . 'Christians
> awake! Salute the happy morn . . .' Thank God for even my wa-
> vering faith—during these last days I [have] found my religion
> an unspeakable comfort—I am not brave enough to manage
> without it. Somehow this Christmas has seemed more full of
> meaning than any other far happier ones: in a way it has been
> the happiest & certainly the most thankful. Everything else
> seems unimportant beside the joyful news that darling Papa is
> getting better, & that he & Mummie are together & Sarah &
> Randolph in lovely sunshine.

Christmas Day was rowdy, fun, and very hard work, as according
to hallowed army tradition the officers waited on the other ranks for
early morning tea, breakfast, and luncheon! Somewhere church parade was fitted in. We officers had our feast at 4:30—"very filling &
delicious," I greedily noted—but there was no letup, as the NAAFI
had to be decorated for the battery dance, which went on late into
the night. Of course, we were fully manned at all times (and mostly
sober!), the only concession in the command post being a strategically
placed sprig of mistletoe.

On Boxing Day I took Molly Oakey with me to join Gil Winant
at the American Embassy: he wafted us down to Chequers, where the
Christmas party was in full swing, despite the absence of the "principals," with Diana acting as hostess: Duncan and their three children were there, along with Uncle Jack, Aunt Nellie Romilly, Pamela

and "Baby" Winston, and Clarissa and Peregrine; neighbours were asked in, as were the officers from the Coldstream company on guard. "Monty" Lamont had decorated the great house as beautifully as ever, and the Christmas tree in the Great Hall was a present from the White House.

We soon began to receive daily detailed accounts of my father's progress, and of the comings and goings at the Carthage "White House," from my mother via the official pouch to the private office. Despite his still being very ill, and his (now several) doctors' orders, my father soon began seeing papers and resuming his hold on affairs. Official bulletins were issued almost daily from No. 10, while my mother attached to her splendid circular letters for the family at home her own "Health Bulletin by CSC (not the doctors)." The one for Sunday, 19 December, read: "Papa much better today. Has consented not to smoke, and to drink only weak whisky and soda. In fairly good spirits. New cook arrived. Food much better and Papa enjoyed good luncheon and dinner, though appetite is not very good." The following day: "Papa very refractory and naughty this morning and wants to leave this place at once. All doing our best to persuade him that complete recovery depends on rest and compliance with regulations. Progress continues."

The position of the villa was hardly ideal from a security point of view, and my mother described how

a little gun boat patrols up and down in front of the house in case a German submarine should pop up its nose and shoot up the Villa. Of course if the enemy knew we were here they could wipe out the place with dive bombers from the airfields near Rome. It is only less than one hour from Palermo in Sicily.

Fortunately secrecy prevailed.

To our intense relief my father began to improve, but the pneumonia had been accompanied by episodes of "auricular fibrillation," so progress was a little uneven, and Christmas Day was the first time he lunched out of his room. On Boxing Day my mother wrote to us: "Yesterday we all of us thought of the party gathered at Chequers, and of Mary in her battery. We had the most extraordinary Christmas ourselves. All the, what Americans call 'high ranking Generals and other notabilities' converged here, and Christmas day was spent by them and Papa in a series of Conferences." The five commanders-in-chief and their staffs were my father's guests at luncheon, which he attended "(having just had a two-hour military conference in his bedroom) clothed in a padded silk Chinese dressing-gown decorated with blue and gold dragons)."[2] On Boxing Day too came the excellent news that the *Scharnhorst,* Germany's last battle cruiser, had been sunk, and on 27 December my father was well enough for them all to go to Marrakech for his convalescence, where they stayed at the Villa Taylor, the residence of the U.S. vice-consul.

As a Christmas present I had given my father a complete set of Gilbert and Sullivan operas, which I knew he enjoyed—he would often, when in a jovial mood, sing ditties from his favourites. Quite fortuitously it proved to be a wonderfully apt present, for some of them had been sent out to him to divert him during his convalescence. I was so touched and overjoyed to receive this letter written in his "own paw" on 2 January:

> Darling Mary,
> Last night we played through 2 of yr records 'Pirates of Penzance' &
> 'Patience'. I read, and brooded on the flowing music. On the whole one of
> the happiest hours I have had in these hard days! How sweet of you to have
> had the impulse! How clever to have turned it into action & Fact. Your ever
> loving Father. W.

On Tuesday, 18 January 1944, I

woke early with that *special* feeling—Left W5 [the gun site] at 0815 . . . found the Annexe in expectant confusion. Diana &

Duncan & Uncle Jack all rolled up about a quarter past nine. We were first at Paddington—w/cabinet & etc soon arrived—and AT LAST the train rolled in [they had come by sea and docked at Plymouth]. Dashed inside & was seized with mistiness & choking—a whirl—Mummie, Sarah, Jock & then Papa—who for one cold despairingly calm moment I'd thought never to see again—Papa home!—I was so much more glad than I could ever write . . . Back to Annexe—talk—talk—talk . . .

I dashed back to the battery for a lecture and returned in time for "a dinner party at Annexe with Christmas food & crackers & candlelight & champagne. M & P, Diana & Duncan, Sarah, Beatrice & Anthony & Nicholas [the Edens' elder son], Uncle Jack, Nana, self & Brendan. Great fun—& Oh! they're home!"

THE FIRST THREE MONTHS of 1944 and the end of April saw a resumption of spasmodic night raids on London. They became known as "scalded cat" raids, and although they were not on the scale of the "Big Blitz"—in terms of either the numbers of aircraft involved or the loss of life and damage resulting from them—nevertheless they were disruptive, and apart from the casualties gave Londoners and their fire brigades and other air-raid services (already tired by four years of war) many disturbed nights; they also kept all of us in the anti-aircraft defences on our toes round the clock.

I described one night when I had been out in a small party given for me by Admiral Sir Bruce Fraser, who had been Third Sea Lord when my father was at the Admiralty, and with whom I had made friends. We had been to a show, and as we arrived at the Savoy for dinner

the sirens wailed . . . Heavy barrage. We were all removed to the downstairs ballroom . . . we out sat the band & finally all dashed back & visited the battery. [This of course was only permissible owing to my host's elevated rank.] ... A second stand-to was just finishing—the gun barrels were still warm from action. Drinks & so on in the mess. Molly & I retired to bed at 0230 with visions of 5 hours heavy, heavenly sleep. Not so. W5 [our site] in action with the rest of London in a big way at about 5. The noise was highly impressive & fireworks will seem tame to me after the slowly descending beauty of some of the flares [dropped by the raiding aircraft to illumine the scene—which they did—only too brilliantly]. It was by far the noisiest night I have ever experienced. At six we all went to bed.

Another night, when my section was on duty, I noted: "*Action.* Quite heavy raid . . . was plotting—felt excited & overcome with worry. Dance also [going on in battery] at same time. Quelle Brou-ha-ha!"

The "worry" to which I referred, and which is a recurring feature in my diary during these noisy weeks of frequent raids, was that I might panic at some moment when I was plotting officer or orderly officer in the camp, and fail in my duty—and, above all, not be what was expected of my father's daughter. But if fear is contagious, so are pluck and calm, and the steadiness of the girls, some of whom operated instruments situated in exposed positions on the command post, communicated itself. Also, having a technical task as plotting officer (marking the course of the target to be engaged) called for concentration. I actually found patrolling the camp (when not on duty at the command post) much more testing. Once, as I was carrying a heavy bucket of cocoa from the cookhouse up the narrow and unlit path to the command post, our own guns and the rocket battery cheek-by-jowl with us (manned by the Home Guard) went off in unison at a low angle: I jumped out of my skin and dropped the bucket! Luckily my shame was not witnessed, and I made some feeble excuse when eventually I delivered the refreshments after considerable delay: but I had to get the cooks out of bed again for fresh supplies—so they knew!

Amid all these alarms and excursions on and off duty there were agreeable occasions: such a one was Judy's twenty-first birthday party on 7 February 1944. We were overjoyed to see each other again, and before the festivities began we had a long gossip and catch-up. The party given for her by Victor Rothschild* in a private room at the Savoy Hotel was very special, and a wonderful mixture of genera-tions: Cousin Venetia, my parents, "Crinks" Johnson, Angy Laycock, Brendan Bracken, Jock Colville, and myself. I noted anxiously that "when Papa came in very late he looked so worn & weary it set my heart beating...", but with such jolly company, and food and wine, he cheered up—and was (like us all) simply gripped by a wonderful conjuror who appeared after dinner. After this lovely party Judy and I went back with Victor to his flat (high up in St. James's Street, near Wilton's,† the famous oyster bar—all to be blitzed to bits very shortly after this)—where we "drank gin & orange—gossiped & fried eggs & bacon—& so back to bed about 3.30."

Precious times to remember for me were those spent alone with my father. One such was an evening at the theatre recorded in my diary on 3 February 1944:

> I have just come back from an evening with Papa. We went a deux to see *There Shall Be No Night.*‡ The first scene was 1938—back to Munich. In the interval I said 'It takes one back a bit—we've come such a long way since then.' Papa said 'I knew what would happen then—and I don't now—that is the difference.' The last few times I've seen Papa I've been struck by his anx-ious preoccupation with the future. His uncertainty—I know he foresees so much more trouble & grief and struggling ahead of us than we can imagine.

---

* Victor Rothschild (1910–90), third Baron Rothschild, friend of Venetia and Judy Montagu: a scientist (Ph.D., FRS) and a hero. Worked in military intelligence; awarded George Medal 1944.
† Now in Jermyn Street.
‡ A play written by the American Robert E. Sherwood. The play was originally set in Finland between 1938 and 1940, but in this staging, starring Alfred Lunt and Lynn Fontanne, the setting was removed to Greece.

Another prized occasion—this time with both my parents—was in April. I had been up most of the night, and then had a busy day, but went home in the evening. It had been a lovely spring day, and

> Mummie & I went for a walk in Regent's Park . . . It was like fairyland. Sunshine and green grass & white canvas deck chairs & pink blossoms & white blossoms & the warm evening sun . . . & people relaxing for a little while . . . Back home, we three were alone for dinner—and I felt so brimful of content & happiness & so secure in our love. Papa in very good form—Mummie too—Candlelight. A night I shall always remember . . .

Back at the battery, though, it was "alarms all night"; and it was with evident relief that I recorded twenty-four hours later: "Thank goodness moderately peaceful night."

During this spring and early summer, London—indeed, all southern England—began to seem very overcrowded—for to the Commonwealth and Allied servicemen now were added ever-increasing numbers of Americans. "The Yanks" evoked mixed feelings—the less appreciative of which arose largely from unworthy jealousy at their superior-quality uniforms, higher pay, and capacity to shower their girlfriends with nylon stockings. (A common jibe was that they were "overpaid, oversexed—and over here"!) Underneath these superficial responses, however, was the graver awareness that the invasion of occupied Europe was daily more imminent.

It was during this spring that I saw a lot of a charming young Frenchman—Jean Louis de Ganay, whom I had met at an Aid to Russia dance organized by my mother. He had "disappeared" some months before from his family home at Courances (about forty miles from Paris) and "reappeared" in England—to join the British army, with which he was now serving. His mother was an Argentinian (a Bemberg), and his uncle was the Argentine ambassador in London— and it was with this uncle that Jean Louis stayed when on leave. It was a curious situation, as Argentina was neutral; despite this, I was received there with civility and kindness. Jean Louis was soon to be sent to Indo-China, but our friendship (later enhanced when he married Philippine de Mouchy and I married Christopher) was to prove enduring.

At the end of May I was sent on a messing course to Aldershot. The whole town and nearby roads were an extraordinary sight—D-plus-three-and-four-Day troops were assembled in barracks or under canvas in or near the town, with their tanks, armour-tracked vehicles, and other transport double-parked in all the roads ready to move off. The regiments were giving "farewell" parties nightly, and, girls being greatly in demand, one went from party to party, walking for what seemed like miles, and getting to bed at three or four in the morning more or less sober. It was quite difficult in the circumstances to concentrate on the subject of—for instance—how to make scrambled eggs for five hundred people with powdered egg yolks!

I managed to escape from this hectic and exhausting scene for a couple of days over the weekend of 3–4 June to join my mother at Chartwell—and catch up with some sleep. My father was away on his special train, visiting commanders and troops assembled in preparation for embarkation. My mother confided to me that D-Day was scheduled for 5 June—Monday—and I carried this fateful news clutched to me when I returned to Aldershot late on the evening of the fourth.

Owing to unsatisfactory weather conditions, the invasion was delayed by twenty-four hours: on Monday, 5 June, therefore I waited all day in a concealed fever of anxiety for the news I was expecting to hear. That evening I went to a regimental party: "Great fun—very gay. Got home [to my billet] about three-ish. I don't think I could have been asleep very long—I suddenly awoke, rather chilly, and heard a throbbing continuous roar—and I knew D-Day was here." I remember I seized a dressing gown and rushed down into the garden, and could just make out the forms of aircraft towing gliders thundering overhead: I fell to my knees and prayed as I had never prayed before.

We all spent the next day hanging on news bulletins and paying very little attention to our lectures. In the evening I went to a service in

huge, hideous and yet curiously impressive St. George's church. We sang 'Oh God our help in ages past' and listened to that wonderful lesson 'Only be thou strong and very courageous ...' and then we sang 'Eternal father, strong to save'. How can one pray for those in battle? I do not pray for their *safety*—somehow that would seem a vain prayer. But I prayed that they may not feel forsaken or frightened or uncertain—in all that is ghastly and fearful ... Early that evening we watched more than 400 planes towing gliders, lumber ponderously out. What strange & awe-inspiring days.

A morning or two later we woke to find a virtually empty Aldershot—and not a truck or tank to be seen.

CHAPTER 16

Doodlebugs

LIFE BACK ON THE GUN SITE WAS SOMEWHAT OF AN ANTICLI-max: "After the excitement & atmosphere of Aldershot," I complained to my diary on 10 June, "Hyde Park is deadly dull—and I'm nearly driven mad by all this footling barrack room competition." However, I was not to be bored for long. One week after D-Day, Hitler launched the first of his long-promised (and anticipated by our intelligence) "secret weapons"—the flying bomb, or V1. This hateful weapon was a pilotless aircraft (about the size of the Spitfire) which carried a high-explosive warhead: flying at speeds of up to 400 mph and at heights of between 2,000 and 3,000 feet, the "doodlebugs" or "buzz bombs" (as they were quickly dubbed) presented difficult targets for anti-aircraft guns in urban areas, approaching as they did at an awkward angle: they caused many casualties and massive damage.*

It so happened that I was on duty as plotting officer on the night of 12–13 June, when the first batch reached London. That first night only four of the salvo of twenty-seven reached Greater London, and for the next two days there was an ominous lull—but from 15 June, for over two months, London was the main target for more or less continuous waves of V1s. They were exceedingly frightening and disagreeable. One could hear and see them for quite a long time before the

* Over 6,000 civilians were killed and 18,000 seriously injured by flying bombs.

engine suddenly cut out and the machine plunged earthwards—then there were a few anguishing moments of silence before the sickening explosion, and the slow rising of a huge cloud of dust: the blast damage was particularly severe because the bomb usually exploded before penetrating the ground. On 16 June I recorded: "All day, on & off alarms & excursions persisted. The whole life of the site is of course upside down—we are all tired but in the wildest spirits." Two days later, "Diver (V1s) attacks continue . . . Rushing up & down to the gun park Molly & I boxing & coxing—people snatching meals & baths at intervals. At night the firing has been unbelievable—the whole sky a mass of lights & tracer tracks and the noise is like hell let loose."

My parents at Chequers that weekend were naturally concerned for their daughters (Diana was an air-raid warden) in London. We were in a spell of glorious June weather, and despite this new threat from the air the streets and parks were thronged with people: one evening I had telephoned my mother to tell her that we had been in action that afternoon, watched by an interested crowd who had assembled to watch an American baseball match on a pitch adjoining the gun site. However, for all the bright sunshine and people's sturdy spirits, there were some grievous incidents.

On Sunday, 18 June,

a lovely warm, breezy day, Mummie drove all the way from Chequers to visit me—bringing roses & strawberries. Within 10 minutes of her arrival we were in action [my section was on a brief stand-down] and we together watched a plane [diver] come down—alas—we discovered it fell on the Wellington Barracks chapel [Guards' Chapel]—packed for morning service*— O God. In the early dawn this [same morning] the Command Post had an escape—the brute actually came down in the Bayswater Rd†—but while it was over us it seemed for us alone &

---

* The casualties in this incident numbered 121 civilians and soldiers killed and 141 seriously wounded.
† It fell on the Tyburn Convent, killing and injuring nuns.

Buster [an officer] & 2 spotters fell flat! The whole site spent the afternoon sleeping—an official rest period. And in the evening came the blow—we are to fire no longer—But obviously this is right.*

Work and life on the site continued much as usual, although it seemed unnatural not to be participating as batches of divers appeared well within our range—as I described in my diary, "flopping all over the place—& some quite near W5!" I also reported: "On the whole morale is excellent—but people *don't* like it—& it is frightening & dangerous—I get very scared! At night it's worst." However, good and positive news was imminent: "On Wed (21st) came the wonderful news—we are to move South to help in the defence of London. The Major told us on a muster parade—everyone thrilled and proud."

Our battery was to be part of a new strategy which involved the redeployment of over 400 guns to an advanced line along the North Downs—a formidable operation carried out with extraordinary speed. For our part, a few days later 481 duly packed up—bags, baggage, and guns, plus about 250 elated gunners and gunner girls. We rumbled laboriously to a map reference, which turned out to be a large field in the village of Four Elms in Kent—a mere two miles from Chartwell! Here we were established in tents, and were in constant action immediately, for we were in the area which became known as "Bomb Alley"—the highway for the flying bombs making for London. Our move from central London to the verdant countryside could be described as plunging us from one frying pan into another, and a day or two after our arrival I wrote:

Firing very often. Tonight we've had more than 23 engagements . . . It seems so strange to be encamped in battle order in the fields I remember so well from riding & walking and to

---

* "Right" in the sense that shooting them down over London merely tended to serve the enemy's purpose, since some of them might have missed their targets and fallen in open country.

lumber at dead of night in a 3 tonner down lanes last seen on picnics and school outings.—I landed up at midnight at Old Surrey Hall [on some battery business] . . . and Mr Anderson appeared in pyjamas & macintosh—we confronted each other—last time we wore hunting kit—this time a sleepy Home Guard commander looked at a weary ruffled AT subaltern in battle-dress!

One weekend my parents, who were at Chartwell, paid us a visit, and while they were there our guns engaged a diver. Our operational role had changed: now we had either to deflect them from their course or—best of all—cause them to explode in the air. The latter option was somewhat hazardous as "wounded birds" quite often came down very nearby—indeed, two crashed actually on our site, and we were fortunate in having only two minor casualties when one came down just in front of our guns. But a ghastly episode occurred a few miles away when a diver plunged directly onto Weald House above Crockham Hill, where evacuated children were living, causing many fatalities.

Being so near the village had (for us!) great advantages—there was the corner shop and the village church, and we had some jolly dances in the village hall, walking home across the dark fields afterwards. It was especially lovely for me when I had some hours off as I could bicycle up to Chartwell and see Nana Whyte, and cadge a bath; if I had a night off I joined her sleeping in the boiler room (converted into an air-raid shelter) up at the "big house."

We had been at Four Elms about three weeks when, in a new development involving many batteries, we were ordered to decamp down to the coast. Here 481 found ourselves perched on a clifftop overlooking the centre of Hastings: the other ranks were accommodated in hotels along the front, and the officers were billeted in the houses immediately across the road from our gun site. Our command post was in a hastily converted public ladies' lavatory: there was some local annoyance at the "hijacking" of this amenity.

We were on this exposed clifftop for about six weeks. The weather was glorious and our morale high—for all the anti-aircraft batteries along the coast were now equipped with new radar, new predicting equipment, and new proximity fuses to the shells, and the results were clear for all to see. Those of us off duty by day would sit and watch with relish our guns destroy the divers, and by night put our heads under our pillows to try to get some sleep. I wrote in my diary: "I'm really happy here—really happy in my work, and feeling very glad that although I was born too late for 1066 and all that—I'm not missing 1944 and all this!"

I was billeted with charming people—Mr. and Mrs. Stone—who made sure I could have a hot bath, and (although of course I had all my meals in the Mess) insisted on my joining them for high tea whenever Mr. Stone, who had a friend with a boat, had acquired some fresh fish—a great treat. Other local people abounded in kindness to us despite the noisiness of our presence—not to mention such a major dislocation as the one I recorded on Sunday, 30 July: "Lovely day. The church we were to have paraded to—we unhappily destroyed by shooting down a doodle bug down on it."

I made a new friend when I met Ian Cowper, then a major commanding a light anti-aircraft battery stationed down the coast at Pevensey, who called on our major on some gunnery business. Thereafter he often took me out—either to dinner at some local hotel or restaurant, or, if time allowed, further afield: we went for one or two lovely excursions, a particularly enjoyable one being to Beachy Head, and those awesome cliffs. We met each other's families, but after we both went overseas we lost touch—only to meet again by chance some years later, after I was married, in Westerham High Street. Over sixty years later, we still see each other from time to time.

Sarah came down and stayed two nights (I think the kind Stones put her up)—a wonderful opportunity to catch up. We went to a battery dance at the Queen's Hotel where many of the girls were living; Ian came too, and although Sarah "went to bed earlyish, I rather forgot about bed—and came 'home' at 0600 hrs! . . . I felt so sleepy all Monday [the next day]—but it was well worth it. There is something rather special about talking the stars out and watching the grey, chilly dawn come."

On my short spells of leave in London or Chequers a major priority was to catch up with some sleep, as well as to pack in people and pleasures. On one occasion

I arrived home [the Annexe] about 10.30—Mummie so welcoming. Papa sitting up in bed in his beautiful & brilliant bedjacket—he gave me a peach off his tray. Changed into my own clothes, dripped with pearls (more or less) & felt a good deal better. Went shopping with Mama till lunch time. Papa lunched with the King, so Mummie and I were alone. Slept after lunch for an hour. Fitted at Molyneux. Saw *This Happy Breed**—very, very good. Changed into my turquoise print [and went] to Diana's birthday party. Mummie, Papa, Duncan, Sarah arrived late looking lovely. Diana radiant & peach-like. Such a lovely party. Mrs Landemare had made a luscious cake. Candlelight— and the family—and for me it worked its spell as always.

During those summer weeks I made the resolve during inactive periods when I was on duty at the command post to learn a Shakespeare sonnet or some other piece of poetry. I copied some of them down in my diary—and I find I remember most of them still.

TOWARDS THE END of August my father went on an extensive tour of the battlefront in Italy—his code name for this journey was "Colonel Kent"—and it was from there that I received the following message on 24 August: "Following from Colonel Kent to Subaltern Mary Churchill: BEGINS. Please send me a telegram through my Private Of-

---

* A play by Noël Coward, written in 1939 but not first performed until 1942, about a working-class suburban family in the years between the two world wars.

fice telling me about your affairs. I follow the triumph of your guns with lively pleasure. PAPA. ENDS."[1]

The following day I replied:

PRIVATE OFFICE. 10 DOWNING STREET LONDON.

Please would you send this message to Papa for me. Thank you very much for your message. The Battle of Hastings proceeds according to plan. We are busy and in good heart and proud of our increased usefulness. Hope you're having a pleasant journey. How glorious the news is. Tender love Darling Papa from YOUR DOODLE GUNNER—MARY.[2]

For operational reasons I cannot now fathom (even if I did then), 481 Battery had been abruptly moved in the last week of August from the relative fleshpots of Hastings a few miles eastwards along the coast to Fairlight Cove—where once more we were all under canvas. "The new site is bloody"—I fumed to my diary—"but the view is beautiful. It is dirty, isolated, muddy (clay), roadless, waterless & completely exposed. . . . Actually the next few days . . . have fled by with duty & work & flapping around. The papers tell me Papa is home. Thank God. One more safe homecoming."

I was due for twenty-four hours' leave on 31 August (Thursday), but I was so tired and harassed by getting all my girls settled in our new site that I decided not to go home, and slept like a log until midafternoon. Then, on going to collect my mail in the Mess, I found a long letter from

Mummie about Papa being ill again. It was such a shock. Everything seemed to reel & go black. Also there was a [subsequent] telegram saying 'Ring me—urgent.' With failing heart I rang up. Thank God—O thank God—M said he is all right—but could I go up tomorrow. Yes—of course. Stan & Mollie sweet about it.

My mother had written:

My darling beloved Mary,

*I had a great shock on Tuesday. I went to Northolt to meet Papa. The 'York'
made a lovely landing & taxied right up to where everyone was waiting for
him. Lord Moran emerged and ran across the tarmac to the car where I
was sitting and said: 'He has a temperature of 103—We must get him back
quickly & get him to bed'.*

*Then Papa emerged looking crimpled & feverish—I got him straight
into the car & we rushed away leaving everyone stunned & astonished
including the special correspondents. But all is well I hope. The two beautiful
Nurses from St. Mary's Hospital appeared as tho' by magic—Doctor
Geoffrey Marshall the lung specialist took blood tests and X rays and gave
M&B. It is a slight attack [of pneumonia]—there is a small shadow on one
lung, but in himself he is well & this morning, now 7 a.m. the temperature is
normal.*

*I was sick with fright Tuesday night & yesterday. We hope it will not be
necessary to publish bulletins [it wasn't] & strange to say Lord Moran says
that in about 5 days he can go to Canada by sea. I shall go with him now
Sarah too. I do wish you could but your job is essential.*

*Darling—he says he must see you before he goes so try to come up,
ringing me first . . .*

In fact I went up that evening:

I arrived home [the Annexe] at 9. Sawyers [my father's valet]
told me they were having dinner together in Papa's room. I went
in—just for a moment I wasn't noticed—Papa looking well, sitting up in bed in his glorious many hued bed jacket—M. sitting
by his bed in a housecoat. And then they saw me & were so so
sweet & loving & welcoming—And I was fed & cosseted and felt
once again that all the people I love are secure.

Next day,

Max [Beaverbrook] came to lunch & brought the most delicious
Rhine wine. M & P and Max said they thought I ought to go
into parliament. I got enthused, & visualised myself in distinguished black (with a soupcon of white) making a speech about
drains. I took it all very seriously—& am still wondering—But
somehow—I don't know.

I must say this makes me blush to tell! However, reality returned
speedily: "Back in camp everyone kind & fun. Manned till midnight."

All these events on my home front were happening, of course,
against the background of fierce fighting in Normandy, upon which
our eyes were fixed with anxiety and eager hope: by the third week in
August the battle could be regarded as hard-won. Paris was liberated
on 25 August—a great heart-lifter, and not only to the French. Thrilling and important events succeeded one another in quick succession
in these weeks.

But amid all these exciting events, as I was reading *The Times* one
day I saw that a friend had been killed in action. It was Tony Coates;
he was twenty-four. I had first met Tony when he came to Chequers
with the Coldstream detachment, and we used to go out together from
time to time in London. That spring he had taken me to see Oscar
Wilde's *An Ideal Husband* and afterwards to dine and dance. The news
of his death shook me to the core, and I poured out my feelings to my
diary:

When I read the list and came so suddenly on his name . . . I
felt stunned . . . I will not—I must not exaggerate—there was
nothing between Tony & me—except something intensely
young & gay [old-fashioned meaning]—Someone I shall always
remember with so much happiness and gratitude and perhaps
just a little nostalgia. He's one of the few people who I liked

when I was 17 & who I still loved to go out with now. And of him? He had all the beauty of good looks & health and youth. Intelligent—fun—kind, so very kind.

It so happened that the day after I read this news I went to London and saw Jock Colville, who was Tony's first cousin: "I think too he is grieved about Tony. He told me how it happened. I must confess I gave way at bedtime to some easy futile tears—& tried to write something adequate to his mother." Jock would write in his diary: "Wednesday, August 16th. Saw Mary Churchill who has been shooting down Doodle Bugs at Hastings. She has grown much fatter, but looked gay and handsome. She is very distressed about Anthony."*

SUNDAY, 3 SEPTEMBER 1944, was the fifth anniversary of the outbreak of the war, prompting me to reflect in my diary:

They've flown these 5 years to me—and yet paradoxically they seem a whole lifetime. It's a lovely day—rather chilly, but clear blue skies and brilliant sunshine. We're on duty, and in a minute there's going to be a service in front of the control room. The news is wonderful—I can hardly take it in. Trained never to be downcast by failure—*always* to discount defeat—Ever to perceive light and success in a distance which seemed to be overcome by darkness—This victorious rush—the tumultuous retreat of our vile enemies seems like a huge meal after privation ... We've had our service—it was rather nice—just manning detachments outside the Control Room in the sunshine. We sang 'Through all the changing scenes of life' and 'Onward Christian Soldiers' and 'Now thank we all our God'. And Nick [Nicholson] read the 61st Chapter of Isaiah. I feel so deeply thankful ...

* When Jock published his fascinating diaries as *The Fringes of Power,* he dedicated the book to me "with affection and with penitence for some of the less complimentary references to her in the early part of this diary." This quotation is from p. 503.

A few days later the spell of lovely weather broke: "Rain fell down all day without respite. Wind howled. The site was reduced to a sea of mud. We all got wet—some of the tents leaked. It was HELL. Everyone cold & miserable. After lunch we were given permission to issue rum. So everyone had hot tea laced with rum & felt better." We were inspected by a high-ranking ATS officer, and evidently the conditions were considered to be unacceptable and unnecessary: so, with remarkable speed, all the ATS personnel were transferred back to the Queen's Hotel in Hastings, from where the duty teams were transported to the site as required. I revelled in the "unspeakable luxury of a room and a bath." And our morale was raised further when, a couple of days later, "we all marched to Marine Court where Sir Frederick Pile* told us we'd done well. Our khaki bosoms swelled & we walked back."

By the end of August a combination of anti-aircraft guns, fighters, and balloons had mastered the flying bombs, and in early September the main bombardment of V1s ceased. But now another of Hitler's "secret weapons"—a long-range rocket, the V2—was launched on the Greater London area. Our intelligence knew about this new scourge—and knew too that there was no known means of resisting or destroying them. Their warheads were much the same size as those of the V1s, their launching pads were nearly 200 miles distant, and they sped at 4,000 miles per hour in a giant parabola before descending on their targets. Also, while the noise of the flying bombs had given warning of their approach, these demons came in silence. The first two rockets fell in the London area on 8 September—a week after the V1 attacks had ceased.† Naturally we in the AA batteries were frustrated at having no role to play against this new threat.

The night before my birthday on 15 September I was on duty: so

* Commander-in-Chief, Anti-Aircraft Command.
† Of the 1,190 rockets launched between September 1944 and the following March, when the Allied armies liberated The Hague, from which area most of the rockets were fired, about 500 fell on Greater London, killing 2,724 people and seriously injuring 6,467. On average each rocket caused twice the number of casualties as a flying bomb. (Figures from Winston S. Churchill, *The Second World War*, vol. 6, *Triumph and Tragedy*, p. 47.)

I "woke up on Friday to discover I was 22. Left the Command Post feeling un-birthdayish—& very old. Was relieved early and had bath & titivated—met Ian [Cowper] at the station. When we arrived at the Annexe Nana [Whyte] . . . Sukie [my poodle] & a birthday cake were waiting. Also an array of presents," including a "cheque of great size from Mummie & Papa." My parents were both away in Canada for the Second Quebec Conference; in their absence Diana had organized a birthday dinner party for me at Quaglino's. Ian came; there were several other guests, and Sarah joined us later. "Dinner was the greatest fun—they played 'Happy Birthday' & there was a cake with candles. Oh how sweet of Diana. But it was rather dreadful of me— I suddenly 'flopped' and felt terribly tired & longed for bed. Perhaps we are tireder than we think." After dinner we all walked to a nightclub, the Astor, but "I longed for bed & slipped away with Ian pretty soon. The Astor is rather haunted for me by gay but wistful ghosts—Graham [a naval officer friend of mine recently killed at sea] Jean Louis [de Ganay] where I don't know—but care a little—& Tony [Coates]."

Back at the battery, all was activity and excitement as orders had been received that we were to move back to our London site—so our seaside summer was over. Three days later I wrote in my diary: "Back to London—the girls singing all the way 'If I had my way,' 'She'll be coming down the mountains when she comes,' 'Wrong—Would it be wrong?,' 'Tipperary'—And 'We're here because we're here because. . . .' And here we are back in Hyde Park which is a blaze of snapdragons & paint."

CHAPTER 17

Paris Again

I HAD NOT BEEN BACK IN LONDON LONG BEFORE DASHING OFF
one morning to Euston Station to join a posse of family and colleagues gathered to welcome my parents and Sarah back from the Second Quebec Conference. I had a thorough debriefing from Sarah, and
later in the afternoon from my mother, who walked me back to Hyde
Park by a circuitous route. As always it was a blessed relief after the
inevitable days of anxiety during their sea voyage to have them home.

We had all been fraught in the third week of September as news
came in of the fierce, costly, and unsuccessful battle for the Arnhem
bridges. An appeal was made for blood, so I went to St. George's
Hospital, where a special centre had been set up to take donations,
and wrote in my diary that evening: "they told me it will be flown
to Holland—I longed to say—take more—let me give something for
them out there. . . ." A few days later I learned a piece of news which
saddened me very much when I met Eve Gibson by chance in a nightclub: "Alas—the sweet & gallant Dam Buster is missing—O God." My
father, knowing Guy would always want to be in operations, had taken
him to Canada in September 1943 to do public relations; but of course
as soon as he returned to his squadron he took part in raids again, and
now he had been lost.

But in among the anxiety and the sadness there were times to savour. About now I had a week's leave, and as usual I crammed in as

much enjoyment as possible—including outings to four plays: *Scandal at Barchester, Richard III, Pink String and Sealing Wax,* and *The Last of Mrs. Cheyney.* Ian Cowper came to Chequers for a weekend, and my diary shows that I was much exercised by a tug-of-war in my emotions between him and Jean Louis de Ganay; also that I had some long talks with my mother about (in connection with Jean Louis) living abroad and the pressure I would inevitably feel to convert to Roman Catholicism. "But oh how I wish I could settle for one—I sometimes feel in despair in case I never *really* fall in love," I wailed to my diary.

WITH PARIS LIBERATED, General de Gaulle invited my parents to celebrate Armistice Day as his guests on 11 November—and I was included in the invitation, to act, in my father's words, as his "orderly officer." The others in the "Paris party" were to be Anthony Eden, Pug Ismay, Sir Alan Brooke, John Martin from the private office, and the excellent Tommy Thompson.

On the very day we left, 10 November, Molly Oakey telephoned from the battery to say my "third pip" had come through, making me a junior commander (the equivalent of captain): I was consequently the object of many family "back-pattings" which greatly added to my own pleasure.

It was a very cold, clear day, and I found gazing down on France again during the flight very moving—as did my mother, who wept. We arrived in the late afternoon at Orly, where the airfield, apart from the main runway, was "a sea of mud—pitted & marked with bomb craters," to be greeted by a large party of *personnalités* headed by General de Gaulle. We bundled into cars:

Mummie & I drove with the President de la Chambre [des Deputés] M. Jeanneney—80 and battered by four years of oppression. Just after we started, the car—which was also rather the worse for wear—broke down. However we transplanted into another one & then were driven at breakneck speed as the driver was determined we should maintain our rightful place in the procession. Crowds appeared from nowhere, mystified by the long line of cars.

There had been no public announcement of Churchill's visit on grounds of security—and indeed, the whole idea of it had been subject to serious misgivings right up to the last moment: fighting was still going on in France, and in Paris itself there were still known to be undercover Germans and others who might pose a serious threat. However, my father waved away any suggestion that it should not proceed.

As the guests of the French government, we stayed in the Quai d'Orsay, where the King and Queen had stayed before the war. My diary account lingered lovingly on the splendour of our surroundings:

a contingent of the Garde [Republicaine] awaited, lining with drawn swords the scarlet carpeted staircase. The suite is sumptious [*sic*] and ornate with gilt & lustres & tapestries & Savonnerie carpets. Mummie & Papa's rooms are palatial with bathrooms like Roman Catholic cathedrals & beds a l'Empire. I am in a humbler room and think it is the prettiest of the lot—cream & gilt & watered blue paper & sprigged blue taffeta curtains— and a huge bouquet of white lilac—in November!* Gabrielle, my femme de chambre is charming and she cannot do enough to please me. She is so kind and we had a rather emotional meeting—and both became a little confused & damp.

Dinner I described with equal enthusiasm as.

Anglo-French—English people & French food—both were extremely agreeable. The party was the Duff Coopers[†] & the Edens & CIGS [Sir Alan Brooke] & John [Martin] and An-

* Forced flowers such as these had long since disappeared from English florists' shops.
† Duff Cooper was at this point Minister in Algiers and about to become ambassador to the French government.

thony's private secretary Nicholas Lawford. I sat between him & Anthony. Papa & everyone was in *excellent* spirits . . . It's nearly one o'clock—I'm so excited & feel so wakeful. But I must go to sleep. Pray God tomorrow passes with no mishap—one must not think of it. What a wonderful thing to happen to me—and how grateful I am and *how* lucky.

Although tight secrecy had been observed officially at the beginning of the visit, the news had leaked early on in the British and French press, and public announcements and posters had encouraged people to join in the celebrations on this first Armistice Day since the liberation of Paris. My diary entry for that momentous day was long and detailed:

It was a lovely day, cold, clear and dry. The crowds were really enormous, and processions were forming from very early in the morning till late that evening awaiting their turn to lay wreaths and banners beneath the Arc de Triomphe. M. Massigli* came & collected Mummie & me at half past ten and drove us to our places in Mde de Gaulle's stand [some way down the Champs Elysées]. Elisabeth [de Gaulle] was there, the Corps Diplomatique—all the women that is—I sat between Beatrice Eden & Diana Cooper who looked exotic & beautiful—but [she] nearly died of cold. Mummie looked beautiful in her new black hat. Papa & the General then arrived amid much cheering & excitement. The sight of the crowds was unforgettable—people had clambered into the trees and were clinging to the chimney pots.

After the brief ceremony at the Arc, the General and my father walked together followed by their immediate entourage down to the saluting base.

---

* Monsieur René Massigli, the newly appointed French ambassador to London.

The parade was long & splendid—the Garde Republicaine on horses looked simply lovely. After Papa & the General drove away amid shouts & cheers, we were taken back to the Quai d'Orsay. Unfortunately we were not able to see Papa lay wreaths on Foch's & Clemenceau's tombs. Papa & the boys were lunching together so Mummie & I lunched at the Embassy. Diana [Cooper], Mummie, Mlle Eve Curie,* Virginia Cowles,† 'Blogs' Baldwin,‡ Victor Rothschild, Cecil Beaton.§ Scrumptious lunch. Victor, to whom I am truly devoted, then whisked me off in a car to try and get some scent for Mummie—we didn't get the scent, but it was delightful driving around. He dropped me at the Quai d'Orsay, & I then braced up my courage & rang up Madame de Ganay—who sounded charming & said I might visit her. Mummie & I walked to their house, and I then left Mummie & feeling very nervous called on Mme de Ganay. I was charmed by her & her three other sons—dear dear Jean Louis you have a most delightful family. I now long to have huge sons to comfort my old age. Once back at the Quai I rushed out again to Victor's flat & drank tea & cognac. His cousin Guy de Rothschild arrived . . . also there was Tess¶ who helps Victor with his contre-sabotage.

We dined at General de Gaulle's house in the Bois de Boulogne. Mummie & Papa, the Duff Coopers, the Massiglis, M. Bidault** and M. Palewski†† (between whom I sat), Capitaine de Levis Mirepoix, Elisabeth [de Gaulle] & Lt Guy. It was most enjoyable. Diana Cooper was, I thought awful after dinner. She

---

* Daughter of the Nobel Prize—winning scientist Marie Curie; friend of Duff and Diana Cooper.
† American journalist: friend of Randolph and persona grata with the Churchills.
‡ Son of Earl Baldwin of Bewdley (Stanley), former Prime Minister.
§ Famous and fashionable photographer and designer.
¶ Tess Mayor, MBE—whom he later married.
** Georges Bidault, French Foreign Minister.
†† Gaston Palewski, General de Gaulle's *chef de cabinet* and close adviser.

attacked the seating arrangements at the parade in the morning—hot-making—very. She is a donkey.

Sunday, 12 November, was a lovely sunny morning, and as there were no official arrangements until lunchtime I asked if I might go to church: one of the General's ADCs collected me and escorted me to High Mass at the Madeleine. The church was packed; seated in the front row, I was in a considerable quandary as to when to sit or stand. There was a remarkable sermon by an army chaplain—declaimed without a note—calling the people of France "to throw themselves beneath the figure of Christ & of her *qui a sut se repentir de ses erreurs,* and to arise in strength & spiritual regeneration."

Before luncheon my parents and I went with Beatrice Eden to visit the club she was running for Allied personnel, returning to the Quai d'Orsay for a luncheon given by M. Bidault. Later that afternoon we all proceeded to the Hotel de Ville for another splendid celebratory event:

This was the centre of Parisian resistance & played a tremendous part in the Liberation [of Paris]. All the officials were wearing splendiferous sashes of scarlet & royal blue. The 'girls' all arrived first & we were installed in large *fauteuils.* We walked upstairs & along corridors lined with la Garde Republicaine, and the sight of them & the huge hall where the chandeliers were reflected as pools of light on the parquet floor is something I shall never forget.

Papa arrived & was welcomed by the Prefet de Police M. Luizet and the President of the Parisian Council of Liberation M. Tollet. The room on whose walls were depicted the most bloody & resisting events of French history was full of members of the resistance movement . . . it was very moving. Papa made a great & remarkable speech in French—and I think they all liked it. Then he was presented with the [flag] with the swastika hauled down from the Hotel de Ville & a dagger. Then we retired & drank champagne. On the way back the streets were still lined with people although it was after dark & they could have no reasonable hope of seeing anything. Papa & Mummie dined with Duff & Diana, and Eric [Duncannon]* gave a dinner party for me. I sat between Etienne de Rosier who was gay & entertaining, with Eric on the other side—who is neither, but *very* nice . . .

This agreeable evening marked the end of our wonderful return visit to Paris. But there was to be for me an exciting sequel.

General de Gaulle had invited my father at the conclusion of his Paris visit to accompany him to see the First French Army, which was about to go into action at the Belfort gap in eastern France. My mother was to stay on for a day or two in Paris, but to my intense joy I was to go with my father. Arrived at the special train which was to take our party I found that my wagon-lit compartment

was bursting with white gladioli and tiger lilies—simply *lovely* but rather overcrowded! The party is Papa, General de G & his 2 aides, CIGS [Sir Alan Brooke], plus Capitaine de Levis Mirepoix, Tommy [Thompson], M. Diethelm,† M. Palewski, & M. Mayer,‡ General Juin.§ I left the boys rather quickly to gather strength for tomorrow's excursions. We rumbled across France from West to East & when we woke up it was to find SNOW— with a white heavy sky threatening more to come. I lost control at Breakfast and guzzled an omelette au jambon instead of banting!

* Now serving as Secretary at the British Embassy.
† M. André Diethelm, Commissioner of the Interior.
‡ M. René Mayer, French radical politician; later, in 1953, he served briefly as Prime Minister.
§ Long-standing friend of de Gaulle who had commanded under the Vichy government all the French troops in Morocco; in 1942 he joined the Allies.

On Monday, 13 November, my diary continues:

We arrived at Besancon at 10, General de Lattre de Tassigny*
plus his staff & etc met us. After a guard of honour & bands
we were bundled into a long caravan of cars. I found myself
with General Valuy (General de Lattre's Chief of Staff—I
think)—and a French general whose name I never did get, and
also Commandant Bullitt ci-devant American ambassador to
France, and now in the French army. They were all charming to
me, and I couldn't have had a gayer journey.

It was indeed 'très gai' for as we climbed & climbed the snow
thickened & it got colder & colder. Then a tyre burst on Papa's
car—after that there were continually halts to unditch various
cars which had stuck firmly in the snow. I decided to trade on
my sex rather than my rank, & therefore sat in great comfort
while various generals, colonels and brigadiers heaved & pushed
the cars about. We eventually arrived at Maiche—eight kilometres only from the enemy, & the battle was explained to Papa
& the General in General de Lattre's HQ which was in a most
attractive diminutive chateau.

I remember that during this long drive the men were able to relieve
themselves as and when—leaving me, the only woman, in growing discomfort and considerable embarrassment, as there was no cover of any
kind in the snowy landscape: by the time we arrived at Maiche I made
a determined and desperate rush for the nearest bathroom!
At luncheon

I sat on General de Gaulle's right and next to General Juin. It
was rather nervous work at first—but I hope it was all right. At
the end of lunch Papa made a short & very moving speech, pro-

---

* Imprisoned by the Vichy government in 1942, Tassigny had escaped after four attempts and joined de Gaulle. He was now commanding the First French Army.

posing conjointly the health of the First French Army and its commander 'ce general rusé' [General de Lattre de Tassigny]. General de Gaulle replied shortly & well & said Papa was 'le Clemenceau de cette guerre'... Then Gen. de Lattre made a speech & then our own CIGS, in perfect & graceful French. I was so proud to be at this occasion in this snowbound village and to be able to drink with my whole heart to resurgent France. May God speed & prosper their forthcoming attack.

By the time we had arrived at Maiche the mountain road had become completely blocked, and there was no possibility of reaching the front—however, General de Lattre suggested that we should return to Besançon by way of Valdahon, where there was a large number of French troops encamped. Accordingly we set forth again: now "considerably warmed by cognac & emotion, we bundled into the cars—now fortified with chains [and] we dashed back along the ways we'd so painfully climbed."

We arrived at Valdahon as twilight was falling. It was still snowing & bitterly cold. Papa & the General drove in a jeep right down the assembled parade. After a quick gouter in the equivalent of NAAFI, there was a march past. Most of the troops were Maquis & FFI [Forces Francaises de l'Interieur]* just completing their training. I thought they looked splendid—small, tough & ferocious, and animated with one desire—to confront the enemy.

There was also a battalion of the Foreign Legion who marched by impressively to their own Marche Consulaire. Then in the gathering gloom about 100 tanks rumbled past. It was such a sombre setting—snow, mud, barracks & twilight, and it will remain in my memory forever. I think all of us there

---

* The FFI were formed in February 1944 by the French Committee for National Liberation: they became part of the Allied armed forces and were integrated into the regular armed forces in September 1944.

who loved France, must have prayed for this small but infinitely determined army . . . We all got icy cold, but thank God Papa was all right.

At dinner on the train I again sat between Gen. de Gaulle & General Juin, and it was our last meeting for the present. Dinner was passed in the most genial and friendly spirit. I do really trust & think a real rapprochement has resulted from these last few days—Long may it last. When we all parted it was to say 'Goodbye'. General de Gaulle sent one of his aides, Lt. Guy, along with a little Croix de Lorraine for my uniform. I am so proud of it.

During the night our train divided, part of it carrying the General back to Paris, while our portion took us overnight to Rheims, near where General Eisenhower's* headquarters was located. During the morning, while my father and "Ike" conferred, I went for a walk

with the dreariest possible WAC [member of the Women's Army Corps]—who has been to so many war fronts that this bedraggled & impoverished little French village—Gueux—was not very exciting to her. To me every step seemed significant— I cannot get over being in France again. In the afternoon we flew away over the spacious champagne country dotted with war cemeteries and made so lovely by the soft wet light and the different shades of the *cultures*. I wish I could begin to describe its rather sad beauty . . . And then we arrived back—and Papa's visit to France was over.

WHAT WITH ALL the excitement and emotions of the visit to France, and with no enemy action, at the end of November I was finding bat-

* General Dwight D. Eisenhower (1890–1969): "Ike," Supreme Allied Commander in Europe; later thirty-fourth President of the United States (1953–61).

tery life quite boring; however, writing up my diary on 9 December, I recorded how "rumours began wafting around . . . and finally General Tremlett told the assembled ATS of 137 [Regiment] that we have been chosen for service in North West Europe. *Wild* excitement and enthusiasm. And lots of work preparing for the move to Weybridge [in Surrey] where we 'concentrate.'"

In a letter to Randolph (in Yugoslavia) at this time my father wrote:

All your sisters send their love . . . Mary has been promoted to Junior Commander with 3 pips, equal to Captain. She is back at the Hyde Park Battery commanding 230 women.* Not so bad at 21! The Battery is to go to the front almost immediately, and will be under a somewhat stiffer rocket fire than we endure with composure here. Mary is of course very elated at the honour of going to the front, and at the same time bearing up against her responsibilities. So far we are proceeding on the voluntary basis in regard to young women sent into the fight. If we do not get enough that way, they will have to be directed. Many of them have troubles at home with their papas and Mamas. When Mary sounded her girls as to whether they wished to go overseas, the almost universal reply was 'Not 'alf!' I hope the Battery will produce a record in volunteering. The Battery, I must explain has eight guns of which only four are in Hyde Park, and Mary journeys from one to the other to discharge her manifold duties.

We are well back in the Stone Age now though, as Stalin (pointed out to me), we have not yet reached cannibalism.

God protect us all, especially the young who are reprieving the follies of the past and will, I pray, ward off the worst follies that threaten us in the future.

---

* Molly Oakey had been posted to another battery, so I was the senior ATS officer in 481 Battery.

Before we left Hyde Park again, however, there was my father's seventieth birthday to celebrate on St. Andrew's Day, 30 November. "I rushed home earlyish to say 'Happy Birthday' & to present the usual buttonholes* and his present—some Gilbert & Sullivan recordings."

That evening we had a dinner party in the Annexe flat:

Mummie had made the sitting room ablaze with flowers. The guests were Cousin Venetia [Montagu], Brendan [Bracken] & Max [Beaverbrook] besides the family—the 3 girls, Aunt Nellie, Uncle Jack & Nana. When we were all assembled the candles were lit on the cake—70 of them—Papa looked so pleased and well. At dinner Diana & Sarah sat on either side of Papa—& I sat between Nana & Duncan. Dinner was delicious & ended with peaches birthday cake & real cream (a present!). All Papa's presents were loaded on a table—and there was a magnificent 'bottlescape'. Max proposed Papa's health—not very well—but Papa's reply made me weep. He said we were the 'dearest there are'—he had been comforted and supported by our love. It was short—but I couldn't see the faces at the end—& then very slowly—almost solemnly—he clinked glasses with each one of us.

I WAS ON DUTY over Christmas this year: again, according to tradition, the officers prepared, cooked, and served the troops luncheon, and there was a battery dance in the evening. The next morning I was "liberated," and rushed off to Chequers—to find, to my dismay, that my father had flown off to Athens on Christmas Eve with Anthony Eden, to cope with the crisis which had arisen with the culmination of the Greek civil war in a bitter struggle for the city and the political future of Greece. It was a highly dangerous situation, and my mother

* Stumped as to what to give my father on his birthday, I usually gave him two carnation buttonholes—one for the day, and another for the party in the evening—but this year I had managed something more inventive!

was deeply anxious; but she was gallantly carrying on the festivities with the usual children's party and a film. Sarah was there (we shared a room, and caught up on each other's lives); also there were Uncle Jack and Aunt Nellie; Diana and Duncan, with their three children; the Prof and Gil Winant—and the officers from the camp, who were duly entertained. So we kept our hearts up and the "home fires burning" on this which, we knew with confidence, would be the last wartime Christmas.

CHAPTER 18

Europe Arise!

DURING THE FINAL WEEKS AT WEYBRIDGE PREPARING FOR OUR foray abroad I was able to make off-duty dashes for home. On one such occasion I noted in my diary some treasured time with my father, who with no morning engagements had worked in bed:

> I lunched alone with Papa. A rare and precious occasion for me. He was sitting up in bed resplendent in his bedjacket.* I sat near his bed & we had a delicious lunch on trays. Crab—beef—mince pies with Liebfraumilch to drink. At first Papa read the Manchester Guardian and Yorkshire Post & then talked to me—Greece—Monty—the battle†—the House [of Commons]. He was so kind and I did so love being alone with him. Only I'm always afraid of boring him—so I was careful not to stay too long & went away at half past two—that hour having flown.

Mobilization being at last completed for 481 Battery's "invasion" of Europe, we departed on 25 January 1945 in bitterly cold weather,

---

* WSC always had very splendid bedjackets made of brilliant, mostly boldly patterned, heavy silk.
† Fierce fighting between British troops and communist forces in Greece, including the capital Athens, had continued through December into January.

travelling by foot, train, boat (Tilbury to Ostend, where we spent the night), and finally trucks via Ghent and Bruges. Arriving at our final destination, which was on a hilltop just outside a small village named Huldenberg, not far from Brussels, we settled ourselves in our Nissen-hut quarters, which had been prepared ahead for the main body of the battery. They were pretty primitive, but the advance party had the stove in each barrack room lit and a hot meal ready—and, totally exhausted by the long journey, everyone was soon asleep.

As usual the battery was on two sites—four guns on each—with the officers' mess and quarters and battery headquarters about half a mile away in a commandeered château. It was, as I wrote to Nana on 3 February,

a most elegant and luxuriously appointed one too—if only the luxurious appointments pushed or pulled. However some of them are being slowly brought into action . . . I spend nearly all day slithering around the sites poking my nose into everything . . . For the first few days we wallowed in snowdrifts and now we flounder in mud.

Walking on semi-cleared roads or tracks was a real physical challenge—but cars or trucks simply got stuck: "Every expedition in transport is an adventure—quite 50% of one's time is spent pushing, pulling coaxing & undigging cars."

Two days later a thaw set in. I wrote in my diary: "Drifts of snow have given place to quagmires of mud & slush. The roads, if possible, are worse than ever." To my father I described how the girls "have not confined themselves to the mere feminine task of operating lethal instruments—but have thrown themselves with gusto into laying tracks, duckboards, and clearing rubbish and sawing wood. We all have the appetites of giants, and the rations are very good indeed." They continued to meet these tough conditions with high spirits; as I told Nana, "They have great fun exploring in the villages. The Belgians here are very friendly and hospitable—and for a little coffee or a bar of soap do all one's washing. I think there's hardly a girl or man who hasn't got a Belgian laundress!"

The burgomaster and his wife, Comte et Comtesse Thierry de Limburg Stirum—and his large family of children and cousins—whose home was the château in the village (their other home in the Ardennes had been razed to the ground in the fierce fighting in that area), were in every way helpful, and extended warm hospitality, including most welcome baths, to the officers. (This was genuinely generous, since fuel for heating was hard to come by for the civilian population.) The worst horrors of occupation had largely bypassed this somewhat out-of-the-way village hidden in the fold of a hill, but there was no doubting the popularity of their liberators.

Although we were immured in the countryside, trips by all ranks to Brussels were facilitated by lifts in the constantly to-ing and fro-ing trucks collecting rations and other supplies. Once in the city there were many amenities on hand, including of course YMCA and YWCA canteens and hostels for short periods of leave. I personally remember on my first visit to Brussels standing stock-still on the pavement, transfixed by the window of a large florist, crammed with potted azaleas, cyclamen, and other hothouse plants—a sight long since vanished at home, where fuel was strictly rationed. I was (somewhat priggishly, I fear) shocked by the flouting by all and sundry of whatever regulations existed here, and the widespread use of the flourishing "black market." This had been regarded as almost a "patriotic duty" during the occupation, but it was still going on now—apparently unrestrained.

A surprise and welcome visitor was Captain Noel Chavasse, one of Field Marshal Montgomery's ADCs. Monty had lunched the week before with my parents in London, where he had learned of my posting to Belgium, and on his return to his headquarters he had dispatched Captain Chavasse, bearing a letter to me in his own hand, "to visit you and make certain all is well. I am also sending him a present for your Battery of a case of Bovril and 10,000 cigarettes. Let me know if there is anything I can do for you. I hope your Battery is shooting down the flying bombs. Yrs sincerely, B. L. Montgomery." In fact, as regards our active participation in the defence of Brussels, we were never actually called upon to fire: the battlefront was moving forward fairly fast, and Brussels was no longer a feasible target for enemy air raids.

The news of the whereabouts of a "mixed" battery soon got round, and our girls were invited to many dances with neighbouring British and American units, who sent transport for them; I and my fellow ATS officers found ourselves in the role of "chaperones," one of us always escorting (and carefully counting) our contingent at the end of the evening. At one party where I was duenna-on-duty, a charming American officer, Ed Chandler, asked me if I would like to go wild-boar hunting, an invitation I accepted with enthusiasm: the result was a long and wonderful expedition to the Ardennes near Namur.

We left at about six o'clock in the morning, and our long drive, during which we collected the local *chef de police,* took us through country where the Battle of the Bulge had been turned in early January. I noted in my diary: "Rusting carcases of tanks lay upturned here and there—the fields bore the marks of giant tracks—but otherwise a pale sun gleamed on a peaceful Sunday countryside." We passed through a devastated Rochefort and eventually reached our rendezvous with our shooting party gathered by the roadside.

Mons Hye, le propriétaire (in an elegant shooting ensemble of bottle green), a Burgomaster, a lawyer, some farmers, and a crowd of beaters and a motley pack of dogs—also Mons. l'Inspecteur des Eaux et des Forets, in a shooting garb reminiscent of a Drury Lane production of *Babes in the Wood.* I was given a carbine[!] by Ed, who lent an air of originality to the scene by appearing garbed as if for an airborne invasion, and bursting with lethal weapons.

The shoot went on all day, in a beautiful forest, involving much standing round, but it was a lovely day "and the air was like iced white wine . . . 3 boars were shot—I saw a beautiful fox—I'm glad to say Ed missed it—and I watched a huge boar break cover and gallop across a clearing." One of the beaters captured a *marcassin* (a baby wild boar) which had become separated from its mother, which he presented to me, and which I most unwisely accepted: it looked perfectly sweet, and complete with miniature tusks! At five we adjourned to M. Hye's hunting lodge for refreshments, and then set off for home—where a sense of reality returned: the major was thunderstruck by the infant boar's appearance, "and a long lovely day ended in tears of fatigue and despair as to what to do with a baby wild boar who showed every sign of intractability & violent disposition." I spent a slightly disturbed night with it rampaging in a box in my room. In the morning the major's batman appeared and removed the boarlet to the gamekeeper's cottage, "where," I wrote ruefully to Nana, "I fear only too soon sucking [*sic*] pig will be on the menu. The Major has *begged* me not to go hunting again!"

Early in March I had a lovely surprise when my parents came to Brussels—my father on his way to visit the armies now approaching the Rhine, and my mother to inspect YWCA hostels, in the running of which she was closely involved. I had been given forty-eight hours' leave and was whisked off to meet them at the airfield. My father soon left for the front, but my mother and I stayed at the British Embassy with the ambassador and his wife, Sir Hughe and Lady Knatchbull-Hugessen.

The next day, Sunday, we were all bidden to the Palais de Laeken, on the outskirts of Brussels, to lunch with Queen Elisabeth (the mother of King Leopold III, who was still in exile, and of his younger brother Prince Charles, presently the Prince Regent, who was "holding the fort" pending decision about the return of the King). There was just time before she flew off home for my mother to make a brief visit to the battery.

That evening the Knatchbull-Hugessens took me to dine with M. and Mme. Paul-Henri Spaak (he was successively the Belgian Minister of Foreign Affairs and Prime Minister); there I met their children, Marie and Fernand. Over twenty years later I would meet Marie again in the French capital; by then I was married to Christopher Soames, at that time British ambassador in Paris, and Marie to the brilliant diplomat Michael Palliser; we would all become great friends.

This "starry" weekend also saw the beginning of a delightful friendship with André de Staercke,* the Prince Regent's secretary who was also at the Spaaks' dinner: over the years he was to become a much-valued friend of my parents, and of Christopher and myself. On this particular evening, after dinner de Staercke took us to the Palace, where we were received by Prince Charles; I noted in my diary that "after some halting formal conversation we all started to play ping pong till midnight, which was the greatest fun." To my mother I wrote: "I thought the Palace lovely—and it is easy to see that the Regent is much better 'entouré' than the Queen. All his ADCs look vital, distinguished and are in uniform. The whole atmosphere is very Royal. . . . The Regent himself is a very well preserved 40? Rather good looking and very shy." After several bouts of Ping-Pong "I was breathless! Scrumptious sandwiches and champagne appeared at intervals. I sustained the impression he must work very hard—he said to me 'I have a great deal of reading to do—you see I am new at this job—I've only just taken it on.'" I continued my letter enthusiastically: "During the ping pong he became far less shy and quite gay. He plays very well, and sweetly altered the score on several occasions so that his opponents were not left too far behind! I have been invited to go and play again—and I should love to do so, because he and his entourage are so kind and agreeable." The following morning I came down abruptly to earth again, and returned to my battery!

---

* André de Staercke had joined the Belgian government just before the outbreak of war and in 1942 was summoned to join the Prime Minister, Hubert Pierlot, in exile in London. After the war he served as Prince Charles's chief political adviser until the regency came to an end in 1950 and was subsequently Belgium's Permanent Representative to NATO.

During these weeks of early spring both the weather and our really spartan living conditions improved daily. On 6 February I wrote to my mother:

> Gradually the sites are taking shape. From bare, bleak necessities we are progressing to elementary comforts—electric lighting is being installed in the sleeping quarters—extra food stores are being built and a canteen is slowly but surely taking shape. Paths and roads are being made, and generally chaos and mud are being reduced to at least organised chaos and controlled (more or less) mud. Never have I seen such luscious, glutinous and liquid mud—and in such abundance! . . . The girls are working very hard, and doing quite heavy work too. They are cheerful and I think enjoy the feeling of real usefulness.

About myself I was in no doubt: "I am bird-happy, and more than ever glad I volunteered to come—I should have hated missing all this." Some weeks later I was able to report in a further letter: "On sites life is proceeding with less discomfort—we've managed to organise bigger and better supplies of hot water. A bath a week is now assured."

Meanwhile the Allied armies were advancing with speed. U.S. forces crossed the great barrier of the Rhine on 7 March, and in my diary on Saturday, 24 March, I wrote: "We knew by Friday evening that today was D-Day—we watched the weather anxiously all day: on Saturday—thank God—it was perfect. Our C.O. read out Monty's 'Order of the Day.' About 20 minutes later the airborne armada swept across the sky. We all rushed out and waved them on their way. It was an unforgettable sight."

Our Belgian friends continued to entertain us hospitably: the Burgomaster and his family were real music lovers, and several times took me with them to lovely concerts in Brussels. One quite frequently bumped into friends from regiments who all had "club" houses there, and so it was that I met up again with my friends from the 11th Armoured Division (last seen in Aldershot), who were now forging ahead at the front. I used to call in and catch up with their exact position from the map maintained there, and felt thrilled to see the little flags advancing so fast. All the regiments gave wonderful dances on their brief "pass throughs," where high spirits and champagne flowed in equal proportions: it was truly an exciting time, and one felt the tide of victory flowing.

At the end of March my mother departed for a six-week goodwill tour of Russia on behalf of the Red Cross Aid to Russia Fund, of which she was the very hands-on chairman. During this time my father was the link between her and all our family, and he kept her abreast of our news. One great personal event for me was when I was awarded the MBE (Military) in April, and my mother cabled her congratulations from Stalingrad: I felt quite *bouleversée* and embarrassed, and was truly touched by how nice all my colleagues were about it.

Our three-month stay on the Huldenberg hilltop ended when 481 Battery removed "lock, stock, and barrel" to an airfield just outside Antwerp (which currently required protection from air attack more than Brussels)—necessitating many farewells to our kind local friends. Our new site had its hazards, as sundry aircraft from time to time tried to "drop in"—not realizing the airfield's purpose had been changed— and we would rush out brandishing our arms to discourage them from their intention. Many deficiencies in basic needs and comforts were remedied, I noted gratefully in my diary, by my fellow officer Joan Scully's success "with a mobile [battery's] Major who produces working parties and grease-traps instead of orchids!"

But our time there was not to be long, for after a mere six weeks our role as an active anti-aircraft battery came to an end. During that time events had crowded on each other with bewildering speed; on 2 May I noted that "Hitler '*on dit*' is dead" and that the "German and Italian armies in Italy have surrendered—Thank God. Really the crescendo of news is breath-taking." Hitler had in fact killed himself on 30 April, and the total surrender of the German and Italian armies on all fronts would come on 8 May. That morning, I had arrived in Brussels on forty-eight hours' leave to find the city in transports of relief and joy.

I had no plans, but kind Belgian friends swept me up and I spent the day with them. On my return to my hotel about half past midnight I found my commanding officer Colonel Galloway waiting for me with a message to say I was to fly home—my father had sent for me.

Accordingly, next morning I was whisked home. Arriving at the Annexe, I was greeted by "Papa in his dressing gown with open arms. He had waited lunch for me: he had his on a tray in bed—I at his feet." Looking back, it seems a little sad that at this hour of triumph my father was virtually alone—but my mother cabled him early from the British Embassy in Moscow: "All my thoughts are with you on this supreme day my darling. It could not have happened without you." Duncan and Diana spent the day in his constituency but came to dinner that evening, and Sarah joined us later.

Victory in Europe was celebrated by two days of national holiday, VE+1 and VE+2 (9 and 10 May), when joyful crowds thronged the streets day and night. I continued my account in my diary for Wednesday the ninth: "I just had time to titivate before Papa set out with me in tow to pay diplomatic calls at the Embassies [French, American, and Russian]. How can I ever describe the crowds or their welcome to Papa as he made his way through London," driving in an open car and "escorted by only 4 mounted police to clear a pathway through the streets and a few despatch riders." At luncheon he had talked to me about the Germans: "Retribution & justice must be done, but in the words of Edmund Burke* 'I cannot frame an indictment against a whole people.' Thus he talked to me about it at lunch, and at the American Embassy used it in his short speech to the staff."

After dinner we were told that there was a large crowd in Whitehall:

So Duncan & Diana and I bolted ahead & got a good place in

---

* Edmund Burke (1729–97), British statesman and political philosopher. Opposed British policy over American colonies.

the crowd, & we & everyone else bellowed happily when dear Papa appeared. After Sarah arrived we dashed to the Palace & were not too late—the King & Queen—she resplendent in white & a diamond tiara appeared & we all yelled with happiness and pride. The flood lighting is too lovely—the city is transfigured.

The blackout had ended in the last week of April, but we were still revelling in a once-again lighted city.

Of my father's reaction I wrote: "Papa in the midst of national victories and personal triumphs suddenly looks old & deflated with emotion, fatigue & a heart breaking realisation of the struggles yet to come."

The weather during these victory days was lovely, and on 11 May,

it being a warm still, clear evening, we had dinner together in the garden at No. 10. The dusk deepened around us. We listened to the news & then to some romantic waltzes. The floodlighting came on at about half past ten. Papa was wearing his mauve and black quilted dressing gown over his siren suit and a soft black hat. We walked a little on the [Horse Guards] Parade to look at the lights.* Nelson gazed down on Papa. Smoky the cat slid silently across the lawn to be remotely & coldly polite to Papa.

Among colleagues and friends who "dropped in" there was already talk of an early general election, and indeed on 23 May my father resigned, bringing to an end the great Coalition government which had fought and won the war in Europe: he now became Prime Minister heading a "caretaker" (mainly Conservative) administration to tide us over until final victory in the Far East, and while preparations went ahead for the first general election for ten years.

Meanwhile on 12 May the family got together to welcome my

---

* Again, it is striking how impressive the "lighting up" again was for us.

mother back from her long Russian travels. I commented in my diary: "She is decorated and looks a WOW in uniform." The next day I went with my parents to a great service of thanksgiving in St. Paul's led by the King and Queen. Such was the mood that we were allowed to sing the second verse of the national anthem (usually a real no-no), bidding God arise to scatter the King's enemies ("Confound their politics / Frustrate their knavish tricks . . .").

ON MY RETURN to 481 I found the battery in commotion and change: we were being re-formed into an all-ATS unit. So we said goodbye to "our" boys, and were flown off in troop-carrying Dakotas to a great encampment on a former airfield, Wenzendorf, about twenty-five miles from Hamburg, where we arrived on 1 June. Here German regiments were handing in their guns and other heavy equipment, and our regiment's new role was to assist in its reception, parking and "mothballing" against deterioration.

We had the distinction of being the first ATS east of the Rhine, but our situation near a devastated Hamburg had its problems, well expressed in the very nice letter Monty wrote me on 13 June.

My dear Mary
I hope all goes well in your battery; I send one of my personal Liaison
Officers to ascertain your needs.

I am anxious that the A.T.S. we have in Germany should not feel lonely;
I am sure you all realise that we are living in the midst of a hostile people,
and things cannot be quite the same as in Belgium, France, Holland, etc.
I have given orders that a Y.W.C.A. shall be set up in Hamburg for you
[servicewomen].

Can I do anything else for the A.T.S. at your unit?

Yrs. sincerely,
B. L. Montgomery
Field-Marshal

My letters home told of this dramatic change in my geographical whereabouts, our regiment's new role, and our life as part of an occupying force. On 2 June I wrote to my mother:

We are under canvas again. Fortunately the ground is much better than Antwerp, where whenever there was any rain (which was practically all the time!) all the tents were flooded. This camp is in the depths of densely wooded country on part of Blohm and Voss' airfield. No girl is allowed out unless accompanied by an armed escort who has to sign for her . . . It is uncanny after being in Belgium where every army truck is greeted by waving children and smiling grownups. Here the children look—a few, very few wave, the grownups just walk on—if they looked—it was a short glance, and no expression of either hate or fear showed—or of any emotion at all. But of course the arrival of the A.T.S. created quite an interest. And wherever we passed our own troops there were shouts of welcome and they all waved.

Last night we were all dead tired, having got up at 3 in the morning but to-day we've revived and are busy settling in. Conditions are even more primitive here than in Antwerp, but Engineers have started on cookhouse, latrines and ablutions, and in the meantime we manage with tents and flimsy structures.

Our job, the receiving of vast quantities of disused equipment does not start for about a week. I only wish it did—this place has few charms once divorced from a really full-time absorbing job.

Nearly a week later I drove through Hamburg and wrote again:

Words are inadequate to describe the devastation. The streets are full—full of crowds of people who presumably have no where else to go and little else to do. Long, apparently aimless queues—lots of families trundling their possessions in prams and barrows. I suppose at night they crawl into the cellars beneath the ruins of their city. On the outskirts of Hamburg there are many pre-fabricated houses—very small and fragile—built to receive some of the refugees. People trek to and from the city daily to pick over the piles of rubble—trying to salvage something from the wreckage. Houses—apparently completely unfit for human habitation, are lived in by several families . . . I did notice a great difference between the people in Hamburg and those out in the country. On so many of their faces is a sort of blank, aimless look.

The sight of the terrible revenge has shocked me. Not into any feeling of weak pity, or a conviction that it was wrong or too horrible. But my mind had not grasped the exact extent of the devastation—and with every day that passes I wonder more and more at the toughness of the fibre of human life. Did you feel the same when you saw the destroyed cities of Russia?

Another week on, I was able to write, with some relief:

Our real job here has just started, and I am pleased that it has. Nearly all my girls now have new jobs, and mostly out-door work which is what they really like. The round of gaiety continues undiminished, and although it is rather exhausting, it is great fun, and the men are so truly pleased to see us, and so thoughtful and kind and attentive. What it is to be in a minority! In addition to dances, we are invited to other kinds of entertainments—afternoon parties when the girls are taken for cruises up the Elbe, or regimental sports meetings, or 'Trotting Races' and all these activities followed by scrumptious refreshments and evening frivolities!

At one regimental sports day I met a splendid hero figure—Brigadier Glyn Hughes (three DSOs and an MC!), who commanded the medical arrangements for the Second Army: as I explained to my mother, "He organised the relief of Belsen and was there from the moment of its liberation until the relief system was working smoothly." Thereafter I met him on several occasions and he arranged for some of our officers and NCOs to pay a visit to the site of Belsen, the photographs of which, published in the newspapers after the camp was liberated on 15 April 1945, revealed to a horrified public the full extent of the terror of Nazi rule in the countries they had overrun.*

I described my visit in a letter to my mother:

The actual horror camp had been burnt to the ground—it is a gloomy sight—twisted, burnt and charred remains of huts and structures cover a few acres—here and there symmetrical mounds of smooth earth appear, with a little white notice: 'Grave No. 12—2,000 bodies' and then the date of the burial. The Brigadier reconstructed the ghastly scene for us. On all sides a beautiful pinewood presses in on the camp, the air is full of skylarks singing. We all walked dumbly away from the camp, and were taken to visit the hospital. 16,000 internees are left—of these 7,000 are bed patients. The death rate is down from 500 a day to 10 a day. But there are some very, very ill people there; and an enormously high percentage of T.B. cases. The typhus epidemic is now under control and almost at an end. But the results of starvation are not attractive to look upon. We walked through many wards. The nurses are mainly British with quite a number of Germans and a large number of Belgian medical students to help the doctors, and a small party of serene-faced nuns from the Vatican.

In one women's ward a Polish Jewess sat up in bed and welcomed us in broken French . . . 'We are so happy to receive here to-day' she said 'the daughter of the great man who has made

---

* Bergen-Belsen, originally an internment camp, was from 1943 a concentration camp and by March 1945 held 60,000 prisoners. Typhus and other epidemics took a fearful toll. The liberators found 10,000 unburied dead in the camp as well as mass graves containing 40,000 bodies, and despite all efforts the death rate among the survivors continued for many weeks to be very high (see *Oxford Companion to the Second World War*).

our deliverance possible...' I nearly wept. I've never seen so much human suffering. And then we went to the small Maternity block where a few wrinkled, shrivelled little babies make their way into a strange world from half-starved Mothers— who have little or no milk to feed their children. The doctor in charge is Polish [a Christian Jewess]. Until 1935 she was in a large Berlin hospital—but then, being a Jewess, she was sent to one concentration camp after another. Wherever she went she tried to care for the other prisoners. At Auschwitz any pregnant woman was automatically sent to the gas chamber, and as it was a mixed camp many women became pregnant. This Doctor aborted them in secret by night, and strapped the poor creatures up tightly to conceal the operation. Thus she saved countless women. When she came to Belsen she started a maternity ward—no instruments—no water: but she struggled on until liberation. She is 36 and looks 50. She has a passion for her work—for the pathetic mothers she delivers and the thin, delicate babies she cares for. I have never seen such an ardour for life—such a victorious manifestation of the human spirit.

Then we went to the Sergeants Mess where a party was being given to about 100 pale-faced solemn [German] children. About the first party they've ever had. They were quiet and dazed and I hope just beginning to be a little happy.

There is a—to me—moving sequel to my visit to that horrifying place. Over fifty years later the historian Sir Martin Gilbert, my father's official biographer, wrote to tell me that during one of his lecture tours in the United States he had met a Dr. Luba Frederick, a Polish Christian Jewess, who had endured fearful experiences in a series of internment/concentration camps. She had been in Belsen, where she had managed to protect a group of orphans and help them to survive, when it was liberated by the British army in April 1945; she was the doctor whom I had met and about whom I had written to my mother after my visit there.

Luba Frederick eventually went to America, where she married another survivor from those terrible years and made a new life. When she met Sir Martin after one of his lectures she asked him if he knew me—and so, after over half a century, and in happier times, we are in touch again.

IN THAT SAME LETTER to my mother, I also wrote about the general-election campaign at home, which was by now in full swing:

> I watch with passionate interest the progress of the Election. I think of Papa so much. I know it must be a strain on him and a grief to have to mawl and be mawled. About the girls—I haven't asked many of them for obvious reasons—but I think they will vote Labour or Liberal. The Officer's Mess—R.A.—will I think go Labour—A.T.S. Conservative. Papa's first election address was not received very well I'm afraid. If I collect any more information or tit-bits I will let you know. I think you will find the Army votes will largely go to Labour. You must remember the Daily Mirror is widely read by all Ranks and especially the Other Ranks. But it is very difficult to tell. I do feel gloomy about it I must confess—gloomy and uncertain.
>
> I find too, that I'm not yet re-acclimatised to the slings and arrows of party dissension—which perhaps makes one more shocked and sensitive to the really violent attacks on Papa. I know one should try to feel impersonal about these things and take the detached view—but I can't, I can't. I hate these scathing, unjust, untrue attacks on Papa. Wow—oh wow—I *wish* I could talk to you about it. Miserable Kitten with electionitis . . .

I grumbled to my mother a little time later about having to cast my first (and of course loyally Conservative) postal vote for the long-sitting true-blue member for Sevenoaks (my home constituency), who seemed to me ineffably uninspiring.

Polling day was 5 July, but exceptionally the result was not to be announced until three weeks later, on 26 and 27 July—in order to allow time for the votes of servicemen and women overseas to be collected and counted. During this tantalizing pause my father decided he would take a "proper" holiday—his first in the war years, other than his convalescence after his serious illness in North Africa the previous winter. Through Bryce Nairn, newly appointed British consul general in Bordeaux, whom Winston had met and made friends with in his previous post in Marrakech, it was arranged that my parents would be the guests of a French Canadian resident, Brigadier General Brutinel, in his large and comfortable house, the Château de Bordaberry, on a hillside overlooking the Bay of Biscay and the seaside resort of Hendaye, quite near the Spanish frontier.

My father decided he would like my company: accordingly I was whisked at short notice and without explanation over to London. My conveyance was a Mosquito bomber aircraft not intended for passengers—so I had a thrilling and unconventional flight on a wooden stool right up in front near the pilot. We did some interesting unofficial sightseeing on the way, flying at times quite low to get a good view of the Dortmund-Ems Canal and Walcheren Island—both scenes of wartime actions.

I arrived home to find my parents at dinner, and learned of the holiday plans in which, to my joy (having some leave due to me), I could quite properly be included. After a hectic morning getting myself ready and packed we set off—the party consisting of my parents and myself, Jock Colville* (Private Secretary on duty); Lord Moran and "Tommy" Thompson; two secretaries, Mrs. Hill and Miss Sturdee; and his detectives.

During the flight my father was engrossed by a life of Frederick the Great, for which, I noted in my diary, "M[ama] and I are queuing." He was, I realized, exhausted:

---

* Jock Colville was back in the private office again, having left in 1941 to join the R.A.F. He flew as a pilot officer in D-Day sorties, but WSC, finding him indispensable, had recalled him later in 1944.

He is much worn and battered by the election. He feels the attacks so deeply—so intensely. We all await the results with impatience & anxiety. I hope he will be returned—although it will
be a bitter journey's end—so much can go wrong. He is sitting
now [I was writing up my diary on the flight] transported to the
age of Frederick the Great—occasionally breaking away to tell
Mama something about the book.

At the Château de Bordaberry we soon settled in, and our hospitable host and my father got on extremely well, "their association
being much cemented by their both having heard 'Foghorn Macdonald' *swear* at Plugstreet in the last war." My father was feeling low and
tired, but a visit to nearby St. Jean de Luz, where the Nairns were staying, transformed his mood. I recorded with great relief in my diary:
"Oh joy, [he] has started to paint. He has laid his first picture. We
are all delighted." I went on to describe how my Mother and I spent
that afternoon "being rolled & tossed by breakers at St. Jean de Luz,
while half way up the hill Papa in sombrero and beneath a mushroom
umbrella puffed & painted," and close by Margaret Nairn, a charming
woman and herself a gifted painter, set up her easel. That evening we
all felt "knocked out & happy. Papa from his painting & Mama & I
from the ozone, food & sun!"

Unfortunately my mother's enjoyment was marred when she
stubbed a big toe and cracked it; but once plastered up she was in action again. My diary account continued happily: "Papa is beginning to
feel the benefit of this complete rest. Occasional depressions au sujet
des elections come over him. But between times he is happy & conver-
sational."

Two days later,

Papa came down & bathed for the first time. We had a tent
pitched half way down the beach from which Papa emerged
in shapeless drawers—smoking & with his ten gallon hat on.
Sawyers [his valet] un-crowned & un-cigared him as he took to

the waves. I was so happy to see Papa floating peacefully like a charming porpoise washed by lucent waves. We are all enjoying ourselves very much.

One day while we were all swimming a "determined 'pounce' was made by a woman, la Comtesse de Beaumont, who, so reliable 'on dit' goes, was an enthusiastic and passionate collaborator, and is in danger of being lynched by the people here!" The lady's advances were however parried and defeated by a combination of my mother, myself, and Jock—and a number of French policemen who were providentially on guard (in swimming attire).

One night after dinner

we repaired to the Casino at Hendaye where the Mayor received Papa & Mama on the steps—a large crowd had assembled and the scene was lit by arc lamps and great glints of summer lightning. Then a fandango was danced and then they let loose a 'toro fuego'—a feature of the Basque pays [*sic*]. It is a splendid model bull borne aloft and it is riddled with squibs & the most lovely Catherine wheels & rockets. It 'charges' the crowd who scream and run as it makes its crackling blazing way among them. It was the first time for four years that a toro fuego had been organised. It was all so moving & spontaneous. Papa loved it & the crowds waved & cheered & laughed; and despite the horrors and terrors, the difficulties & dangers of the newly born soi-disant peace, one did feel that a little gaiety was returning at last for France.

CHAPTER 19

Triumph and Disaster

If you can meet with triumph and disaster
and treat those two impostors just the same . . .

—RUDYARD KIPLING, "If—"

OUR LOVELY HOLIDAY SOON CAME TO AN END. MY MOTHER FLEW home, anxious to start making Chartwell habitable once more, while my father prepared to meet Harry S Truman, who had succeeded FDR as U.S. President, and Marshal Stalin at Potsdam for the "Big Three" conference to be held there. I went with my father, on duty again as his ADC.

Although the meeting was known as the Potsdam Conference, the discussions actually took place in Babelsburg, an unravaged residential suburb midway between Potsdam, which had been heavily bombed, and the shambles of Berlin. The "Big Three" and their staffs were accommodated here too; and it was from here that I wrote regularly to my mother about the buildup to the Conference and my impressions of the event itself.

23, RINGSTRASSE

16TH JULY, 1945

My darling Mummy,

Our air journey was, I thought, horribly bumpy—and I felt definitely sick. We arrived in blazing sunshine at 5 o'clock. A band, troops of all three services, and a posse of generals, marshals and so on were assembled to greet Papa . . .

We sped off to our villa along roads posted with smart and beautiful looking Russian soldiers.

The house is lovely. In rose pink stone with grey pointing. The ground floor gives, through French windows, on to a balcony, on which are arranged garden chairs and great tubs full of hydrangeas—blue, pink and white. The lawn slopes away to a romantic looking lake which I am told is unhygienic (but whether from decomposing bodies or drains I am not in a position to state) . . . The rooms are large, light and well-proportioned, and there are some quite good chandeliers. The pantry and kitchens are something to dream of. There is a staff of Mr. Pinfield (Petty Officer who used to be in the 'Renown') and four charming A.T.S.—who are looking harassed—but I think it's the heat. I have a charming bedroom opposite Papa's. The curtains are blue and white and there is a romantic flower-wrought chandelier—tres jeune fille.

Last night Anthony [Eden] dined alone with Papa on the balcony—the rest of us had our dinner in the dining room. And I think this arrangement will probably persist so long as this delicious heat continues.

Anthony is brown from the sun—but beneath it he looks ill—and I think poor Simon's loss* is a bitter grief. My heart bleeds for him—it is such a cruel blow.

This morning Papa paid his first visit to President Truman, who is installed in a monstrously ugly house about 400 yds. down the road. While Papa talked to the President, I, Tommy [Thompson] and John Peck were entertained by the 'court'—only Admiral Leahy remains from the previous

---

* Simon, Anthony and Beatrice Eden's elder son and a pilot officer in the RAF, had been reported missing while on active service in Burma on 23 June 1945.

establishment. Papa remained closeted for about two hours—during which time Anthony joined them, and our circle was enlarged by Sir Alexander Cadogan*—as dry as ever—but I like him.

When Papa at length emerged we decided to walk home. He told me he liked the President immensely—they talk the same language. He says he is sure he can work with him. I nearly wept for joy and thankfulness, it seemed like divine providence. Perhaps it is F.D.R.'s legacy. I can see Papa is relieved and confident.

Archie C-K,† Anthony and Sir Alexander lunched a quatre with Papa. I spent a 'domestic' afternoon snooping in the kitchen, and persuading Mr. Pinfield to put cigarettes in the drawing room and for the ashtrays to be emptied every so often. I also banished 2 hideous black vases, and had them replaced by inoffensive gold and white china candelabra. I am trying to beat my sword into a feather duster!

LATE THIS EVENING

At four this afternoon in sweltering heat, Papa, Anthony, Archie C-K, Sir Alexander—Sawyers and all, tootled off to inspect the ruins of Berlin. They are quite extensive. The utter squalor and dilapidation of the place—the stunned look on the faces of the people are not easily forgotten. We gazed on the ruins of the Chancellery—saw the disordered air raid shelters where Hitler is said to have died. The sun beat down on dust and devastation—the Press rushed around madly photographing—and Sir Alexander complained how badly the tour was organised—which it was. But it was worth it.

General Marshall has been to dinner, and has just left. Papa is reading the evening papers and making plans for tomorrow—which I am accepting with a good deal of scepticism (silent) as I'm sure they'll all be changed in the morning. Papa is sorry you will not come out—and means to have another try!

* Permanent Under Secretary at the Foreign Office.
† "G-men" was a popular nickname for FBI officers; OGPU was the Soviet secret police, a forerunner of the KGB.

I am well and happy and determined to be a 'good A.D.C.'—I've just had another china-clearing campaign—and removed some of the more revolting china 'pieces' that recline on every table. I also have designs on a sofa—but I will have to attack that in the morning.

No more for now.

Tender love and kisses darling Mummie
from your loving Mary

23, RINGSTRASSE,
BABELSBURG
19TH JULY 1945

My darling Mummie,
Yesterday President Truman lunched with Papa. I spent the morning flapping around the chef, Mr. Pinfield and the soldier-gardener (who promised to produce some special flowers, and turned up at half past twelve with some purple dahlias and a few tired dog roses!) I was very nervous that Papa would be late. However, in the end everything worked out beautifully. Papa was actually down at the garden gate five minutes before the President arrived. The Scots Guards formed a Guard of Honour—Ian Colquhoun's* younger son [Donald] was in command . . . We all had delicious iced cocktails on the terrace in the sun, and then Papa took the President to the study, where they lunched à deux. His two aides lunched with all of us in the dining room. This was the menu:

Cold Consommé
Fried Sole & Tartar Sauce
Roast lamb, Mint sauce, Mashed Potatoes, Green peas
Ice Cream
Melon.

* Sir Ian Colquhoun of Luss. I had been a maid of honour when he was high commissioner in Edinburgh in spring 1943.

At three the President left to go and visit Uncle Jo, and when they arrived there they found another enormous lunch awaiting them. So they must have felt pretty full by the time the Conference began!

Then—at seven—I dined with General Marshall, General Arnold and their Staff in General Marshall's mess. This was great fun, and afterwards we all went on to a very funny American Army revue.

Papa dined alone with Uncle Jo—and he told me this morning that everything had passed off very agreeably.

Please give my fondest love to all the family,

> Tender love and kisses darling from your
> Mary

P.S. Beatrice [Eden] arrived last night and I've just paid her a visit.

POTSDAM

21 JULY 1945

My darling Mummie,

On Thursday (July the 19th) Papa worked in bed all morning, and lunched alone still 'digesting' Conference papers.

I asked Donald Colquhoun to lunch with all of us, and in the afternoon he and a brother officer took me to swim in a most romantic lake about ten miles from Berlin. It is surrounded by pinewoods, and strewn with water lilies, and it is deliciously warm, and mysteriously deep. After dinner I attended a sort of party, and got involved in an orgy of toasts with 2 Russian generals. Meantime, while the A.D.C. (local, acting and temporary) was gambolling among water lilies and frisking with Bears—the Conference proceeded with its usual intensity.

On Friday Papa had Mr. James Byrnes* and the Prof. to lunch. Poor Prof, I'm afraid he is not very comfortable—he has to share a bathroom with someone else.

---

* U.S. Secretary of State.

This afternoon Beatrice [Eden] and I sallied forth with a very good interpreter and a Russian escort to tour in great detail the wreckage of Berlin. The Russian was a Capt. Kotikoff—who announced that he had accompanied you throughout your tour—that he loved it—that you were a wild success . . . This was an excellent start to our afternoon—and throughout our peregrinations he was charming—easy and very kind. We clambered over ruins, and gathered an extraordinary collection of souvenirs until half past six, when we came home and refreshed ourselves with drinks.

Just before dinner Anthony came dashing over (he and Beatrice were invited anyway) and went up to Papa. It was to tell him that Simon's aircraft had been found and everyone in it was dead.

Anthony and Beatrice both came to dinner nevertheless, and dined on the balcony with Papa and Lord Moran [and myself]. I have never seen two people behave with such noble dignity.

To-day, Saturday, there was the great victory parade. It was a thrilling, moving sight. Afterwards Monty and Alex and Admiral King* came to lunch.

In the afternoon Beatrice and I, again accompanied by that good looking and delightful Captain K. and Mr Morrow our nice interpreter, set off on a mammoth sightseeing tour of the royal palaces at Potsdam. It was very enjoyable, and there were very good guides and not jostling crowds—so we saw a lot.

. . . To-night Papa dined chez Uncle J. Beatrice and I Anthony's two P.P.S.s had dinner in the delegation mess. Beatrice has been so nice to me—I am devoted to her and I think she is such an unusual and lovely creature.

Darling Mummie, your letter arrived to-day and I was so glad to hear from you . . .

Fondest love and kisses from your devoted Mary

---

* Admiral Ernest King, U.S. Chief of Naval Operations.

Darling Mummie,

The whole of yesterday was coloured by the prospect of the great party in the evening. 'Cranky'* was wonderful, and took immense trouble—a special table was constructed to get the necessary number of guests in.

Papa entertained the Chiefs of Staff and Anthony to luncheon. As soon as they'd finished—Cranky—Tommy—Mr. Pinfield—a horde of furniture movers and myself descended like a swarm of locusts on the rooms and a scene of disorder and scramble ensued, which I can leave to your imagination.

I had undertaken (very nervously) to arrange the flowers—and for most of the afternoon I sat amid a heap of rather sodden wind blown sickly-pink hydrangeas, and wondered what I could possibly do with them. However eventually I sorted something out. Then I rushed like a whirlwind through the reception room, casting out furniture—banishing statues, and trying to remember what you always say about chairs 'talking' to each other.

When Papa said 'Have you got a pretty dress here?' and I said 'Yes I had.' 'Go and put it on', said Papa.

So, I wore my printed crepe de chine, and clanked with your lovely aquamarines. At last the guests started to arrive, all our Chiefs of Staff and Field Marshals and of course American and Russian opposite numbers— then a fleet of cars swooped up and out skipped Uncle Joe attended by a cloud of minions, (the house had already been surrounded and laid siege to an hour earlier by what appeared to be half the Red Army).

Uncle J. wore the most fetching white cloth mess jacket blazing with insignia. Close on his heels the President arrived, having walked from his house.

When they all went in to dinner I went off and dined at the mess with the private office. Afterwards we returned through cordons of G. Men and Ogpu,† and I slipped into the dining room (on Papa's instructions) and sat

---

* Lieutenant Colonel Sir Eric Crankshaw, KCMG, Secretary of Government Hospitality Fund.
† "G-men" was a popular nickname for FBI officers; OGPU was the Soviet secret police, a forerunner of the KGB.

on a stool behind his chair, and this was lovely because I heard many of the
toasts, and was able to watch the proceedings from a very good vantage point.
The party appeared to be a wild success—and presently Uncle Joe leapt up
and went round the room autograph hunting! The evening broke up at about
midnight in a general atmosphere of whoopee and goodwill.

Tomorrow I shall be home. I long to see you darling Mummie . . .

But the person I've really lost my heart to is 'Alex'—who is quite
definitely my fav'rite Field Marshal. Moreover he is one of the few people
I fell for when I was 17, who have stood the stern test of time, increasing
discrimination and the decreasing vulnerability of my sentiments!

Tender love and kisses from the Conference kitten
Mary

THE POTSDAM CONFERENCE was not due to end until 2 August, but on
the afternoon of 25 July my father, I, and his immediate entourage
flew home, as the results of the general election would be announced
the following day.

On Friday, 27 July, I wrote up my diary account of the preceding two days—dramatic days for the country politically; dramatic and
painful days for my father and all of our close-knit circle of family,
colleagues, and friends.

I am writing in the sitting room of the annexe—it is just before dinner. Mummie is with Papa. There is an atmosphere of
finality throughout the flat—the Private Office dark and un-
tenanted—an unusual feeling of unhaste and quiet—for after
all there is no hurry now—no decisions—no meetings—no minutes—no telegrams.

I will try to recount accurately and calmly the crashing
events of the last 2 days.

I will try, if only as a mental exercise, to keep my recital
of these hours, which to Papa and those who love him, have

brought a bitter and overwhelming defeat, I will try and keep this account beyond the sway of my emotions, and free from any trace of the tears, which seem to spring unbidden to my eyes.

On Wednesday 25th July, Papa conferred in the morning and we all met at the airfield at one o'clock. We had an uneventful flight home. I think we were all feeling soberly confident that Papa would return on the 27th having a workable majority. This view was supported and indeed chiefly derived from the reliable estimates of both big parties. Our farewells at Potsdam were therefore light hearted and of a very 'au revoir' nature. Little did we then guess what lay within the sealed ballot boxes.

Mummie was at the airfield. Papa on his return proceeded straight to work. R came to dinner and then caught the night train to Preston [his constituency in Lancashire]. He was very confident. Duncan & Diana came in after dinner—they were both gloomy—D. was certain he was 'out'. Robin [Maugham] whisked me off to Michael Parish's house—friends there v. confident.

THURSDAY 26TH JULY 1945

Felt v. excited when I woke up. At breakfast M told me Papa was suddenly feeling low about the results, and feared a stalemate perhaps. M & I drove down to the constituency (Woodford) and were admitted to the court. Here the first inkling of a setback occurred. Mr Hancock—a crackpot and non-representative polled 10,000, and early reports from London showed 44 Labour gains to 1 Conservative gain. We drove home rather silently and went to the Map Room, where all had been prepared to record and tabulate the results. On our way we met a gloomy Jock [Colville] with black looks 'It is a complete debacle' he said 'like 1906'.* We went in—Papa, David Margesson†

---

* 1906 saw a landslide general-election victory for the Liberals.
† Secretary of State for War, 1940–42, and former Chief Whip for the government during the 1930s.

and Brendan [Bracken] and the results rolling in—Labour gain, Labour gain, Labour gain.

It was now one o'clock and already it was quite certain we were defeated. I watched Papa taking it in—grasping defeat—savouring the humiliation. Every minute brought news of more friends out—Randolph, Bob [Boothby], Brendan out— Anthony [Eden] in—Fitzroy [Maclean] in—Leo Amery out— Ralph Assheton out. Duncan out.

Hot tears came and had to be hidden. Everyone looked grave and dazed.

We lunched in Stygian gloom—David Margesson, Brendan, Uncle Jack . . . Sarah arrived looking beautiful and distressed. We both choked our way through lunch. M maintained an inflexible morale. Papa—what can I say? Papa struggled to accept this terrible blow—this unforeseen landslide. Brendan and David looked unhappy.

But not for one moment in this awful day did Papa flinch or waver. 'It is the will of the people'—robust—controlled—the day wore very slowly on—with more resounding defeats. All of the Staff and all our other friends looked stunned and miserable.

Papa spent the afternoon watching the results—M went to rest. I wandered from the sitting room to the Private Office— from the kitchen (where Mrs Landemare moved unhappily among her saucepans) to the Map Room and then back again. Finally I could bear it no longer and went for a long purposeless walk. It was a relief to feel the sun on my face and the wind in my hair to walk rapidly through the streets.

Back in the annexe Robin rang me up.

Dinner—Uncle Jack (so thin and ill looking),* Venetia (battered by her illness but such a kind and supporting friend),

---

* He would die early in 1947.

Duncan, Diana, Sarah looking aggressively beautiful—Brendan and Anthony. Papa was in courageous spirits—Mummie riding the storm with unflinching demeanour—Sarah only a little less brave. Diana pale but philosophic—I am ashamed to say I think, I of them all, was the least composed. But I struggled— I truly did. But I could not gaze at Papa or talk to his devoted friends without feeling overwhelmed with sadness.

After all but Brendan and Duncan had gone away Robin came to see me bringing with him Michael Parish. When Papa came from the dining room he sat down and talked to them. His stature seems to grow with every hour of this bitter personal calamity. He talked to us of the new government 'give them a chance . . . let's see what they can do . . . Only this—let them try to tamper with the Constitution and we will be at their throats—But now is your chance (to Robin and Michael) keep in touch—keep alert—you are our hope . . .' Sombre— noble words and witty ones too.

Papa: '. . . I've thrown the reins on the horse's neck.'
Michael: '. . . but you won the race.'
Papa: 'And in consequence I've been warned off the turf'.

And then the future—his future—painting—writing—He looked at the picture he did at Hendaye. And presently he went off to discuss with Brendan.

Of course—at 7 he'd been to the Palace and laid down his burden taken up in darker days.

Robin and Michael swept me off to the purple, soothing gloom of the Orchid Room. Here were Toby and Miles Hillyard all grieved and shocked at the defeat—all sweet and comforting to me.

God, what a long, long day. I felt stunned, numbed, incapable of thought or action—dried up even of prayers.

FRIDAY 27 JULY

In many ways Friday was worse than Thursday. Cares and anxieties and the tedium of moving descended in their full force on M. Papa woke up to no boxes—no cabinet. Letters began pouring in—sweet—consoling friendly letters. Expressing love and indignation and loyalty.

Randolph arrived from Preston and is even now on the search for a seat. We both went and had drinks at the Ritz with Ally [Alastair Forbes]—Lunch—Randolph—Judy.

M for first time looks tired and shattered—but she set to work with Hambone. Judy & I spent the afternoon together—saw Hugh Fraser he is IN—Met Ronnie and swept him off to give us tea at Gunters. It was rather a relief to giggle freely—Had drinks with Robin—Robin Sinclair, Kate Mary and Bobby [Bruce]—Jane Forbes—the Hillyards and Ally. Dined alone with M & P. A sad dinner on the whole. Papa said 'Yesterday seems years ago'. I thought so too—the days seem endless. After dinner Robin and the Hillyards came and I went off to Jane's flat—We sat in the cool darkness of the garden. But conversation was only an inquest—my resolve for complete calm and dignity was broken once or twice—Home too late—too tired and too sad.

On the following day I returned to my diary:

SATURDAY 28TH JULY 1945

Visited Holding Unit and fixed to return next Wednesday—Bought two pairs of cami-knickers to try and boost my morale. Letters and messages continue to pour in—Mummie and Miss J beetled off to an Aid to Russia tennis match. I remained with Papa. He talked to Jack—and then we went over to the garden at No. 10, Papa read the papers in the friendly quiet of the Cabinet room, and then we sat in the sunshine in the garden looking at the lovely herbaceous border and watching white butterflies flirting with the flowers.

While Papa perused the evening papers I sat and thought of the times we'd lunched or dined en famille in the garden—thought of the Old Admiralty House days, and then our move—and scenes and people drifted through my mind.

This morning Mummie had Leslie [Rowan] and then John [Peck] in for sherry and to say adieu—for they were both off to Potsdam with the Prime Minister. It was for us both a painful farewell—very little was said, but I know Mummie was deeply moved and I think they are sorry too.

Papa and I went about half past four to see the house at Hyde Park Gate.* It is charming and he has fallen for it. We paddled round and I felt he was visualising his life there—and even finding it agreeable.

Back at the Annexe—and then to tea with Diana. She and Duncan are lending their flat in Westminster Gardens to M & P until such time as a house is ready.

M returned from Wimbledon and we all repaired to Chequers for the weekend.

LAST WEEKEND AT CHEQUERS

The party is—Uncle Jack, Tommy, Jock. Papa seemed fairly cheerful all through dinner. M went to bed. We all saw newsreels of the beginning of the Conference and Ike's documentary film 'The True Glory'. As we came downstairs I noticed Papa looked very gloomy—he said to me 'This is where I miss the news—no work—nothing to do . . .' It was an agonising spectacle to watch this giant among men—equipped with every faculty of mind and spirit wound to the tightest pitch—walking unhappily round and round unable to employ his great energy

---

* 28 Hyde Park Gate SW7. My parents bought the house later that summer: it would be their home until WSC's death.

and boundless gifts—nursing in his heart a grief and disillusion I can only guess at.

This was the worst moment so far—unavailingly we played Gilbert & Sullivan—but finally French and American marches struck a helpful note—'Run Rabbit Run' raised great attention & 'The Wizard of Oz' was a request number. Finally at 2 he was soothed enough to feel sleepy and want his bed. We all escorted him upstairs.

Dear Sgt Davies (Inspector Hughes & Sgt. Green left him sorrowfully this morning) had waited up—O darling Papa— I love you so, so much and it breaks my heart to be able to do so little. I went to bed feeling very tired and dead inside me.

On 29 July my diary continued the account of that last Chequers weekend. I noted that Jock and I went to church but "I could not concentrate." The Prof came to luncheon, along with Mr. Pennruddock, the Secretary of the Chequers Trust.

After lunch Jock and I walked for the last time to Beacon Hill and looked at the beautiful English landscape. We talked much of Papa. Duncan & Mummie were playing croquet. Mr White (the Rector of Ellesborough) came to tea to say good-bye, & later Mrs Randag (wife of the Dutch born farmer who was the Chequers' tenant) and about 6 of her brood visited us. Randolph, Gil Winant, Sarah, Diana all arrived & we were all outside on the sunlit lawn. I played hectically with the children who are very sweet. Mr Bevir (Private Secretary) and Brendan [Bracken] also arrived.

We sat down 15 to dinner. Papa seems almost gay again. Awful film. Afterwards I've left them. Sarah is playing records for Papa. It has been a peaceful evening—Randolph was pleasant and quiet and has twirled Sarah and me round waltzing.

Gil is sweet and sympathetic. Jock is sense and loyalty, intelligence and good company personified.

We've all signed on one page of that memorable visitors' book where you can follow the plots and stratagems of the war from the names there.

Papa has signed at the bottom of the page and beneath his name has written 'Finis'.

BACK IN LONDON my parents visited other flats, but the 28 Hyde Park Gate house seemed more and more the solution to their house hunting. Later that Monday, my diary records,

> Papa and I drove down to Chartwell. When we arrived he went straight off for a tour of inspection of the house, the rose and water gardens and the lakes. Papa said how lovely the overgrown gardens are—'. . . like the Sleeping Beauty'. It is lovely and peaceful beyond all words. A flood of memories came rushing to my mind with every step we took.
>
> At half past nine Nana [who was cooking for us just now] gave us and Mrs Hill a delicious dinner.
>
> I sat with Papa till midnight—alone . . . He said I was 'sweet and valiant'—indeed I will try to be . . . Then we remembered this time last week—his 'banquet' [at Potsdam]. He said this had been the longest week in his life. It has been so in my life too. Only a week—only a week. It is difficult to grasp. I was feeling so very tired when I went to bed.

Pending their move into Duncan and Diana's flat my parents were perching (as I put it in my diary) "in film-starry luxury in Claridges penthouse apartment." On the last night of my leave I went with them to see Noël Coward's *Private Lives*:

> Mummie and I went ahead to the theatre. Papa arrived in time. The audience stood up and applauded him. Papa simply loved *Private Lives*—so did M & I. But it was an overwhelming joy to

see Papa so happy and laughing . . . at the end John Clements came forward and made a most moving and charming little speech to Papa—and a crowd cheered him off . . . Back at Claridges we dined à trois gazing out over the lights of London. God knows when I shall see Mummie & Papa again—how I long to come home to them.

The next morning, a lovely summer's day, my mother walked with me across St. James's Park at about a quarter to six to the centre to which servicemen and women returning to their European units reported.

I arrived back at my battery to find a bustle of expectation, as Monty was scheduled to inspect us the next day. His visit passed off well; as he was leaving he summoned me to speak to him, and, as I wrote later that day in my diary, he "asked me so kindly about Papa and Mummie. I was deeply moved and touched by his genuine solicitude for them and his thoughtful kindness to me."

I HAD HARDLY BEEN back with my battery for three weeks when I received a letter from my mother which deeply concerned me. I had written to tell her that our regiment was soon to be disbanded, and that therefore I felt I could apply for a posting back in England. In her reply she wrote:

what really excited & relieved me was that you say you [my regiment] may soon be disbanded & that you will apply for a post in England. Now my Darling please ask for a job at the War Office, so that you can live at home in your lovely bed-sitting room at Hyde Park Gate. Because I am very unhappy & need your help with Papa.

I cannot explain how it is but in our misery we seem, instead of clinging to each other to be always having scenes. I'm sure it is all my fault, but I'm finding life more than I can bear. He is so unhappy & that makes him very difficult. He hates his food, (hardly any meat) has taken into his head that Nana tries to thwart him at every turn. He wants to have land girls & chickens & cows here [Chartwell] & she thinks it won't work & of course she is gruff & bearish. But look what she does for us. I can't see any future. But Papa is going to Italy & then perhaps Nana & I can get this place straight. It looks impossible & one doesn't know where to start . . . Then in a few days we shan't have a car. We are being lent one now. We are learning how rough & stony the World is.

This letter galvanized me into action. Having been driven the 240 miles return journey to our regimental headquarters by a kind army chaplain to whom I had confided my anxieties, I had an interview with the "Queen AT." She was most understanding about my situation, and thought it perfectly proper in the circumstances for me to ask for a posting to London. This was arranged quite quickly, and by the middle of September I was posted as an administrative officer to the War Office Holding Unit in Radnor Place in central London. The ATS officers lived in formerly luxurious houses in nearby Gloucester Square which had been commandeered for their use. This was ideal: my parents' new house was just the other side of Hyde Park, so that even when I had only a few hours off I could visit them quite often.

CHAPTER 20

"Civvy Street"

———

As soon as the war ended my father began to receive invitations from the erstwhile occupied countries to visit them and receive their thanks for the great part he had played in their deliverance. My mother was of course invited too—and so, on several occasions, was I. Having already witnessed the ecstatic welcome he had received in Paris, I would now accompany him to Brussels in mid-November 1945 and to The Hague and Amsterdam the following May; later that summer Randolph and I went with him to Metz, driving from there to Luxembourg.

It was the most wonderful and unforgettable experience to be with my father on those occasions and to see the vast crowds which everywhere gathered to hail him. One realized that they were seeing the incarnation of that voice to which so many of them—often at danger to themselves—had listened in the dark years of their occupation by the enemy.

Back at home my mother was trying to organize—or rather, reorganize—our family life both at Chartwell and in London. I see from my diary that during some leave I had in mid-September she and I spent time "beetling to Chartwell where we live in the cottage and push furniture about in the big house." At the same time I noted that "happy contented news comes from Sarah in Italy," where she was keeping my father company in the villa Field Marshal Alexander had lent him on

Lake Como. After a few days, he picked up his brushes and—to the joy of us all—started to paint again.

On 15 September I celebrated my twenty-third birthday at Chart-well with my mother and Nana. It was a happy day; but I was in fact at the beginning of what was to be a difficult and unsettled period in my life. I was finding my desk job quite tiresome—"processing" for demobilization ATS arriving back from overseas—and my excursions into life with my own contemporaries were proving disappointing. At the various parties to which I was invited I knew very few people: the young men who (through no fault of their own) had not "done the war" seemed hopelessly juvenile to me.

I described in detail in my diary one party given by the Marlbor-oughs at the Dorchester for Caroline (my cousin and near contem-porary) and Sunny Blandford, her brother (a good deal younger). Apart from one, "I knew none of the other Y[oung] M[en]—who were all in blues and looked very young and well bred." Dinner—though itself not very satisfactory—was to prove by far the best part of the evening for me. I had arrived, I wrote, "full of hope and plea-surable anticipation," wearing "my short blue and white striped dress [and] Mummie's diamond brooch." After dinner,

> we waited for le monde to arrive—the 'gals' bench very quickly emptied. I sat trying not to look like the wallflower I was and felt. Everyone was in long and some of them in lovely eve-ning dresses—and everybody appeared to know everyone else. M[ummie] arrived—I would like to say she found me twirling with a fascinating parti—she did not. David Bruce danced with me—He is sweet but he bores me—and I him. I liberated him to dance with his pin-up Angela Jackson—she is very pin-uppable.

I had one or two more dancing partners and caught sight of some-one I fancied who sadly

> didn't catch sight of me—and alas and alack was taken pity on by Giles [my cousin]. We gyrated slowly round the floor in si-

lence. I felt more and more miserable and downcast. I felt *jeune fille* and stale and faded all at once. I felt mortified and conspic-uous. At last unable to contend with events any longer I bolted. I told Caroline I had a headache and that Ally was taking me home—said my au revoir to Cousin Mary [Marlborough] and bolted from the place.*

Outside a huge full moon poured light on the city—I walked quickly home. Spoilt, angry, mortified tears burst from me. Someone tried to pick me up—A kind Canadian soldier said 'Was I ill?'—'No . . . no' I muttered striding on—realising sud-denly I must look a little strange dashing about alone sobbing! Westminster Cathedral was my goal—there I could cast myself down in incensed gloom and calm lights and before the merci-ful majesty of my God lay all my silly, hurt pride—my idiotic grief. My feet were so tired in high heeled shoes I almost fell against the door. It was locked.

At last I got home. I don't know when I've been in such a passion of misery. It was a mixture of many things—mortified pride, disappointment, hurt vanity—a dreadful desolation at the knowledge that I can be a success and have been—except in what is meant to be my own milieu . . . I was acutely conscious of how much I must be lacking. But O God what depths to plumb of tears and unhappiness and all over a party! La folie humaine où va t-elle donc se nicher?

The next day, Sunday, "I woke feeling crushed and headachey. Mummie sweet. She and I went to a lovely comforting service at the Grosvenor Chapel. Lunched together—and here I am back at Glouces-ter Square."

I am happy to relate that not all my social outings were such a dismal failure—but the months following my return to England were, I see in retrospect, not on the whole happy ones. I was not due for demobiliza-

---

* My mother must have left earlier.

tion for some seven months yet, and meanwhile I was in a quandary as to what I should do with my life after that. I was markedly lacking in any ambition, and had no qualifications for a career. In my heart of hearts I earnestly longed to meet "Mr. Right" and live happily ever after! But pending this desirable outcome I fully intended not to be idle.

DURING THE LATE SUMMER of 1945 my parents had a delightful holiday in Switzerland. A gift to my father from the Swiss people, it took the form of the loan of a charming house—the Villa Choisy—between Geneva and Lausanne, standing in its own grounds, with the lawn sweeping down to Lac Leman. It was fully equipped and furnished with lovely furniture lent by many admirers. They would be there for about a month, and—until my mother had an unlucky accident in a boat in early September, resulting in some fractured ribs which caused her much pain—it was a great success. I was with them, and other members of the family and some close friends all came for visits. Painting expeditions, sightseeing, and picnics were all organized by M. Charles Montag, a painter friend of my father, and my father explored the opportunities offered by very large canvases and experimented with painting in tempera.

It was during these holiday weeks that I made a long expedition into France to see my beloved French holiday governess of the prewar years—Mme. Gabrielle L'Honoré. I had managed to keep in touch with her intermittently; she was now living in a Maison de Bon Repos near La Frette in Isère, and it was there that I went to see her—and had a pleasant surprise, as I recorded in my diary:

I expected to find an old, shattered invalid—perhaps a little wandering. Instead, I found her sitting up in bed looking much the same as I remember her. Despite poverty, loneliness and illness she is still sparkling with gaiety and vitality . . . We talked and laughed and remembered and wept a little too. She told me she is 'croyante' now—'comme je ne l'etais pas autre fois'.

I drove away in the evening "feeling humble, and so so happy to have seen her, and to have been received by her with such love and joy . . . all my life I shall remember her with loving and tender and grateful feelings."

A week later I turned twenty-four; the evening before I recorded in my diary my birthday text, which I had found while reading the *Gazette de Lausanne:* "Je suis trop petite, O Dieu, pour toutes tes grâces et toutes tes fidelités."

The plan had been for my parents to be received officially in Geneva, Berne, and Zurich; but, most disappointingly for her and for our hosts, my mother was still in too much pain from her ribs to take part in these events, and had to stay and be cared for at the beautiful Château de Lohn near Berne, which was our base for several days. Meanwhile, on 16 and 17 September successively I went with my father to witness his receipt of tumultuous ovations from massed crowds in Geneva and Berne, and then on to Zurich on the eighteenth, where we stayed at the Dolder Hotel (my mother remaining in painful seclusion at Lohn).

On 19 September—our last day in Switzerland—my father addressed the students of the University of Zurich from a balcony in a speech that has since become famous for his theme—"Europe arise!"—and which came to be regarded as the clarion call for a united Europe. That night we dined as the university's guests at an old and lovely house called "Schipf": here, as I recorded in my diary, "we were greeted by the students lining the long, steep stairway to the house bearing aloft lighted torches. We dined by candlelight in a room where Goethe once was entertained."

During these wonderful days my father made a series of inspired speeches—some (as he would say) "off the unpinioned wing." His theme through all of them was his concern for "the life and happiness of thousands of humble people who are constantly trampled and mauled by these fearful wars—and he quoted that bitter, moving cry from the days of the Jacquerie:* 'Cessez, cessez gendarmes et pié-

---

* The rising up of French peasants against their *seigneurs* in 1358.

tons de piller et de manger le bonhomme—qui depuis longtemps se nomme—le bonhomme.'"

On my father's previous visit to Brussels in November 1945, Prince Charles had suggested that he should make another visit with the express purpose of painting. This had been duly arranged, and towards the end of September 1946 I once more accompanied my father to the Belgian capital, where we were the guests of the Prince Regent in the Palais Royal. Winston had some lovely painting days, which I happily noted in my diary: in Dinant he was "watched by an admiring but respectful crowd," and the next day in Bruges "Papa settled down to paint in the Béguinage":* here he was attended by charming Benedictine sisters and received a visit from the Bishop. Meanwhile the rest of us went for a lightning sightseeing tour of some of the sights and treasures of that beautiful city.

At some point during these days the U.S. Secretary of State, Mr. Byrnes, had arrived in Paris, and through the American ambassador sent a message to say he would much like to see my father: consequently our plans changed, so that instead of flying back to London in the Prince Regent's plane we would go on to Paris. Our last hours at the Palace were marred for me by the confusion and embarrassment caused by the idea, being canvassed in several newspapers in London and Brussels, that Prince Charles and I were to become engaged. At the farewell luncheon "I sat next to Prince C. But all ease had vanished. I felt suffocated and wretched. . . . Prince Charles was kindness and calm and understanding personified. And my heart warmed gratefully to his gentleness."

On the afternoon of 28 September my father and I flew to Paris, where we stayed with Duff and Diana Cooper at the embassy. The following day my father went off to see Mr. Byrnes, and Diana's social secretary, Penelope Lloyd Thomas, was instructed to find some kind member of the diplomatic staff who would entertain me to luncheon.

* The Béguinage in Bruges was for several centuries the home of the *béguines,* women who wished to pursue a religious life without taking the binding vows of nuns. Since 1937 it has been the home of the city's Benedictine sisterhood.

I was in Penelope's office (now the Salon Or) while she was telephoning round, when in came a tall, thin young man—Christopher
Soames—with whom she was lunching, and who had wearied of waiting downstairs (Christopher never did like to be kept waiting): we
were briefly introduced before he took her off for their date. Later that
afternoon my father and I flew home to London.

To my surprise—for I had thought nothing more of our meeting—
some weeks later Christopher rang me up to say he was coming home
on leave and hoped very much we could see each other. I was pleased
to hear from him—although a little puzzled—but I had to tell him
that I was about to leave for Rome, to be with Sarah, who had been
filming there and had been taken ill with a kidney affliction; she was
now recovering, but I was being dispatched by my parents to join her
and to keep her company during her convalescence. I felt somewhat
disappointed that I should miss seeing Christopher and getting to
know this impetuous person, but my plans were now made and I was
eager to be with Sarah. So I duly left early on Tuesday, 22 October,
for my long journey to Italy. My diary entry that evening records what
happened next:

> At Calais a message awaited me from Christopher to say he
> would be coming to Rome on the same train—he was getting
> on at Paris. Sensation! At Paris we duly met, and the long jour-
> ney that followed was most enjoyable, completely unexpected,
> and most memorable. I tried mild reproaches to C. for boarding
> this train, but in the end I had to admit I couldn't possibly have
> been more glad!

> Dinner à deux that evening was most pleasurable and our wagon-
> lit compartments were next door to each other, so in the morning we
> could open the door between them and resume our now-blooming
> acquaintance—which had progressed so swiftly that "as we emerged
> from the Simplon tunnel, C. asked me to marry him—I said NO."

On arriving at Milan, I was truly grateful for an efficient as well as

an agreeable travelling companion, because our part of the train was delayed for eight hours. Christopher took a room for the day at the Continental Hotel, where we could rest, have baths, and generally tidy up.
It was a fine sunny afternoon and we did some mild sightseeing, visiting the cathedral. Sitting in the Galleria, we were spotted by one of our
mutual French acquaintances—a great gossipmonger—who, strolling by,
must have been much astonished to see us. Our "secret" would now be
radioed throughout the capitals of Europe. My diary recorded the last
stages of our day: "Played gin rummy in the hotel. Dined well and ro-
mantically with music. Back to our train and off to Rome at 11.30 p.m."

The following day I spent mostly in my cabin,

being read to or playing gin rummy or talking to Christopher.
He managed to contact some of his Italian friends from his
SOE days* who met us at a station en route with delicious pic-
nic food and wine.

... Arrived in Rome to a great reunion with Sarah who looks
pale and thin and is very weak. I am in a room next door to
her—I am so happy to be here. C and I dined with her in her
room. Long gossips and bed.

I at once addressed myself to Sarah and her state of health, seeing
her doctors and keeping our parents informed. She was on the mend,
but needed to rest and put on weight in order to stabilize her "floating
kidney" (the layman's term for her condition). Christopher and Sarah
took to each other instantly, and he sent her flowers with this verse:

> *I have seen men die with smiling faces*
> *And second class horses win classic races;*
> *And now a kidney floating in empty spaces*
> *So I have hope!*

---

* When he was helping to get British prisoners of war back into France after the Italian
surrender on 7 September 1943.

At this point we were joined by Gil Winant, who had come to Rome to be with Sarah. As I have explained earlier, Winant was the American ambassador to Britain, having succeeded the defeatist and anti-British Joseph Kennedy in 1941. Inevitably a frequent guest at Chequers, he had rapidly established the friendliest of relations with my parents and all our family; he and Sarah, however, became particularly close, and were soon lovers. But at that time neither of them was free to marry—nor did either of them want to cause the inevitable commotion in their respective families. Their desire to keep their relationship out of sight was fortuitously aided by their living near each other: Sarah had for many years a flat in 55 Park Lane, and Winant's own private house was a few blocks north in Aldford Street.

During these days Christopher again asked me to marry him—and this time I said "yes."

Having assured myself that Sarah was "on the mend," and knowing Gil would certainly keep an eye on her, I returned home by train on 3 November—via Paris, where Christopher joined me. We went straight to Hyde Park Gate and I presented him to my parents. My father and Christopher took to each other immediately—but my mother was not such an easy conquest. Years later, when she was dining with us one night, Christopher charged her with this: my mother held out her hand across the table and said, "No, darling—but I made up for it later!"

OUR ENGAGEMENT WAS announced on 8 November, and our wedding planned for early February 1947. The months of our engagement were not particularly happy or easy, mostly owing to the bitter divisions between Christopher's parents, Arthur Soames and Hope Rhys.* Also, we could not spend much time with each other as Christopher

---

* Charles Rhys (who became Lord Dynevor on his father's death) had eloped with Hope Soames (as she then was); they were married after Arthur Soames divorced her in 1934.

was not due any more home leave for a while. At least my mother and I were able to make a visit to Paris, staying as usual with the hospitable Duff and Diana Cooper at the embassy.

Christopher and I were married on a freezing February day in St. Margaret's Westminster, where my parents had been married. That winter was to set records for icy conditions. For more than two months the country suffered the heaviest snowfalls of the twentieth century: road and rail links were paralyzed, causing a desperate shortage of coal, and there were draconian power cuts, reducing offices and homes alike to living by candlelight. Nevertheless, unheated St. Margaret's, which still bore the marks of interior war damage, was packed: the reduced lighting was boosted by candlelight and someone was standing by to blow the organ by hand if necessary. My dress was made by Molyneux and my tulle veil was held in place by a coronet of orange blossom. My one bridesmaid was my dear faithful friend and cousin Judy Montagu, wearing flame-coloured chiffon. The choir could not rise to anything more elaborate than "Jerusalem," but the essentials were there—and our promises and prayers would be wonderfully fulfilled.

A large crowd gathered despite the arctic conditions, and cheered the arrivals (although afterwards I learned to my embarrassment that the Attlees, who were kind enough to come, were loudly booed).

The reception at the Dorchester was largely candlelit, which was very pretty—and also made the room warmer! We stayed in London that first night, leaving the next morning by the Golden Arrow for Paris and Lenzerheide, the small Swiss resort where my mother and I had skiied together in 1937: here we thought we would have privacy, but the press descended and put paid to that—as well as making skiing quite difficult. After a few days a friend of Christopher's appeared, sized up the situation, and advised us to move to St. Moritz—which we duly did. This—a bigger fishbowl!—was much more fun.

Shortly before we were due to go home Christopher was taken alarmingly ill with what turned out to be a duodenal ulcer, as a result of which he would shortly be discharged on medical grounds from the army. My mother flew out to be with us—which caused a certain level of visible merriment among our fellow guests—and Christopher dispatched me to Paris to close up his apartment there.

By a most fortunate coincidence the farm below Chartwell came up for sale just now, and my father bought it: it included a small house which they now offered to us, and on 10 May we moved in with skeletal furnishings; over the next few months we would spend much time visiting local salerooms. For the first ten years of our married life, during which four of our five children were born, Chartwell Farm would be our home.

Acknowledgments

I AM GRATEFUL TO HUGO VICKERS FOR SENDING ME THE LETTER I wrote to the Duke of Marlborough on 24 July 1931, to the Hon. Robert Lloyd George for sending me the letter I wrote to David Lloyd George on 20 September 1937, and to the Library of Congress, Washington, D.C., for permission to quote from my letter to W. Averell Harriman of 13 May 1941.

I would like to thank Sally Gaminara of Transworld Publishers for her guidance on overall strategy and for her great patience; Sheila Lee, the picture editor, for her skill in tracking down so many evocative photographs; and Gillian Somerscales, my copy editor, for her eagle eye and invaluable suggestions. And, as always, my thanks to Nonie Chapman, my private secretary, who keeps my life on an even keel.

M.S.

Notes

CHAPTER 3: *Sisters and Cousins*

1. Sarah Churchill, *Keep on Dancing: An Autobiography,* ed. Paul Medlicott (London: Weidenfeld & Nicolson, 1981), p. 14.
2. Ibid., p. 36.
3. Ibid., p. 2.

CHAPTER 5: *Family Affairs*

1. Angela Culme-Seymour, *Bolter's Grand-daughter* (Oxford: Bird Island Press, 2001).
2. Mary S. Lovell, *The Mitford Girls: The Biography of an Extraordinary Family* (London: Little, Brown, 2001), pp. 162, 185.
3. Ibid., p. 205.

CHAPTER 6: *A Bright Life and a Darkening Horizon*

1. Shiela Grant Duff to WSC, 19 June 1937, quoted in Shiela Grant Duff, *The Parting of the Ways* (London: Peter Owen, 1982).
2. Winston S. Churchill, *The Second World War,* Vol. 1, *The Gathering Storm* (London: Cassell, 1948), p. 253.
3. Maze Papers, quoted in Martin Gilbert, *Winston S. Churchill,* Companion Volume V, Part 3, *The Coming of War* (London: Heinemann, 1982), p. 1592.

CHAPTER 7: *Clearing the Decks*

1. Churchill, *The Gathering Storm,* p. 389.
2. Ibid.

CHAPTER 8: *A Year to Remember*

1. John Colville, *The Fringes of Power: Downing Street Diaries 1939–55* (London: Hodder & Stoughton, 1985), pp. 120–21.
2. Martin Gilbert, *Finest Hour: Winston S. Churchill, 1939–1941* (London: Heinemann, 1983), p. 361.
3. Ibid., pp. 486, 500.
4. Winston S. Churchill, *The Second World War,* Vol. 2, *Their Finest Hour* (London: Cassell, 1949), p. 162.
5. Quoted in Colville, *The Fringes of Power,* p. 185.
6. Ibid., p. 176.
7. Ibid., p. 219.

CHAPTER 9: *At Chequers*

1. Churchill, *Their Finest Hour,* p. 332.
2. See Norma Major, *Chequers: The Prime Minister's Country House and Its History* (London: HarperCollins, 1996).
3. Colville, *The Fringes of Power,* p. 247.
4. Ibid., diary entry for Saturday, 12 October 1940, pp. 262–63.
5. Letter to the author from Professor R. D. Keynes, CBE, FRS, and attached Royal Society Biographical Memoir of Charles Frederick Goodeve by F. D. Richardson FRS, quoting Gerald Pawle, *The Secret War, 1939–45* (London: Harrap, 1956).

CHAPTER 10: *Decisions . . . Decisions . . . Decisions*

1. Recounted in John G. Winant, *A Letter from Grosvenor Square: An Account of a Stewardship* (London: Hodder & Stoughton, 1947). The quotation is from the Book of Ruth.
2. The President's personal instruction to Harriman: see Gilbert, *Finest Hour,* p. 1020.
3. Gilbert, *Finest Hour,* p. 1059; Mary Soames in conversation with the author, October 1982.
4. Colville, *The Fringes of Power,* p. 387.
5. MC to W. Averell Harriman, 13 May 1941, Library of Congress; Rudy Abramson, *Spanning the Century: The Life of W. Averell Harriman, 1891–1986* (New York: William Morrow, 1992).

CHAPTER 12: *Battery Life*

1. WSC, "Address to the Central Council of the Conservative Party," published in *The Times* (London), 27 March 1942.

2. Hugh Trevor-Roper, ed., *Hitler's Secret Conversations* (New York: Farrar, Straus & Young, 1953), 27 June 1942, p. 141. I am much obliged to Andrew Roberts for this nugget.

CHAPTER 14: *"Subaltern George"*

1. Gilbert, *Finest Hour,* p. 484, n. 6.
2. I am indebted for a reminder of this story to Gerald Pawle, *The War and Colonel Warden* (New York: Knopf, 1963), pp. 249–50.
3. Sarah Churchill, *A Thread in the Tapestry* (London: André Deutsch, 1967).

CHAPTER 15: *Testing Times*

1. From Irwin Shaw, *The Young Lions* (Chicago: University of Chicago Press, 1948). I am grateful to Ken Perkins for the reference.
2. Harold Macmillan's description, quoted in Gilbert, *Finest Hour,* p. 622.

CHAPTER 16: *Doodlebugs*

1. Copy of telegram courtesy of Churchill College Archives Centre, Churchill College, Cambridge.
2. Ibid.

Bibliography

Abramson, Rudy. *Spanning the Century: The Life of W. Averell Harriman, 1891–1986.* New York: William Morrow, 1992.

Churchill, Sarah. *A Thread in the Tapestry.* London: André Deutsch, 1967.

———. *Keep on Dancing: An Autobiography.* Edited by Paul Medlicott. London: Weidenfeld & Nicolson, 1981.

Churchill, Winston S. *The Second World War.* Vol. 1, *The Gathering Storm.* London: Cassell, 1948.

———. *The Second World War.* Vol. 2, *Their Finest Hour.* London: Cassell, 1949.

———. *The Second World War.* Vol. 6, *Triumph and Tragedy.* London: Cassell, 1954.

Colville, John. *The Fringes of Power: Downing Street Diaries, 1939–55.* London: Hodder & Stoughton, 1985.

Culme-Seymour, Angela. *Bolter's Grand-daughter.* Oxford: Bird Island Press, 2001.

Gilbert, Martin, *Winston S. Churchill.* Companion Volume V, Part 3, *The Coming of War.* London: Heinemann, 1982.

———. *Finest Hour: Winston S. Churchill, 1939–1941.* London: Heinemann, 1983.

Grant Duff, Shiela. *The Parting of the Ways.* London: Peter Owen, 1982.

Ingram, Kevin. *Rebel: The Short Life of Esmond Romilly.* London: Weidenfeld & Nicolson, 1985.

Lovell, Mary S. *The Mitford Girls: The Biography of an Extraordinary Family.* London: Little, Brown, 2001.

Major, Norma. *Chequers: The Prime Minister's Country House and Its History.* London: HarperCollins, 1996.

Oxford Companion to the Second World War. Oxford: Oxford University Press, 1995.

Pawle, Gerald. *The Secret War, 1939–45.* London: Harrap, 1956.

———. *The War and Colonel Warden.* New York: Knopf, 1963.

Trevor-Roper, Hugh, ed. *Hitler's Secret Conversations.* New York: Farrar, Straus & Young, 1953.

Winant, John G. *A Letter from Grosvenor Square: An Account of a Stewardship.* London: Hodder & Stoughton, 1947.

Photograph Credits

———

Acknowledgments read clockwise from the
top left-hand corner on each page/spread.

MC = *Mary Churchill*
CSC = *Clementine Churchill*
WSC = *Winston Churchill*

FIRST SECTION

Page 1: MC as a baby: Churchill Archives Centre, The Papers of Randolph
Churchill, RDCH [9/2/4B], reproduced with permission of Curtis Brown,
London, on behalf of the Estate of Randolph S. Churchill, copyright © Ran-
dolph S. Churchill; MC with CSC: Mary Soames collection.

Pages 2–3: MC and WSC: Churchill Archives Centre, The Broadwater Collection, BRDW [1/1/95], reproduced with permission of Curtis Brown Ltd,
London, on behalf of the Broadwater Collection; MC with her parents: Mary
Soames collection; MC with a bucket: Churchill Archives Centre, The Papers
of Clementine Spencer-Churchill, CSCT [5/2/42]; MC on a pony: Churchill
Archives Centre, The Papers of Clementine Spencer-Churchill, CSCT
[5/5/5]; MC with her doll: Churchill Archives Centre, The Papers of Clementine Spencer-Churchill, CSCT [5/2/43]; MC with Sarah Churchill: Churchill
Archives Centre, The Broadwater Collection, BRDW [1/1/95], reproduced
with permission of Curtis Brown Ltd, London, on behalf of the Broadwater
Collection; Chartwell in 1922: Topfoto/TopFoto.co.uk; portrait of MC by
Neville Lewis: private collection; MC with Diana Churchill: Churchill Archives Centre, The Papers of Clementine Spencer-Churchill, CSCT [5/2/38].

Pages 4–5: MC and WSC bricklaying, 1928: Getty Images; *Tea at Chartwell* by
WSC, 1927: reproduced with permission of Anthea Morton-Saner on behalf

of Churchill Heritage Ltd/Copyright © Churchill Heritage Ltd; *Mary's First Speech* by WSC, 1929: reproduced with permission of Anthea Morton-Saner on behalf of Churchill Heritage Ltd/Copyright © Churchill Heritage Ltd/ photo Topfoto/TopFoto.co.uk; MC head and shoulders and MC in fur coat: both Churchill Archives Centre, The Papers of Randolph Churchill, RDCH [9/2/4B], reproduced with permission of Curtis Brown, London, on behalf of the Estate of Randolph S. Churchill, copyright © Randolph S. Churchill; Churchill family, Westerham, June 1928: Mirrorpix; MC in the snow: Churchill Archives Centre, The Papers of Randolph Churchill, RDCH [9/2/4B], reproduced with permission of Curtis Brown, London, on behalf of the Estate of Randolph S. Churchill, copyright © Randolph S. Churchill.

Pages 6–7: MC at the Scamperdale Pony Show: Churchill Archives Centre, The Papers of Clementine Spencer-Churchill, CSCT [5/2/79]; MC skating: Churchill Archives Centre, The Papers of Clementine Spencer-Churchill, CSCT [5/2/91]; MC with CSC skiing: Churchill Archives Centre, The Papers of Clementine Spencer-Churchill, CSCT [5/2/97]; MC with Fiona Forbes: Churchill Archives Centre, The Papers of Clementine Spencer-Churchill, CSCT [5/2/83]; CSC's bedroom at Chartwell: © AP/Topfoto; MC and WSC at the circus: Churchill Archives Centre, The Papers of Clementine Spencer-Churchill, CSCT [5/1/27]; MC and WSC on horseback: Mary Soames collection.

Page 8: MC by Cecil Beaton: all Cecil Beaton/Vogue © The Condé Nast Publications Ltd, photo Churchill Archives Centre, The Papers of Clementine Spencer-Churchill, CSCT [5/4/60–62 and 87].

Page 9: MC by Antony Beauchamp: Churchill Archives Centre, The Papers of Clementine Spencer-Churchill, CSCT [5/2/74].

Pages 10–11: CSC in Admiralty House, c. 1939: Churchill Archives Centre, The Papers of Clementine Spencer-Churchill, CSCT [5/2/94]; bedroom in the Annexe: Mary Soames collection; WSC, CSC, and MC arriving at the Free Trade Hall, Manchester, Jan. 1940: Daily Mail/Rex Features; CSC launches the *Indomitable,* March 1940: Churchill Archives Centre, The Papers of Clementine Spencer-Churchill, CSCT [5/3/9]; MC in her coming-out dress, 29 Feb. 1940: Churchill Archives Centre, The Papers of Clementine Spencer-Churchill, CSCT [5/4/89]; WSC and CSC at Queen Charlotte's Ball for debutantes, 29 Feb. 1940: Press Association; Pamela Digby and Randolph Churchill at their wedding; MC and Randolph at his wedding, 4 Oct. 1939: both Churchill Archives Centre, The Papers of Clementine Spencer-Churchill, CSCT [5/2/68]; dining-room downstairs at No. 10: Mary Soames collection.

Pages 12–13: MC outside Ditchley Park: Churchill Archives Centre, The Papers of Clementine Spencer-Churchill, CSCT [5/4/20]; MC at Westerham War

Weapons Week, 1 Feb. 1941: Churchill Archives Centre, The Papers of Clementine Spencer-Churchill, CSCT [5/4/10]; MC at Queen Charlotte's Ball, 22 March 1941: Press Association; Gil Winant, unknown man, MC, and Averell Harriman, Cardiff, 12 April 1941: Churchill Archives Centre, The Papers of Clementine Spencer-Churchill, CSCT [5/4/22]; MC, CSC, and Nana Whyte, 1941: Mary Soames collection; MC at Stoke Mandeville, June 1941: Mary Soames collection; Chequers: Alamy; "Prison Room," Chequers: ITV/Rex Features.

Pages 14–15: MC at training camp, 28 Sept. 1941: Popperfoto/Getty Images; MC and Judy Montagu carrying a dustbin: Churchill Archives Centre, The Papers of Clementine Spencer-Churchill, CSCT [5/4/66]; MC and Judy Montagu at training camp, 1941: Churchill Archives Centre, The Papers of Clementine Spencer-Churchill, CSCT [5/4/65]; MC and WSC on board the *Duke of York,* Dec. 1941: Mary Soames collection; CSC, MC, and Dudley Pound, 1941: © Hulton-Deutsch Collection/Corbis; MC and friends cleaning shoes: Churchill Archives Centre, The Papers of Clementine Spencer-Churchill, CSCT [5/4/71]; MC and friends hanging up washing: Churchill Archives Centre, The Papers of Clementine Spencer-Churchill, CSCT [5/4/67].

Page 16: "Some of Pip Section": Churchill Archives Centre, The Papers of Clementine Spencer-Churchill, CSCT [5/5/42].

SECOND SECTION

Page 1: MC at an infantry inspection by WSC, 28 Dec. 1942; AP/Press Association Images.

Pages 2–3: CSC, WSC, Sarah, and Mary driving to Mansion House, 30 June 1943: Daily Mail/Rex Features; *Friday Night, Control Room,* by Bryan de Grineau, 22 Oct. 1943, printed in *Illustrated London News,* 30 Oct. 1943: *Illustrated London News* Ltd/Mary Evans; the Queen visits MC's battery, Hyde Park, 5 July 1943: Mary Soames collection; same occasion: Churchill Archives Centre, The Papers of Clementine Spencer-Churchill, CSCT [5/5/90]; MC and WSC, Downing Street, 3 July 1942: Getty Images; WSC and MC outside Mansion House, 30 June 1943: Getty Images.

Pages 4–5: CSC and MC entering City Hall, Quebec, 23 Aug. 1943: Skadding/AP/Press Association Images; WSC and MC, Niagara, Aug. 1943, CSC, WSC, and MC on the *Renown* returning from Quebec, Sept. 1943, MC celebrating her birthday on *Renown:* all Mary Soames collection; WSC and MC on train observation platform, Niagara, Aug. 1943: British Official Photograph (Crown copyright)/Mirrorpix; CSC and MC, Quebec, 1943: Mary Soames collection; Brendan Bracken, General Ismay, and MC on the train: Imperial War Museum/H32957.

MARY SOAMES is the youngest and only surviving child of Winston and Clementine Churchill. She was born in 1922 and brought up at Chartwell in Kent. In 1941, aged eighteen, she joined the ATS and served in mixed anti-aircraft batteries in England and Europe. She accompanied her father as his ADC on several of his wartime overseas journeys. In 1945 she was awarded the MBE (military). In 1947 she married Captain Christopher Soames, Coldstream Guards, later Lord Soames, PC, GCMG, CH. She has also written her mother's biography, *Clementine Churchill,* and edited *Speaking for Themselves,* a collection of the personal letters between her parents.